Oriental Manuscripts Worldwide

Oriental Manuscripts Worldwide

By

Dr. Amjad Ali

Deputy Librarian

Aligarh Muslim University, Aligarh

&

Chairman

Central Sectional Committee for Oriental Libraries

Indian Library Association, New Delhi

Ess Ess Publications

4837/24, Ansari Road, Darya Ganj,

New Delhi-110002

✆ : 23260807

Fax : 23274173

E-mail: info@essessreference.com

url:http://www.essessreference.com

First Published 2005

ISBN : 81-7000-421-7

Price : Rs. 675/-

Published by :

Ess Ess Publications

4837/24, Ansari Road, Darya Ganj,
New Delhi - 110 002
Phone : 23260807
Fax : 23274173
E-mail: info@essessreference.com
url:http://www.essessreference.com

Laser Typesetting:

Mukesh Graphics

L-2/8, DDA Market,
Mangolpuri, New Delhi
Ph. : 27924405
E-mail:mukeshgraphics29@hotmail.com

Printed at :

Print Line

Dedicated to My
FATHER

CONTENTS

PREFACE

Human beings learn through experiences and pass the skill so earned to their posterity. Manuscripts are the manifestation of such experiences into physical form recorded by hand at different times. The materials and methods for recording and reproduction of manuscripts changed as per the availability of techniques but they always remained useful to the society. Manuscripts represent the selected fragments of time, which help in recreating the past and deciphering the history of mankind.

Looking at the World history, one finds that the East has always had an edge over the West in respect of the richness of culture. About all leading civilizations of the past belonged to the East popularly known as the Orient. Egypt, Greece, Rome, Mesopotamia and India have a bright and recorded past. Plenty of manuscripts were produced in these civilizations, which remained the personal property of kings and nobles for many centuries and were gurded by political might. A large number of such manuscripts have been lost with political instability from time to time still we have them in great quantities.

The political stability and prosperity of nations promoted the creation and prerservation of manuscripts and their collections expanded with the spread of kingdoms. The centres of powers became the abode of manuscripts such as in case of Greece, Egypt, Turkey and England, which hold most of the precious manuscripts available on the earth.

In this book, an attempt has been made to provide general introduction to the major representative collections of oriental manuscripts available worldwide. Only the larger and popular organizations holding manuscripts have been included in the survey keeping in view that it would not have been possible to accommodate all such collections in a single volume. Material for this book was collected from all possible sources including traditional as well as the current electronic media. It was found that the information available in print was outdated in most of the cases whereas the same although current was brief on the World Wide Web. The entries of institutions in the book have been made in alphabetical order except for the last two chapters which relate to a different category.

The collections of manuscripts available in some major oriental languages manily Arabic, Persian, Sanskrit, Tamil, Tibetan, Turkish etc. have been presented in this book since it was felt that no such work already exists. However the East Asian and South East Asian languages and the languages of Non-Arab Africa have not been included in this survey. It is expected that the book will be useful for any person who has interest in history and also for the librarians and students of library and information science.

I am highly indebted to Professor Irfan Habib Saheb, an eminent historian of our times who spared his valuable time to see the manuscript of this book and provided valuable guidelines. Some very important institutions might have been left uncovered had he not seen it. I am also thankful to a number of individuals and organizations who have hosted information about manuscripts on the World Wide Web which I referred to for accomplishment of this work. My thanks are also due to Mr. Sumit Sethi of Ess Ess Publications, New Delhi who allowed me enough time to revise and update the manuscript a number of times before undertaking its publication.

Dr. Amjad Ali

E-mail: amjad_alig@yahoo.co.in

140-Nai Abadi, Kela Nagar

Aligarh- 202 002 (UP) INDIA

FOREWORD

The strength of a nation primarily depends upon three factors; its military power, economic prosperity and intellectual superiority. The intellectual superiority is the key to progress, prosperity and dominance. It affects all the other aspects of a nation and takes it ahead of the others. Greece, Egypt and Britain dominated over the world scene because of their advance level of knowledge.

History tells us that libraries played pivotal role in the social, cultural and intellectual development of the society. Libraries were established with the primary objective of preserving the wisdom transformed into physical objects such as manuscripts and books and also for extending the facilities for studying the resources so collected and organized by individuals and organizations. Based on these human assumptions, libraries came into existence in varied forms ranging from the one holding clay tablets to the electronic gadgets of our own time.

In fact, the emergence of libraries in a society signifies the dawn of its intellectual era. Its documentary heritage provides an insight into the past and a vision for the future. The human races, which protected their heritage dominated the world scene. Examples may be drawn from the ancient civilizations of Egypt, Greece, Persia, and India. From the very beginning, Islam emphasized on seeking knowledge and the rise of Muslims was mainly attributed to their respect and love for wisdom. In Islam further emphasized the acquisition of knowledge from whatever sources it was available and from cradle to grave.

The advent of Islam witnessed an unprecedented growth in the quantity of knowledge and gave birth to a healthy tradition of reading, writing and preservation of the thoughts contained in documents. This led to the promotion of libraries and development of the art of papermaking. Paper substituted tree bark, leaves, animal skin and bones as medium for recording, reproduction and preservation of knowledge which further accelerated the rate of generation of manuscripts and books. It ultimately led to the rise in number of libraries.

During the reign of Caliph Haroon al-Rasheed, the city of Baghdad had about 300 libraries. The Bait-ul-Hikmah (House of Wisdom) 786-809 A.D. established at that time still reminds us the bright historical past of Muslims. They promoted libraries in every period and as a natural requirement to man these institutions, the profession of librarianship emerged emphasizing on preservation, copying, classification and indexing of the intellectual work.

Archaeological evidences suggest that books were being produced in India in the 4th century A.D. The materials used for writing generally included, tree barks, palm leaves, copper plates, mud and stones since animal skin and bones were considered as impure objects by Hindus. For this reason only, the documentary heritage of Hinduism, Buddhism and Jainism is recorded and preserved on these materials, which are found in every corner of the country. The oldest account of the existence of libraries in India is traced from the writings of a Chinese traveler, Fa Hi Yan. Similarly, the evidence of libraries in later centuries is found in the account of the other foreign travelers. Libraries were established and destroyed with the rise and fall of the ruling dynasties through out the history and what has been descended to us today tells about the glory as well as the devastation of mankind at different times.

The invention of printing press was the second major achievement after the art of papermaking, which contributed to an unprecedented growth of knowledge. The moveable type further accelerated the rate of growth. It also paved way for establishment of new libraries in an ever-increasing number. Prior to this, entry to libraries was generally restricted to the elite only and the common man was deprived of the benefit of using them.

For the purpose of safety and security, books were kept in chains. The printing press liberated them and opened new avenues for the seekers of knowledge to come to libraries and consult the resources.

Unlike the art of papermaking, which was rapidly adopted by Muslims, the printing press took centuries to be popularized among the Islamic states. Till such a time, manuscripts remained the main source of information for kings, nobles and learned personalities. So long as the Islamic states maintained a scientific approach, contributed to the expansion of knowledge and adopted new discoveries, they remained powerful rulers. But they legged behind in utilization of the power of printing press and subsequently the history witnessed their downfall.

The Western countries adopted the moveable types as early as in the 15th century whereas the Islamic states made its use from the 18th century onwards. In a way this contributed to increase in the number of manuscripts since they remained the main source of information till that time. As a result, the number of oriental manuscripts available internationally is very high compared to their occidental counterparts.

In India, the availability of paper is traced in the 13th century but it could not be used as a popular medium for a long time. The documentary heritage is not found on paper till the 16th century when publishing industry started in the country. Like the Islamic states, the delay in opting the printing technology permitted the increase of published items in abundance. It is said that India is having the second largest number of manuscripts available in a single country of the world and is next to Egypt only.

The present book Oriental Manuscripts Worldwide by Dr. Amjad Ali is a successful attempt to keep intently into the vast treasure of man's knowledge preserved in the form of handwritten documents mainly in Arabic, Persian, Turkish, and Sanskrit languages. The libraries which have been covered in this book preserve more than 10,000 manuscripts and other documents.

The compiler deserves our complements and appreciation for this useful contribution and also for providing all the necessary information in a very organized and scientific method. This was expected of him as he is a devoted library professional and has authored several books on various aspects of library and information science. We hope that he will continue his studies and shall work on smaller libraries also which although have lesser number of manuscripts but are equal if not greater in value.

Dr. M. Ziauddin Ansari

Formerly: Director

Khuda Bakhsh Oriental Public Library, Patna

1
ASIATIC SOCIETY, KOLKATA

The Asiatic Society is a premier oriental institution of the Asian continent. It was founded in 1784 by Sir William Jones (1746-1794) who dreamt of a centre for Asian studies including almost everything concerning man and nature within the geographical limits of the continent, the history, civil and natural, the antiquities, arts, sciences and literature of Asia. In the dim hours of the genesis of the Asiatic Society, William Jones for all his efforts could not procure even a slice of land wherein to house his Asian dream. The Society which in no time was to be regarded as the first and best of its kind in the whole world had no permanent address, no fixed place for holding its meetings and, which was most disconcerting, no funds.

Sir William Jones arrived in Calcutta on 25 September 1783 as a Puisne Judge of the Old Supreme Court.While still on board of the frigate Crococlile carrying him from England to India, he prepared a memorandum detailing his plan of study. This included 'the laws of the Hindus and Mahomedans; the history of the ancient world; proofs and illustrations of scripture; traditions concerning the deluge; modern politics and geography of Hindusthan; Arithmatic and Geometry and mixed sciences of Asiaticks; Medicine, Chemistry, Surgery and Anatomy of the Indians; natural products of India; poetry, rhetoric and morality of Asia; music of the Eastern nations; the best accounts of Tibet and Kashmir; trade, manufactures, agriculture and commerce of India: Mughal constitution, Marhatta constitution etc." This memorandum could easily be regarded as an early draft of the memorandum of the Asiatic Society itself. The Society, which was still in the embryo of a dream was actually born within four months of Jones's arrival in India.

William Jones was, however, not the earliest among the Orientalists of the East India Company to arrive in India. About a decade earlier came Charles Wilkins (1770), Nathaniel Brassey Halhed (1772) and Jonathan Duncan (1772): Warren Hastings's "bright young men",who had paved the way for the two future institutions- The Asiatic Society and the College at Fort William. All the Orientalists who became famous in history clustered around either the Society or the College or both. The Society, of course, was the pioneer and first in the field.

While others were thinking in terms of individual study and research, Sir William Jones was the first man to think in terms of a permanent organisation for Oriental studies and researches on a grand scale in this country. He took the initiative and in January 1784 sent out a circular letter to selected persons of the elite with a view to establishing a Society for this purpose. In response to his letter, thirty European gentlemen of Calcutta including Mr. Justice Hyde, John Carnac, Henry Vansittart, John Shore, Charles Wilkins, Francis Gladwin, Jonathan Duncan and others gathered on 15 January 1784 in the Grand Jury Room of the old Supreme Court of Calcutta. The Chief Justice Sir Robert Chambers presided at the first meeting and Jones delivered his first discourse in which he put forward his plans for the Society.

Asia, he said, was the "nurse of sciences" and the "inventress of delightful and useful arts." He proposed to found a Society under the name of The Asiatick Society. The name went through a number of changes like The Asiatick Society (1784-1825), The Asiatic Society (1825-1832), The Asiatic Society of Bengal (1832-1935), The Royal Asiatic Society of Bengal (1936-1951) and The Asiatic Society again since July 1951.

The pioneering activity of the Society was praised abroad and even compared with that of the Italian Humanists of the *quattrocento*. But the first two decades of the Society's existence remained precarious. The original plan of holding meetings every week had to be discarded, and even monthly meetings were not possible. When William Jones died in 1794, the Society was just an orphan of ten, having no roof overhead and no assured funds to defray normal running expenses, not to speak of having in its proud possession, as it has today, an invaluable Asokan rock edict or precious old coins. There was hardly any hint at that time that Jones's dream of a world centre of Oriental studies in Calcutta was going to survive.

In the beginning, the Society was very loosely organised and had no real Executive Body. It had only two important functionaries: a President who conducted meetings, and a Secretary who kept the minutes. After Jones's death the interest of the members declined considerably and in 1800 a resolution had to be passed urging members to attend meetings more regularly. Financial conditions were so bad, and there were so many defaulters among the members, that the first Treasurer of the Society, Henry Trail resigned in desperation in 1799. After the turn of the century things began to look up.

The collaboration between the Society and the Fort William College increased, and this collaboration was symbolised in 1807 when Henry Colebrooke became the President of the College Council as well as the President of the Asiatic Society. Already in 1805 the Secretary of the Society, William Hunter had been made the Secretary of the College. In 1808 Colebrooke as President of the College transferred a section of the Fort William College Library to the Society.

The publication of the *Asiatick Researches* became assured when Hunter's Hindoostan Press took up its printing responsibility. Ram Comal Sen, the 'native' manager of Hunter's Press, later on became the 'native' Secretary of the Asiatic Society itself. In 1846, two years after Ram comal Sen's death, Rajendralala Mitra, then a young man, joined the Asiatic Society as its Assistant Librarian. The Indian Renaissance was made possible and in fact was accelerated by the quiet but far-reaching work going on at the corner of Park Street despite all odds and adverse circumstances.

In 1837, only four years after Wilson's departure, James Prinsep, the new Secretary of the Society, deciphered the Brahmi Script and was able to read the Asokan Edicts. It was a world event that revolutionised all future Oriental studies and contributed to the growth of Comparative Philology.

The Transactions of the Asiatic Society were first published under the title of *Asiatick Researches* in 1788, the subsequent four volumes being published in 1790, 1793, 1795 and 1797 respectively. At first the publication was private, undertaken by Manual Cantopher on the condi- tion that each member of the Society would purchase one volume at a price of Rs. 20. Later on, the Society itself undertook the responsibility of the publication. The publication *Asiatick Researches* was so much in demand in the literary and scholarly world that a pirated edition of the first volume came into circulation in England in 1798, and some of the volumes of the *Asiatick Researches* were translated into German as well as in French. Through its published Transactions the Society now came in touch with several distinguished scholarly Associations abroad such as the American Philosophical Society of Philadelphia, the Linnean Society of London, the Royal Society of Edinburgh, and the Society of Antiquities of England.

The Society also proved to be a pivotal centre of Oriental studies and research and extended its helping hand to the other two major centres of activity that paved the way to the Indian Renaissance, namely, the College at Fort William and the Serampore Mission of William Carey. In 1805 a proposal came to the Asiatic Society from the Serampore Mission to publish classical Sanskrit works with their English translations, and the first book chosen for this was the Sanskrit epic, Ramayana. For this purpose the Society spent from its fund five thousand and five hundred rupees. From 1788 till its cessation in 1839 the journal *Asiatick Researches* ran into twenty volumes and was superseded by the *Journal of the Asiatic Society*, henceforth the official organ of the Society. The Society also started in 1905 a new serial entitled the *Memoirs* which was discontinued in 1933. The nucleus of the Society's own library was formed soon after the building was completed in 1808. The Fort William College which was helped a lot academically by the Society, presented books to the Society from its own collection, and another valuable collection of books came from the Palace Library of Tipu Sultan in 1808.

It may be mentioned that two decades before Ram Mohan Roy's first tract on *Sati* it was H. T. Colebrooke who proved from the early texts that the practice of *Sati* was a gross deviation from the authentic tradition. The founding fathers of the Asiatic Society were responsible for the rediscovery of India and her past.

Sir Charles Wilkins (1750-1 833) translated the *Bhagavadgita* into English in 1785, deciphered a number of Sanskrit inscriptions published a translation of *Hitopadesa* (1787) and a *Grammar of the Sanskrit Language*. Sir William Jones translated Kalidasa's Sakuntala (1789), Jayadeva's *Gitagovinda* (1789) and *Manusamhita* (1794), and edited *Ritusamhara* (1792). Jones also translated a Persian work *Laila Majnu*. The works initiated by Wilkins and Jones were continued by Colebrooke (1765-1837) and Wilson (1784-1860). Colebrooke was the President of the Society from 1806 to 1815 and contributed nineteen papers to the Transactions of the Society. He published an English translation of Jagannath Tarkapanchanan's celebrated work on Hindu law, the *Vivadabhangarnava* under the title *Digest of Hindu Law on Contracts and Successions* (1798). He also published a critical edition of the Sanskrit lexicon *Amarakosha* (1808). Wilson was Secretary to the Asiatic Society from 1811 to 1833 and published Kalidasa's *Meghaduta* (1813) and got the eighteen principal *Puranas* also translated into English. He also published an edition of Kalhana's *Rajatarangini* (1825). Sir John Shore (1751-1834) who succeeded William Jones as President of the Society in 1794, published from a Persian version an abridged English transalation of the *Yoga Vasistha* and contributed six papers to the *Asiatick Researches*.

Most of the works of the Society are research-based and research-oriented, and have not been loudly spectacular. But its publication, the Bibliotheca Indica, consisting of a series of several hundred Oriental texts in Sanskrit, Arabic, Persian, Bengali, Tibetan and other Asian languages, both in original and translation, has earned the Society a rare reputation among scholars all over the world. Its Monographs were supplemented by several new series such as Public Lectures, Monthly Bulletins, Seminar Proceedings, Memorial Lectures and Memoirs (1905-33). These are in addition to the Society's Journal, Journal of the Asiatic Society, formerly, *Asiatick Researches (1788-1849), Journal of the Asiatic Society of Bengal (1832-1904), Proceedings of the Asiatic Society (1865-1904), Journal and the Proceedings of the Asiatic Society (1905-1934), Journal of the Asiatic Society of Bengal (1935-1952) and Journal of the Asiatic Society (since 1953).* A cursory glance at the contents of the publications of the Asiatic Society will show how great many historical Monographs and Oriental studies, all fruits of original research, were brought out in them. Archaeological and Geological surveys, census reports, treatises on law and revenue systems, all these prepared the solid basis for all future researches on Asia and the Orient.

Library of the Society

The Library of the Society is the grand stay, glory and honour of the Society. Its importance lies not in numerical strength but in its rich and unique contents. The collection has been built up mainly with gifts received from the members, dating back to 25 March 1784, when the Society received with thanks seven Persian manuscripts from Henri Richardson. The next gift came from William Marsden, F.R.S., his book, History of Island of Sumatra (1783) on 10 November, 1984. Since the foundation of the Society, books, manuscripts, drawings, coins, antiquarian and other objects of historical importance were exhibited to the

Society's meetings, and kept in the custody of the Secretary. As the Society had no habitat of its own, the risk of loss was serious. After the demise of the founder, the question of a permanent house for the Society was strongly felt for transacting its academic activities and for keeping and preserving for the posterity books, records, art, antiquarian and museum objects. The Society moved into its own building in the early part of 1808 and the Library was thrown open to the members and the public in the same year. Thus the Society laid the foundation of the first Academic as well as Public Library in India. The books that had been received till then formed the nucleus of the collection. Since then, gifts were pouring in from heads of States (e.g. Emperor of Russia), Institutions, Societies and individuals. Robert Home who was for some time Secretary of the Society and the first Library-in-Charge (1804), donated his small but very valuable collection of works on Art. The first accession of importance was a gift from the Seringapatam Committee (3 February 1808). being a selection from the palace library of Tipoo Sultan. The Collection contains many old and rare works. Special mention may be made of an illuminated manuscript of the Quran an old text of Gulistan, and manuscripts of Padshanamah bearing an autograph of Emperor Shahjahan. Similarly, Surveyor-General Colonel Mackenzie's collection of manuscripts and drawings were recived in December 1822.

Collections of the Library

The collection has been grouped into three Departments; e.g.

(1) Printed Books and Periodicals

(2) Manuscripts and Archives and

(3) Museum Objects.

The Printed Books Depatment has four sections, including European, Indian, Perso-Arabic, Urdu and Sino-Tibetan and South-Asian Departments

On the abolition of the College at Fort William, a much larger collection of historical and other works relating to India, the whole of its Sanskrit, Arabic, Persian, and Urdu works, mostly in manuscript, were placed under the custody of the Society, subject only to two conditions, namely, safe and careful preservation, and unrestricted accessibility to the public at all reasonable hours. Exchanges of publications were also made with institutions and learned Societies. Duplicates in the Library were exchanged with books in possession of private individuals, and members retiring from India sometimes presented or sold selections of their libraries to the Society. A collection of some illustrated works on Botany was received from Dr. N. Wallich in June 1817, which was subsequently sent to the East India Company's Botanical Gardens at Sibpur.

Acquisition by purchase has always been very insignificant. The Society's supplier in the days of Willian Jones was Peter Elmsly of London. Since 1806, the Society appointed agents in England from among its members who offered gratuitous service (e.g. Dr. Francis Gladwin, H. T. Colebrooke, Dr. H. H. Wilson and others) to select, purchase and forward all important books of Science and Oriental literature together with the leading scientific and other periodicals published in Europe. In the 20th century Dr. N. Annandale, Dr. B. C. Law (on Buddhism), Dr. C. W. Gurner (on Greek and Latin Literature), R. P. Chanda (on Indian History and Culture), C. R. Cama (on Indo-Muslim literature and history), Bengal Club (on European History and Politics) and Dr. Pratap Chadra Chunder Literature (Nirmal Chandra Chunder's Library) and many others made gifts of large and special collections. Ananda Bazar Patrika presented a very valuable collection of about 12,000 volumes to the memory of Prafulla Chandra Sarkar. Among the institutions of foreign countries, which donated a large number of books to the Society's Library mention should be made of the Smithsonian Institute of America, Institut Danois des Exchanges, and Japan Foundation. Prof. Nirmal Kumar Bose bequeathed his library to the Society.

This filled in many gaps in the collection of the Society. Jnananjan Niyogi's collection of books now forms a part of the Library. Space does not permit to record the names of other distinguished donors.

The periodical collection of the Society is unique in Asia, especially in its holdings of learned journals from all over the world. Even the journals of the Societies established long before the foundation of the Asiatic Society are available here. Most of these have been acquired by way of gift or by exchange with Society's publications which were, and are still, held in high esteem by the learned world. Of course, its collection in Asian languages is comparatively weak. Nevertheless, there are some unique journals in Indian languages which are not available elsewhere. There are about 5,000 titles of learned journals of which about 100 titles only are subscribed and these run into 1,12,000 volumes or thereabout. Scholars from all parts of India and abroad visit this library for consultations of this unique collection.

Rare Book Division

In 1978 the Council decided to open a Rare Book Division. The preliminary screening of the collection has since been started. Among the earliest printed books mention may be made of the following: Julii Firmici Astronomicorum libri octo integri (Venice 1499), Kitabal-Qanun (Arabic/Romae 1595), Kripar Sastrer Arthabhed (Bengali in Roman Character, Lisbon 1743); S. Purchas's Purchas : His Pilgrimage (London, 1 61 4), N. Halhed's Grammar of the Bengali Language, (Hooghly, 1778), Malabar and English Dictionary, (Madras, 1779), Rasamanjari (Sanskrit, Banaras, 1791), Ram Ram Bose's Lipimala (Bengali. Serampore, 1802), The Ramayana 3 vols, (Bengali, Serampore, 1803), Hitopadesa (Sanskrit, Serampore, 1804), Colebrooke's Grammar of the Sanskrit language Vol.1 (Serampore, 1805).

Manuscripts Collection

The Asiatic Society holds rare and invariable collection.

It is varied and rich, and covers most of the Indian languages and scripts and even several Asian ones, e.g., Assamese, Bengali, Gujarati, Gurumukhi, Kanarese, Urdu, Marathi, Modi, Nagari, Newari, Oriya, Rajasthani, Sarada, Armenian, Sinhalese, Arabic, Persian, Pushto, Javanese, Turki, Burmese, Chinese, Siamese, Tibetan etc. The materials used for the manuscripts are also varied; palm and palmyra leaves, barks of different trees, papers of various grades.

The four sections devoted to the manuscripts are as under:

(a) Sanskritic Section : This Section comprises of manuscripts in Sanskrit and Modern Indian Languages, which range in date from the 7th Century A.D. and number about thirty thousand. Rich and varied in textual contents the collection is an epitome of India's achievements in diverse spheres of life and learning. Some of the manuscripts have fine miniature illustrations, the earliest of which belongs to the 10th Century A.D.

(b) Islamic Section : This Section comprises of manuscripts in Arabic, Persian, Turkish, Pushto, Urdu, etc. numbering more than seven thousand, ranging in date from the first quarter of the 12th Century A.D. Some of the manuscripts belonged to the Mughal Imperial Library, Tipu Sultan's Library and Fort William College Library. Some are extremely rare and some are rich and varied in textual contents. They cover every branch of Islamic history and learning. In some, the calligraphy is most excellent while a few others bear miniature paintings of high quality and style, some of them being autographed.

***(c)* Sino-Tibetan and South-East Asian Section :** This Section comprises of manuscripts and Xylographs in Burmese, Chinese, Tibetan, Siamese etc. Chinese manuscripts relate to Chinese translations of the Indian Buddhist texts, while the Tibetan group includes the entire set of the *Kangyur* and the *Bstangyur*, besides also individual Xylographs and manuscripts. Manuscript works in Burmese, Siamese, Javanese, etc. are interesting for studies in the history and culture of these countries and also for study of Buddhism.

(d) English Section : This Section comprises a few English manuscripts in the Society. These are from Nathaniel Halhed, James Prinsep, Buchanan Hamilton, Alexander Csoma de koros and others.

Sanskrit

The manuscripts cover the period from 7th c. A.D. down to the 19th century. These are useful source materials to illustrate the development of the Indian scripts (especially Bengali, Nagari etc.). The colophons and post-colophons contain information relating to socio-economic conditions of the people. Besides, they help us to fix the chronology of the Royal dynasties of India. Where the inscriptions fail to ascertain dates and chronology, the manuscripts may throw some light, provided a thorough critical study of these and their colophons and postcolophons were made.

Some of the rare Sanskrit manuscripts may be mentioned here. *Brihati (from Kavindracharya's collection), Amrita Vindu (11th c.), Kiranavali, Charucharya, Nartaka Nirnaya, Parasika-prakasa, Sanskrita-ratnakara, Lalitavistara, Horoscope* of a muslim of the Mughal Court (1640 A.D.) *A Deed of Mortgage (1639), Ramayana (Bengali) of* Ramananda Yati, *Vajrayana* text *(11th c.),* a text on *Buddhist Nyaya, Rigveda Padapatha, Laghu-Kalachakra-tika, Kalachakravetara, Kuttanimatam, Vajravalinama mannadalopayika, Ramacharita* of Sandhyakar Nandi, *Bhattikavyatika of Srinivasa, and Paragali Mahabharata.*

The manuscript of *Kubjikamatam* is of the 7th Century A.D. The manuscript of *Rigveda Padapatha*, copied in 1362 A.D., is perhaps "the oldest manuscript of the Rigveda."

Islamic

Of the many Islamic Manuscripts there are some which are extremely rare and unique. Of these only a few may be mentioned: *Tahdhib Sharh As-Sab' at Mullaqat (early 12th c. Arabic), Qalaid al-Iquian wa Mahasin al-Ayan (12th c.), Kharidat al-Qasr (12th c.), Al-Jam Baynas as-Sahihin* abridged version with autograph, *(13th c.), A-Madkhul(13th c.), Tafsir-i-Quran (Persian, 13th c.,* important also for calligraphy*), Tuhfat al-Ahbar fi usul at Hadith wa'l Akhbar (15th c.), Kitab al-I'lan (18th c.), Saha' if-i-Shara' if* or *Duraral Mansur (Persian, 19th c.,* an autographed copy*),* and *Adab-i-Alamgiri (18th c.).*

Illustrated Manuscripts

There are large numbers of illuminated and illustrated manuscripts of different schools, many of which are unique for their calligraphy, delicacy of their lines, and elegance of composition and charming colour schemes. These miniatures still afford glimpses of India's past achievements, Of these unique manuscripts (earliest belonging to the 10th Century A.D.) mention may be made of a few: Astasahasrika Prajnaparamita, Aparimitayurnama Mahayana sutra, Pancharaksha, Paramarthanama Sangati, Devimahatmya, Viveka Panchamrita, Bhagavatgita, Shahnama, Kulliyat-i-Saadi, Suwaru'l aqalim, Farhang-i-Aurang Shahi, Ain-i-Akbari, Diwan-i-Makhfi, Qissa-i-Nush-Afarin, Jamiut-Twarikh, Amir nama Tutinama, Iyar-i-Danesh, Bihar-i-Danesh, Tarjuma Mahabharata, Tafrihul-Imarah (by Silchand, dedicated to J. H. Lushington), and Imaratut-Akbar (by Chitarmal for James Duncan).

Many scholars are using the collection for editing their texts and for translation in modern languages.

Archives/English Manuscripts

In the Library there are preserved a large number of old letters some of which date back to1784, just after the Society was founded. These letters were received by the Society from persons belonging to different walks of life, requesting information on such subjects as old and rare manuscripts, ancient monuments, coins etc. Some among the writers of these letters were persons well known for their literary, scientific and other cultural accomplishments. These old files constitute important documents relating to the history of the Society, as also of many other scientific and humanistic organisations that were established in India either in the 19th or in the 20th century.

Other Collections

Urdu

The Society has a fine collection of about 234 Urdu manuscripts many of which were received as a gift from the Fort William College (founded in 1800). Fort William College decided to award prizes, at the instance of J. S. Gilchrist, for standard original and translated works in the Hindusthani language, produced in the College.

Sino-Tibetan and Burmese

The Society has a complete set of Kanjur and Tanjur texts of the Buddhist scriptures and some extra-canonical works. These were collected by B. H. Hodgson and A. Csoma de koros. A section of the collection has been catalogued. There are over one hundred titles of Chinese books, some of which are rare and valuable for Chinese studies. These cover almost all the subjects relating to Chinese Culture, Civilization and Science and Buddhism. Subjects covered include Classical Literature, Language. History, Geography, Topography, Philosophy, Religion, manners and customs, biography of scholars, sciences (Botanical, Astronimical, Zoological).

Bengali Manuscripts

Other than Sanskrit, a few Bengali manuscripts have been found written by Bengali Brahmins residing in Varanasi. Parageli Mahabharat, Chuti Khan'sAsvamedha Parva, and many other important manuscripts were purchased. Mss. donated by Justice Ramaprosad Mukherjee and Sri A Roy enriched the collection. Now we have 703 Bengali Mss. and 12 Assamese manuscripts in the collection of the Asiatic Society. It comprises Asiatic Society's own collection, Government collection, Indian Museum collection and donors' collection. At present, the collection of Bengali manuscripts in the possession of Asiatic Society is rich in respect of number and rarity. The Society has manuscripts on Ramayana, Mahabharata, Srimadbhagavat, Mangala Kavyas, treatises on Vaisnava faith and its allied subjects. Folk literature, erotic verses and Vaisnaba Sahajiya Cult etc.

Rajasthani

The Society possesses very rare, valuable and important Raiasthani Manuscripts which date the pre-middle and middle years. Under the guidance of Dr. Sukumar Sen, the Society prepared and brought out a descriptive catalogue, Part 1, of the same in 1957.

Except a few short treatises on genealogies of Rajput warriors or Jain monks, the bulk belongs to eulogistic literature known as *Prashasti Kavya*. A few manuscripts are on traditional and Puranic themes, such as the story of the Goddess Karani, Krishna and Rukmini, Rama and Siva. Of special interest are the romances unique to Rajasthan and its literaure. The best known amongst them is the story of Dhola and Maru. There are other manuscripts which throw ample light on the rulers of Rajasthan.

2

BERLIN STATE LIBRARY, BERLIN

The Berlin State Library was initially founded in 1661 by the Grand Elector, Friedrich-Wilhelm of Brandenburg. From 1701 to 1918 it served as the Royal Library. Between 1918 and 1945 it was called the Prussian State Library. During World War II the holdings were evacuated into all parts of Germany. After the war they were divided between the German State Library, Unter den Linden, and the State Library - Prussian Cultural Foundation, Potsdamer Strasse. Since the beginning of 1992 the libraries were reunified under the name: Staatsbibliothek zu Berlin - Preussischer Kulturbesitz, (Berlin State Library).

The Oriental Department was founded in 1919 as a separate department of the Preussische Staatsbibliothek. It took its present structure on 1 January 1992 when the Department of Asia and Africa of the Deutsche Staatsbibliothek and the Oriental Department of the Staatsbibliothek Preussischer Kulturbesitz were amalgamated.

The Staatsbibliothek's Oriental collection is one of the largest in Europe; the scope and importance of the collection of Oriental manuscripts and blockprints means it is held in high esteem the world over. The Oriental Department collects books, periodicals, manuscripts, blockprints, microfilms and an increasing amount of electronic media on countries and peoples, cultures and religions (in particular Hinduism, Islam and Judaism), languages and literature, also in the respective languages, of the following regions: the Early and Christian Orient, Africa, Near and Middle East (including European parts of Turkey, Israel, the Caucasus, Islamic Central Asia), South Asia,

Southeast Asia, Oceania as well as what were temporarily Islamic regions of Europe.

Handwritten and printed works in Oriental languages had already formed part of the library's original stock in the middle of the 17th century. As the collections were expanded by extensive acquisition in the ensuing years, the drive towards appropriate administration of material and a growing public interest in the Orient led to the establishment of the Oriental Department in 1919, and the pening of the Oriental Reading Room at the Preußische Staatsbibliothek (Prussian State Library) in 1924. A generous acquisition policy in the first two decades earned the department its status as an internationally ecognised collection of oriental literature. Work was brought to a temporary standstill by World War Two and the relocation of all books and manuscripts during these years.

Some of the collections relocated during the war were brought to the Oriental Department (in 1969 named the Asia-Africa) Department of the Deutsche Staatsbibliothek (German State Library) in Berlin (East), others initially to Marburg and Tübingen and later to the Oriental Department of the Staatsbibliothek Preußischer Kulturbesitz in Berlin (State Library, Prussian Cultural Heritage) in Berlin (West). Some elements of the collection were either destroyed during the conflict and post-war years, or later traced to Eastern European libraries. Both departments developed independently of each other until 1991, but contact between the two was never completely broken off in the years before German reunification. In its own way, each section continued in the tradition of the Oriental Section of the Preußische Staatsbibliothek. While the Asia-Africa Department concentrated primarily on the collection and more specifically the presentation of modern literature and current sources of information, the Oriental Department focused on the collection, conservation and presentation of valuable oriental manuscripts. After the merging of the two libraries in 1992, the separate departments began their own process of unification, culminating in their spatial union in the Potsdamer Straße in November 1997.

The Oriental Department's responsibilities include:

Acquisition and cataloguing of printed materials in Asian, African and European languages originating in or concerning following areas and subjects:

* Ancient Near East and Ancient Egypt
* Islamic countries of the Near and Middle East, from North Africa to Afghanistan and Central Asia (inclusive of those parts of Europe which were in the past or still are Islamic)
* Caucasus (in co-operation with the East European Department)
* Africa
* Israel (as well as Hebrew Studies and Judaica)
* South Asia
* South-East Asia
* Pacific Ocean

Special collections

Oriental Studies in general, and South-East Asia (part of the special collection East and South-East Asia, for which the East Asia Department bears overall responsibility)

Acquisition, management and utilization of manuscripts and woodblock prints from all regions of Asia and Africa.

Printed Materials

Printed materials and microforms, which are acquired by the area/subject specialists of the Oriental Department, have always been part of the general holdings of the Staatsbibliothek, irrespective of language. Thus older acquisitions (published before 1956) are for the most part to be found at the site Unter den Linden , more recent acquisitions (published since 1956) at the site Potsdamer Strasse . Information concerning the exact distribution of the Orientalist holdings between the two sites can be had from the Services Department. The total holdings of the

Staatsbibliothek concerning the regions and subjects in the responsibility of the Oriental Department exceed 600.000 volumes (monographs, periodicals and microforms).

Together with the East Asia Department, the Oriental Department maintains a special reading room. Access to the Oriental Reading Room is limited to specialist readers.

The reference collection in the reading room contains approximately 30.000 volumes, primarily general and specialist bibliographies, reference and primary information materials concerning states, people, cultures, languages and literatures of Asia and Africa. The holdings are systematically arranged; they are listed partly in a separate catalogue, partly in the online public access catalogue StabiKat .

Printed books not in open shelves can be ordered by using the general ordering and lending system (Ausleihe). The library's Regulations on Fees and Usage for readers apply with regard to loans as well as reproductions; these regulations can be downloaded (heading "Benutzungsordnung", A-Z, homepage, Staatsbibliothek zu Berlin).

Collection of Manuscripts

The Oriental Department is custodian of all Oriental (including Far Eastern) manuscripts of the Staatsbibliothek, as well as its Tibetan and Mongolian woodblock prints. It also holds numerous photographs and microfilms of Oriental manuscripts in other collections.

The manuscripts holdings at present consist of more than 42.000 volumes and woodblock prints, as well as more than 180.000 microfilms. Most of these are copies of manuscripts in Nepalese collections. The Oriental Department is also responsible for administration and conservation of approximately 40.000 fragments of manuscripts which are part of the Berlin Turfan collections, owned partly by the Berlin-Brandeburg Academy Sciences and Humanities, partly by the Prussian Heritage Foundation. (Some further fragments are to be found in the Museum of Arts.

The manuscript collection encompasses some 80,000 originals and of these some 40,000 Turfan fragments from the Berlin-Brandenburgische Akademie der Wissenschaften (Berlin-Brandenburg Academy of Sciences) also administered by the Oriental Department. It also holds more than 180,000 microfilmed manuscripts, the bulk of them from Nepal. The use of such valuable materials is only possible in the Oriental and East Asia Reading Room and is subject to special conditions detailed in an information sheet available on site. Visitors are requested to acknowledge their acceptance of these conditions by signing a file card. Both the Oriental and East Asia Departments share the Oriental and East Asia Reading Room, which is open to specialist researchers. The reference library contains some 30,000 volumes, contains general and specialized bibliographies, as well as key reference books on the countries, peoples, cultures, languages and literatures of Asia and Africa. The Oriental manuscript collection contains pieces of enormous scholarly and historical importance, as well as of great artistic quality.

The oldest written document in the Staatsbibliothek is a fragment of an Egyptian Book of the Dead from the New Kingdom (c. 12th century B.C.). Other highlights include a codex of the Book of Proverbs in Achmimic-Coptic dialect from the 3rd century A.D., magnificent volumes from the Near East, as well as illuminated manuscripts from Persia, India and Southeast Asia. The "Saray Albums" were acquired in 1817 with the collection of the diplomat H.F. von Diez. They contain examples of central Asian and Persian book illustrations from the 14th and 15th centuries, bound together for an Ottoman sultan at a later date. The "Jahangir Album" is also highly significant in the history of Islamic-Indian book illustration. It was made between 1608 and 1618 for the Mughal Emperor Jahangir, and contains selected miniatures and calligraphies, framed with opulent gold ornamentation and drawings. Also of particular note is a group of Mamluk manuscripts from Egypt (14th and 15th centuries),

Koran fragments in Kufi script (dating from the 7th-10th centuries, among them seven pages of one of the oldest known Koran manuscript), Imperial Ottoman documents as well as several opulent Hebrew manuscript volumes including the Bible "Erfurt 1" – the largest known Hebrew parchment manuscript dating from 1343, prayer books such as the "Hamilton Siddur" (Spain, 13th century), and the celebratory prayer book according to the German ritual from the 15th century. Last but not least, there are the manuscript fragments from Central Asia in the Berlin Turfan Collection. These texts in more than 20 scripts and languages were discovered at the beginning of the 20th century, and have not yet been completely deciphered or published.

Digitisation of Manuscripts

The Oriental Department has begun to digitise manuscripts selected from its holdings. In co-operation with the University of Frankfurt and the Tamai-Foundation all Tocharian fragmentsfrom the Berlin Turfan collections have been digitised. This project aims at presenting digital images together with transcriptions and transliterations of the texts.

In co-operation with the Berlin-Brandenburg Academy of Sciences all Middle Iranian and Uighur fragmentsare being digitised; the project is sponsored by the German Research Foundation (Deutsche Forschungsgemeinschaft). The Oriental Department also participates in the Shahnama Project. This project is being financed by the British Academy; working-groups in Cambridge and Edinburgh are recording and digitising all illustrations contained in manuscripts of the Iranian national epic. The digital images will be presented in an on-line database together with information on the individual manuscripts. The Oriental Department is co-operating with the Max-Planck-Institute for the History of Science, Berlin, in the digitisation of some of its manuscripts which are of importance for the history of science.

Restoration

The Conservation Studio of the Staatsbibliothek has for some years been working on the restoration of a two-volume Hebrew bible, badly damaged during the Second World War (Ms or fol 1210/1211). This is the largest known Hebrew manuscript on parchment, also known as "Erfurt 1".

The Oriental Department's collections are partly listed in the library's central catalogue (including StaBiKat – http://stabikat.de –INCLUDEPICTURE "A:\\Staatsbibliothek zu Berlin Departments_files\\link_intern_666666.gif" * MERGEFORMATINET —), and partly in the department's own catalogues. Some of the older printed works and their relevant catalogues are located at the Unter den Linden site. The special collections, for example manuscripts or blockprints, have their own catalogues. Many of the manuscripts from the Staatsbibliothek collections are listed in the "Verzeichnis der Orientalischen Handschriften in Deutschland".

Catalogues

"Katalogisierung der Orientalischen Handschriften in Deutschland" (The Union Catalogue of Oriental Manuscripts in German Collections, or KOHD): founded in 1957, initially funded by the Deutsche Forschungsgemeinschaft (German Research Foundation). Since 1990, the project has been pursued by the Akademie der Wissenschaften zu Göttingen (Göttingen Academy of Sciences), in conjunction with the Oriental Department in Berlin, and is funded by the German government. Researchers publish the "Verzeichnis der Orientalischen Handschriften in Deutschland" (Union Catalogue of Oriental Manuscripts in Germany, or VOHD); 111 catalogues and 49 supplementary volumes have been produced to date.

The director of the Oriental Department has also been the director of the Union Catalogue of Oriental Manuscripts in Germany (Katalogisierung der Orientalischen Handschriften in Deutschland, KOHD), since its foundation, in 1957, under the auspices of the German Orientalist Society (Deutsche Morgenländischen Gesellschaft). The project was financed until 1989 by the German Research Foundation (Deutsche Forschungsgemeinschaft). Since 1990, it has been a research project of the Göttingen Academy of Sciences.

Most of the printed catalogues of Oriental manuscripts in the Staatsbibliothek were published in two monograph series:

* Die Handschriften-Verzeichnisse der Königlichen Bibliothek zu Berlin (23 volumes, 1853-1914)
* Verzeichnis der Orientalischen Handschriften in Deuschland (VOHD; at present 111 volumes of catalogues and 49 supplementary volumes, since 1961)
* Survey of the groups of special materials in the Oriental Department according to shelf numbers
* Published catalogues listed by languages

The Library has brought out catalogues of its manuscript's holdings available in various languages including Ethiopian, Arabic, Armenian, Burmese, Chinese, Georgian, Hebrew, Indian, Nepalese, Persian, Javanese, Turkish, Sanskrit. Urdu etc. and also some others on the basis of geographical regions. But the collection being discussed here mainly focus on the language of the Far East.

Arabic manuscripts:

* Wilhelm Ahlwardt: Verzeichniss der Arabischen Handschriften der Königlichen Bibliothek zu Berlin. 1-10. Berlin, 1887-1899. (Handschriften-Verzeichnisse. 7-9, 16-22)
* Rudolf Sellheim: Arabische Handschriften. Reihe A: Materialien zur arabischen Literaturgeschichte. 1.2. Wiesbaden, Stuttgart, 1976-1987. (VOHD 17,A,1.2)
* Ewald Wagner [et al]: Arabische Handschriften. Reihe B,1. Wiesbaden, 1976. (VOHD 17,B,1)

* Gregor Schoeler: Arabische Handschriften. Reihe B,2. Stuttgart, 1990. (VOHD 17,B,2)
* Rosemarie Quiring-Zoche: Arabische Handschriften. Reihe B,3. Stuttgart, 1994. (VOHD 17,B,3)
* Rosemarie Quiring-Zoche: Arabische Handschriften. Reihe B,5. Stuttgart, 2000. (VOHD 17,B,5)
* Hars Kurio: Arabische Handschriften der "Bibliotheca orientalis Sprengeriana" in der SBPK. Berlin, Freiburg, 1981. (Islamkundliche Materialien. 7)

Indian and Nepalese manuscripts:

* Albrecht Weber: Verzeichniss der Sanskrit-Handschriften. Berlin, 1853. (Handschriften-Verzeichnisse. 1)
* Albrecht Weber: Verzeichniss der Sanskrit- und Prakrit-Handschriften der Königlichen Bibliothek zu Berlin. 2,1-3. Berlin, 1886-1892. (Handschriften-Verzeichnisse. 5)
* Walter Schubring: Die Jaina-Handschriften der Preussischen Staatsbibliothek. Leipzig, 1944. (Verzeichnis der Handschriften im Deutschen Reich. 3,1,1)
* Klaus L Janert: Indische Handschriften. 1. Wiesbaden, 1962. (VOHD 2,1)
* Klaus L Janert, N Narasimhan Poti: Indische und nepalische Handschriften. 2. Wiesbaden, 1970. (VOHD 2,2)
* E R Sreekrishna Sarma: Indische Handschriften. 3. Wiesbaden, 1967. (VOHD 2,3)
* Klaus L Janert, N Narasimhan Poti: Indische und nepalische Handschriften. 4. Wiesbaden, 1975. (VOHD 2,4)
* Klaus L Janert, N Narasimhan Poti: Indische Handschriften. 5. Wiesbaden, 1979. (VOHD 2,5)
* Klaus L Janert, N Narasimhan Poti: Indische Handschriften. 6. Wiesbaden, 1980. (VOHD 2,6)

* N Narasimhan Poti: Indische Handschriften. 7. Stuttgart, 1986. (VOHD 2,7)
* N Narasimhan Poti: Indische Handschriften. 8. Stuttgart, 1987. (VOHD 2,8)
* N Narasimhan Poti: Indische Handschriften. 9. Stuttgart, 1990. (VOHD 2,9)
* Klaus L Janert: Indische Handschriften. Generalregister A für 2,1-6. Wiesbaden, 1982. (VOHD 2,10)
* Klaus L Janert: Indische Handschriften. Generalregister B für 2,7-9. Stuttgart, 1991. (VOHD 2,11)
* Gerhard Ehlers: Indische Handschriften. 13. Stuttgart, 1999. (VOHD 2,13)
* Gerhard Ehlers: Indische Handschriften. 15. Stuttgart, 2003. (VOHD 2,15)
* Siegfried Lienhard, Thakur Lal Manandhar: Nepalese Manuscripts. 1: Nevari and Sanskrit. - Stuttgart, 1988. (VOHD 33,1)

Islamic manuscripts:

* Ernst Kühnel, Hermann Götz: Indische Buchmalereien aus dem Jahangir-Album der Staatsbibliothek zu Berlin. Berlin, 1923. (Buchkunst des Orients. 2)
* M S Ipsiroglu: Saray-Alben. Diez'sche Klebebände aus den Berliner Sammlungen. Wiesbaden, 1964. (VOHD 8)
* Ivan Stchoukine [et al]: Illuminierte islamische Handschriften. Wiesbaden, 1971. (VOHD 16)
* Max Weisweiler: Der Islamische Bucheinband des Mittelalters nach Handschriften aus deutschen, holländischen und türkischen Bibliotheken. Wiesbaden, 1962. (Beiträge zum Buch- und Bibliothekswesen. 10.)

Japanese manuscripts and woodblock prints:

Eva Kraft: Japanische Handschriften und traditionelle Drucke aus der Zeit vor 1868.[1.] Wiesbaden, 1982. (VOHD 27,1)

Middle Iranian manuscripts:

* Mary Boyce: A catalogue of the Iranian manuscripts in Manichaean script in the German Turfan Collection. Berlin, 1960. (Deutsche Akademie der Wissenschaften zu Berlin, Institut für Orientforschung. Veröffentlichung. 45)

Persian manuscripts:

* Wilhelm Pertsch: Verzeichniss der Persischen Handschriften. Berlin, 1888. (Handschriften-Verzeichnisse. 4)
* Wilhelm Heinz: Persische Handschriften. 1. Wiesbaden, 1968. (VOHD 14,1)

Sanskrit manuscripts from Turfan:

* Ernst Waldschmidt [et al]: Sanskrithandschriften aus den Turfanfunden. 1-3. Wiesbaden, 1965-1971. (VOHD 10,1-3)
* Lore Sander, Ernst Waldschmidt: Sanskrithandschriften aus den Turfanfunden. 4. Wiesbaden, 1980. (VOHD 10,4)
* Lore Sander, Ernst Waldschmidt: Sanskrithandschriften aus den Turfanfunden. 5. Stuttgart, 1985. (VOHD 10,5)
* Klaus Wille: Sanskrithandschriften aus den Turfanfunden. 6-9. Stuttgart, 1989-2004. (VOHD 10,6-9)

Tibetan manuscripts and woodblock prints:

* Hermann Beckh: Verzeichnis der tibetischen Handschriften der Königlichen Bibliothek zu Berlin. Erste Abteilung: Kanjur. Berlin, 1914. (Handschriften-Verzeichnisse. 24.)
* Manfred Taube: Tibetische Handschriften und Blockdrucke. 1-4. Wiesbaden, 1966. (VOHD 11,1-4)
* Dieter Schuh: Tibetische Handschriften und Blockdrucke sowie Tonbandaufnahmen tibetischer Erzählungen. 5. Wiesbaden, 1973. (VOHD 11,5)
* Dieter Schuh: Tibetische Handschriften und Blockdrucke. 6. Wiesbaden, 1976. (VOHD 11,6)

* Friedrich Wilhelm, Jampa Losang Panglung: Tibetische Handschriften und Blockdrucke. Teil 7. Wiesbaden, 1979. (3-515-02819-6)
* Dieter Schuh: Tibetische Handschriften und Blockdrucke. 8: Sammlung Waddell. Wiesbaden, 1981. (VOHD 11,8)
* Peter Schwieger: Tibetische Handschriften und Blockdrucke. 9. Stuttgart, 1985. (VOHD 11,9)
* Peter Schwieger: Tibetische Handschriften und Blockdrucke. 10-12. Stuttgart, 1990-1999. (VOHD 11,10-12)
* Manfred Taube: Die Tibetica der Berliner Turfansammlung. Berlin, 1980. (Berliner Turfantexte. 10.)

Turkish manuscripts:

Alttürkische Handschriften / Old Turkish manuscripts:

* Dieter Maue: Alttürkische Handschriften. 1: Dokumente in Brahmi und tibetischer Schrift. Stuttgart, 1996. (VOHD 13,9)
* Gerhard Ehlers: Alttürkische Handschriften. 2: Das Goldglanz-Sutra und der buddhistische Legendenzyklus Dasakarmapathavadanamala. Stuttgart, 1987. (VOHD 13,10)
* Simone-Christiane Raschmann: Alttürkische Handschriften. 5-6: Berliner Fragmente des Goldglanz-Sutras. Stuttgart, 2000-2002. (VOHD 13,13-14)
* Jens Wilkens: Alttürkische Handschriften. 8: Manichäisch-türkische Texte der Berliner Turfansammlung. Stuttgart, 2000. (VOHD 13,16)
* Jens Wilkens: Alttürkische Handschriften. Teil 9: Buddhistische Beichttexte. Stuttgart, 2003. (VOHD 13,17)

Ottoman manuscripts:

* Wilhelm Pertsch: Verzeichniss der Türkischen Handschriften. Berlin, 1889. (Handschriften-Verzeichnisse. 6)

* Barbara Flemming: Türkische Handschriften. 1. Wiesbaden, 1968. (VOHD 13,1)
* Manfred Götz: Türkische Handschriften. 2. Wiesbaden, 1968. (VOHD 13,2)
* Hanna Sohrweide: Türkische Handschriften und einige in den Handschriften enthaltene persische und arabische Werke. [3.] Wiesbaden, 1974. (VOHD 13,3)
* Manfred Götz: Türkische Handschriften. [4.] Wiesbaden, 1979. (VOHD 13,4)
* Hanna Sohrweide: Türkische Handschriften. 5. Wiesbaden, 1981. (VOHD 13,5)

Urdu manuscripts:

* S Mujahid Husain Zaidi: Urdu-Handschriften. Wiesbaden, 1973. (VOHD 25)

3 BIBLIOTHEQUE NATIONALE, PARIS

Bibliotheque Nationale is one of the most pretigeous libraries of the world. It is located in France. The collections of Bibliotheque Nationale are very rich on oriental subjects and scholars from all over the countries refer their resources, especially on the subject of history.

The beginning of the Bobliotheque Nationale can be traced to the year 1368 when the personal library of Charles V moved into the Louvre, in the Tour de la Fauconnerie. At that time, the inventory drawn up by Gilles Malet, guardian of the library, showed that the collection contained only nine hundred and seventeen manuscripts. In those days, however, royal collections were transient in nature as they were irretrievably dispersed on their owner's death. It was not until Louis XI, who reigned from 1461 to 1483 and was the true founder of the Bibliothèque Nationale, that continuity was established - reflecting the continuity of the royal dynasty. His son Charles VIII, followed by Louis XII, subsequently added more early manuscripts as well as the first printed books brought back from the Italian campaigns. The collection was never again to be dispersed.

The Bibliotheque was transferred to Amboise and then to Blois, where it was incorporated into the new "*Librairie*" set up in Fontainebleau by François I in 1522 and entrusted to the care of Guillaume Bude, scholar in the humanities. On the 28th December 1537, the king introduced a new principle by royal decree, whereby all printers and booksellers were ordered to deposit copies of any printed book put on sale in the kingdom with the Château de Blois library. This obligation was known as the "*Dépôt Légal*" (legal or copyright deposit) and its creation marks a fundamental date in the history of the library, even though the decree was by no means uniformly enforced in the early stages. A 1622 inventory still lists only 4 712 manuscripts and printed works. In the second half of the 16th. century, the library was transferred to Paris and sustained considerable damage during the Wars of Religion.

The Library's hitherto greatest period of expansion came under the auspices of Colbert, the leading French statesman under Louis XIV, whose ambition was to make the *Bibliothèque* an instrument testifying to the glory of his sovereign. Colbert moved its contents to a Paris quarter which it still occupies to this day, by transferring the royal collections for which there was no more space at the Louvre into two small houses which he owned in the rue Vivienne. He actively implemented a collection-improvement policy, purchasing or receiving as gifts a large number of private collections such as the one on French history belonging to Loménie de Brienne, or the collection belonging to the orientalist Gilbert Gaulmyn.

Within a few decades, the Bibliothèque had become Europe's leading library. The number of books had grown to such an extent that librarians could no longer rely on their memory to locate them. Nicolas Clément, who had entered the service of the *Bibliothèque du Roi* (the royal library) in 1670, established a classification system for printed material whose guiding principles endure to this day. The works are divided into twenty three categories, each of which is represented by a letter of the alphabet : the first four for religious subjects, two for law and jurisprudence, ten for history, four for philosophy, science and art, and three for literature. Manuscripts are classified according to language and subject. It was the Abbe Bignon, who became Librarian to the King in 1719, who brought the library to the peak of its splendour. In 1720 he organised the library into five departments, each one supervised by a guardian : Manuscripts, Printed Books, Titles and Genealogy, Engraved Plates and Prints, Medals and Stone Engravings. Bignon continued his predecessors' work in improving the collections, and was particularly anxious to acquire all major works by European scholars. Aiming to widen access to the wealth of the library, he opened up larger parts of its collections to scholars and also to those merely wishing to satisfy their curiosity in various fields. In 1720, it was decided by Council decree that as well as allowing scholars to consult the collections, the library would also open to the public "once a week, from eleven in the morning to one hour after mid-day". Finally, in 1721, Bignon made the first transfer of the royal library collections to the Richelieu buildings.

The French Revolution

The Revolutionary period was a time of profound upheaval for the library. Legal deposit provisions were abolished for three years, and library staff came under suspicion. Yet during that time the library, which had become the *Bibliothèque Nationale* instead of the *Bibliothèque du Roi*, found its holdings considerably increased due to the confiscation of property in France and abroad : church property, collections belonging to emigrants, private princely collections, etc. In this way, private collections owned by Louis XVI, Marie-Antoinette and Madame Elizabeth found their way into the national collections. It has been estimated that some two hundred and fifty thousand books, fourteen thousand manuscripts and eighty thousand engravings came to the library during this crucial period in the constitution of the national heritage of France.

19th. to 20th. century : new means and resources

The sudden influx of material resulting from confiscation policies during the Revolution brought still greater urgency to the problems of lack of space already besetting the library. The first half of the nineteenth century was a time of prolonged trial and error. While large numbers of people were pressing for the library to be housed elsewhere, others were becoming impatient with the accumulating backlog in cataloguing its material. In 1858, a commission chaired by Prosper Mérimée drew up a report on the changes needed in the organisation of the *Bibliothèque Impériale*, as it had then become. The conclusions of this report were adopted in part by Napoleon III, who entrusted the rebuilding of some of the library's premises on the same site to the architect Henri Labrouste. Labrouste restored the Hôtel Tubeuf and the Galerie Mazarine, landscaped the Vivienne garden, and built new premises along the rue de Richelieu and the rue des Petits Champs on the Hôtel Chevry site. Labrouste is particularly remembered for the Printed Books reading room (1868) which features a triumph of cast-iron work. Resources were also allocated to continue the work of printing catalogues. These advances continued under Léopold Delisle, the medievalist and administrator general of the library from 1874 to 1905. Delisle was responsible for initiating work on the Master Catalogue of Printed Books (*Catalogue général des livres imprimés*), of which the Authors section was only completed in 1981. After Victor Hugo's celebrated bequest in 1881, Delisle gave the first impulse to a policy promoting the acquisition of authors' manuscripts.

Extension and modernisation

The library continued to expand throughout the twentieth century, with three annexes built in Versailles in 1934, 1954 and 1971, the opening of a new catalogue and bibliography room (1935 - 1937) and a periodicals reading room (1936), the installation of the Engravings department next to the Hôtel Tubeuf (1946) and the transfer of maps and plans to the Hôtel Tubeuf (1954). In 1958, the central printed materials stockrooms were raised and a specialist Oriental Manuscripts department created. New premises were built at 2, rue Louvois in Paris to house the Music Department and Sound Archives (1964). Administrative departments were housed in a new office building in1973, and in 1985, several buildings on either side of the Galerie Colbert at 2-4 rue de Vivienne were converted to accommodate the computer department and administrative facilities for incoming printed material.

Digitisation of both printed books and graphic material is well under way. For technical and economic reasons, documents have been processed primarily in image mode to begin with. Most of the texts selected for digitisation are out-of-copyright material making up an encyclopaedic collection on the human and social sciences which includes original material, peer reviews, reference works and a collection of journals which are either major research references or difficult to find elsewhere. The 100000 digitised images are drawn from document collections held outside the Bibliothèque nationale de France and from patrimonial collections selected among its own departments. The digitised collections are distributed through the internal Bibliothèque nationale de France network, but once the various technical and legal problems involved in on-line communications have been resolved, all digitised documents will be available through the various "information highways".

Like many other libraries, the Bibliothèque nationale de France provides free access to the Internet through its reading room workstations (though not to fee-paying data bases). The library also offers free introductory sessions to Internet searching, as well as a selection of Internet sites chosen for their quality and relevance to disciplines covered by the library's various thematic holdings.

The first version of the Bibliothèque nationale de France Web site was launched onto the Internet in 1996, providing descriptions of its collections, practical information, news, programmes of events and professional information. Thanks to private sponsorship, 1 000 illuminations from 11 painted manuscripts were digitised to form a searchable data set focusing on the life and times of Charles V, entitled Charles V et son temps (1330-1380). Finally - and perhaps most importantly as access statistics show - the site provides free access to the BN-OPALE and BN-OPALINE data bases containing more than 2.5 million bibliographic references, which may be searched in Telnet mode. As the new integrated information system becomes fully operational, readers will be able to search the library's entire catalogue covering printed material from Gutenberg to the present as well as sound recordings and audiovisual material, totalling some 8 million references.

Gallica an Internet server was first set up to test on-line searching of Bibliothèque nationale de France digitised collections, together with fixed image collections produced jointly with the Musée de l'Homme, the Maison Pierre Loti and the National school of civil engineering document centre. By October 1998, the pilot set of material made available in October 1997 will have been expanded to include 5 000 books and periodicals, including 900 ($$illisible) from the Frantest data base produced by the CNRS (National centre for scientific research), and 20 000 fixed images. Although Gallica currently focuses on the 19th century in France, the material to be added by 1999 will provide a much wider historical perspective, with a total of 50 000 documents covering the Middle Ages through to the eve of the First World War and including a wide range of disciplines : science and the history of science, economics, law, politics, philosophy, literature and travelogues, history and ethnology. Gallica thus provides students, researchers and the general public with opportunities to consult contemporary editions, reference texts and monographs, rare periodicals and early images (prints and photographs), many of which had previously been difficult to locate. Data base contents may be searched via an indexed bibliography, or in full text through monograph and journal contents lists. Users may also access the contents through a chronological subject-based overview of the entire data base. For non specialists in particular, navigating is greatly facilitated by the hypertext links provided in a general introduction to the Gallica collection.

Oriental Manuscripts

The Department of Manuscripts (Eastern Division) of the Bibliotheque Nationale holds a large number of oriental manuscripts. They have been collected over the last many centuries by different enthusiastic persons. François I had already some manuscripts in Arabic and in Hebrew in his "Bookshop", but, to speak about a collection about Eastern manuscripts, it is necessary to await the reign of Louis XIV and the vigorous policy of acquisition inspired by Colbert according to two major axes: the purchase of collections of scholars or amateurs in France and the sending of missions of acquisition in the East.

The library of the King grew rich then by several collections: that of Gilbert Gaulmin, 588 manuscripts in Hebrew, Arabic, Persian and Turkish bought in 1667; the following year, an exchange with the library of the College of the Four-Nations, heiress of the collections of Mazarin, gets to the king more than 2 000 manuscripts (of which first Chinese books entered to the library). In same time, the Vansleb father, sent by Colbert to Raising, forwards to the library nearly 600 manuscripts in Arabic, Persian, Turkish, Hebrew, syriaque, copte or Ethiopic, bought between 1671 and 1675 in Cyprus, Aleppo, Cairo and Constantinople.

Widened in India and China, acquisitions continue throughout XVIII E century, according to the policy initiated by Colbert, whose personal collection, more than 6 000 manuscripts acquired by the Library of the King in 1732, enriches the Eastern collections by 637 volumes. The Revolution, while nationalizing the goods of the clergy, brings to the young national Library a thousand of Eastern manuscripts, 500 in Hebrew, 340 in Arabic, resulting for the majority from the libraries from Saint-Germain-des-Prés, the Oratory and the Sorbonne.

During the 19th and 20th centuries, the purchases, the legacies or the gifts of significant collections and the product of the scientific expeditions constitute the principal sources of increase. The purchases on sale public are added to it, near booksellers or of private individuals.

For this period, among remarkable acquisitions, one can quote:

* **the collection Asselin de Cherville** , 1515 Arabic manuscripts especially, bought in 1833;
* **the Schefer collection** , 791 manuscripts of very first order in Arabic, Persian and Turkish, bought in 1899;
* **the Goupil-Aubin collection** , 385 manuscripts Mexican, posthumous gift of Eugene oupil in 1898;
* **the collection Antoine d' Abbadie** , more than 200 Ethiopian manuscripts bequeathed to the Institute, deposited with the national Library in 1902;
* **collections brought back by the mission Paul Pelliot in China and Central Asia in 1910:**
    * several thousands of manuscripts former to the XI century, in Chinese, tibétain, Sanskrit, in koutchéen, khotanais some, in sogdien and ouïgour;
    * a whole of 3 000 sheets of concise stampings of inscriptions;
    * a collection of Chinese books of more than 2 000 titles (more than 30000 booklets);
* **the Griaule collection** , 366 bought Ethiopian manuscripts with Gondar in 1932 by the Dakar-Djibouti mission which Marcel Griaule directed;
* **the sinological library of Paul Pelliot** , more than 30 000 volumes in all languages, 1946.

The policy of acquisition of the previous centuries continues through purchases, gifts and exchanges. The enrichment of the databases, printed or periodic, in all languages and concerning all the cultural surfaces of the old East constitutes the essential axis of it.

The very high number of old copies, *unica,* scientific texts, decorated manuscripts and manuscripts with paintings confers on this collection a very particular interest and puts it at the row the best.

* Manuscripts: 45 000 volumes
* Xylographes: 60 000 volumes
* Stampings: 4 000 sheets
* Printed: 100 000 volumes
* Microforms: 8 000 reels

They are classified in about fifty categories by language or collection:

* *Africa and the Middle East*: African, Arab, Armenian, Assyrien, Berber, Copte, Egyptian, Abyssinian, Abyssinian of Abbadie, Géorgien, Harari, Hebrew, Persian, Sabéen, Samaritan, Syriaque, Turk
* *South Asia* : Indian, Faded, Sanskrit
* *Asia of South-east* : Indochinese, Vietnamese
* *The West Indies and Oceania* : Austronesian
* *Central Asia and Eastern*
* *Melt Pelliot of Central Asia* : Chinese Pelliot, Chinese Pelliot Douldour-âqour, Pelliot khotanais, Pelliot koutchéen, Pelliot ouïgour, Pelliot ouïgour cave 181, Pelliot Sanskrit, Pelliot sogdien, Pelliot tibétain, Pelliot xixia, Pelliot various
* *America* : American, Angrand, Mexican
* *Various collections* : Asselin various, Burnouf Papers, Papers of orientalists, Papers Leon Feer, Chinese Smith-Lesouëf, Japanese Smith-Lesouëf, Smith-Lesouëf manuscripts, Vietnamese Smith-Lesouëf

Successor to the old Bibliothèque Royale, the Bibliothèque Nationale has assembled collections of Islamic manuscripts formed over the centuries and regularly augmented by purchases and gifts; these collections rank among the most important in Europe and cover nearly all subjects (total ca. 12,000). Especially noteworthy are some Qurânic manuscripts of the first centuries after Hijra. These are kept in the Départment des Manuscrits, Division des Manuscrits Orientaux.

4
BODLEIAN LIBRARY, OXFORD

Oxford is a unique and historic institution. As the oldest English-speaking university in the world, it can lay claim to nine centuries of continuous existence. There is no clear date of foundation, but teaching existed at Oxford in some form in 1096 and developed rapidly from 1167, when Henry II banned English students from attending the University of Paris.

Oxford early on became a centre for lively controversy, with scholars involved in religious and political disputes. John Wyclif, a 14th-century Master of Balliol, campaigned for a bible in the vernacular, against the wishes of the papacy. In 1530, Henry VIII forced the University to accept his divorce from Catherine of Aragon. During the Reformation in the 16th century, the Anglican churchmen Cranmer, Latimer and Ridley were tried for heresy and burnt at the stake in Oxford. The University was Royalist in the Civil War, and Charles I held a counter-Parliament in Convocation House.

In the late 17th century, the Oxford philosopher John Locke, suspected of treason, was forced to flee the country. The 18th century, when Oxford was said to have forsaken port for politics, was also an era of scientific discovery and religious revival. Edmund Halley, Professor of Geometry, predicted the return of the comet that bears his name; John and Charles Wesley's prayer meetings laid the foundations of the Methodist Society.

The University assumed a leading role in the Victorian era, especially in religious controversy. From 1833 onwards The Oxford Movement sought to revitalise the Catholic aspects of the Anglican Church. One of its leaders, John Henry Newman, became a Roman Catholic in 1845 and was later made a Cardinal. In 1860 the new University Museum was the scene of a famous debate between Thomas Huxley, champion of evolution, and Bishop Wilberforce. Frm 1878, academic halls were established for women, who became members of the University in 1920. Since 1974, all but one of Oxford's 39 colleges have changed their statutes to admit both men and women. St Hilda's remains the only women's college.

During the 20th century, Oxford added to its humanistic core a major new research capacity in the natural and applied sciences, including medicine. In so doing, it has enhanced and strengthened its traditional role as an international focus for learning and a forum for intellectual debate.

The University of Oxford's total student population numbers over 17,000 (students in residence, 2002-2003). Almost a quarter of these students are from overseas, and more than 130 nationalities are represented among our student body. Over 5,600 students are engaged in postgraduate work. Of these, around 3,000 are working in the arts and humanities. Every year 16,500 people take part in courses offered by the University's Department for Continuing Education. Our admissions office is in contact with more than 5,000 schools and colleges across the UK, and our admissions staff visit a school, college or Higher Education Fair nearly every working day of the year.

Oriental Collections

The Department of Oriental Collections is diffused in its organisation, and comprises six distinct units distributed between five different locations. Some of these individual libraries are historically separate, and have only recently been incorporated into the Bodleian. Furthermore, coverage of many of the major subject areas is not restricted to a single location.

The Bodleian Library is the main research library of the University of Oxford. It is also a copyright deposit library and its collections are used by scholars from around the world. The buildings within the central site include Duke Humfrey's Library above the Divinity School, the Old Schools Quadrangle with its Great Gate and Tower, the Radcliffe Camera, Britain's first circular library, and the Clarendon Building.

In addition, the Bodleian consists of nine other libraries, in separate locations in Oxford: the Bodleian Japanese Library, the Bodleian Law Library, the Hooke Library, the Indian Institute Library, the Oriental Institute Library, the Philosophy Library, the Radcliffe Science Library, the Bodleian Library of Commonwealth and African Studies at Rhodes House and the Vere Harmsworth Library.

In addition, the Bodleian consists of nine other libraries, in separate locations in Oxford: the Bodleian Japanese Library, the Bodleian Law Library, the Hooke Library, the Indian Institute Library, the Oriental Institute Library, the Philosophy Library, the Radcliffe Science Library, the Bodleian Library of Commonwealth and African Studies at Rhodes House and the Vere Harmsworth Library.

The Library has acquired Oriental printed books and manuscripts since its refoundation in 1598 by Sir Thomas Bodley, himself a Hebraist. The Department's current acquisitions largely reflect the teaching and research undertaken in the University in Hebrew, Islamic, South Asian and Far Eastern studies, and important collections are also maintained in areas such as Central Asia, Southeast Asia and Tibet.

The Department comprises six libraries on five separate sites, with holdings of some 500,000 volumes. Many of its collections have an importance that is truly international, and are being made accessible to scholars through both published and automated catalogues.

5
BRITISH LIBRARY, LONDON

Britain is one of the richest countries of the world as far as the availability of the cultural resources is concerened. Since it ruled the largest part of the land, the records of human history were accumulated in its libraries and museums.

The British Library is relatively young. Its immediate roots lay in the report of the National Libraries Committee under the Chairmanship of the late Lord Dainton issued in 1969, followed in 1971 by a White Paper recommending the setting up of a national library for the UK ('the British Library'). In 1972 The British Library Act was passed by Parliament bringing the Library into operation with effect from 1 July 1973.

Under the Act the following institutions were administratively combined to form the British Library: the library departments of the British Museum (which included the National Reference Library of Science and Invention), the National Central Library, and the National Lending Library for Science and Technology (the centre for interlibrary lending, located at Boston Spa in Yorkshire). In 1974 the British National Bibliography and the Office for Scientific and Technical Information joined the UK's new national library.

Two additional institutions subsequently became part of the Library increasing the breadth of its collections: the India Office Library and Records (1982) and the British Institute of Recorded Sound (1983).

Constituent parts

Library of the British Museum

To the library community and the public at large, the best

known component of the new national library consisted of the library departments of the British Museum. The Museum's Department of Printed Books was founded in 1753, the year of the foundation of the Museum itself. Over the intervening two hundred years, the library of the British Museum had grown into one of the largest in the world, sustained by its privilege of legal deposit whereby it was entitled to a copy of most items printed in the United Kingdom - not only books and periodicals, but newspapers, maps and printed music. In addition, the Museum's comprehensive holdings of non-legal deposit items had reportedly earned it the accolade from Lenin of possessing (in the 1900s) a more comprehensive collection of Russian books than libraries in Moscow and St Petersburg.

Lenin was one of those privileged to use the Museum's spectacular domed reading room. Designed in the 1850s at the instigation of Sir Anthony Panizzi, then Chief Librarian, the reading room and surrounding bookstacks were constructed in the courtyard of the British Museum providing its library with impressive premises in the heart of what was already an overcrowded building. The Reading Room had been thrown open to all for a short period at the time of its opening in May 1857, thereafter admission was by pass only, giving access to its collections an aura of selectivity and exclusiveness. In addition to Lenin (who used the pseudonym Jacob Richter), the roll call of those holding reader passes included Karl Marx, Charles Dickens, George Bernard Shaw and Virginia Woolf.

Patent Office Library (from 1962 National Library of Science and Invention)

Another constituent part of the British Library was the library of the Patent Office. Its origins lay in the Patent Law Amendment Act of 1851 which required "true copies of all specifications to be open to the inspection of the public at the office of the commissioners", the Patent Office library itself opened in 1855. For the remainder of the nineteenth century this was housed in cramped accommodation and it was not until 1902 that purpose built premises were opened in Southampton Buildings off Chancery Lane - an impressive 'Galleria' style structure by the architect Sir John Taylor. As with the Museum's library, despite new premises, the Patent Office collections soon suffered severe shortage of space.

The Second World War highlighted the need for a comprehensive scientific and technological network in the UK, specifically for a national library of science and technology. In the late 1940s and 50s there was considerable debate among the Scientific Community whether the collections of the libraries of the British Museum or the Patent Office should serve as the nucleus of this: the position was resolved in 1959 when a Working Party on the issue recommended that the proposed library should be based on the collections of both libraries and put under the control of the Museum Trustees. The National Reference Library of Science and Invention (as it was called) was set up in 1962, administratively as part of the British Museum library.

National Central Library

National Lending Library for Science and Technology

The third major component of the British Library consisted of the National Central Library or NCL which began operation in 1916 in London and the National Lending Library for Science and Technology (NLLST), in service since 1961 at Boston Spa in Yorkshire. These were amalgamated in 1973 as the British Library Lending Division (BLLD).

The function of the Lending Division was to support the library systems of the UK by providing a loan and photocopy service to other libraries throughout the country.

The NLLST had a stock specialising in science and technology, containing 25,000 monographs and subscriptions to 1,200 serials; its staff numbered 120. Around 600 tons of the NCL stock, which specialised in humanities and social sciences, was transferred to Yorkshire during the Library's first year of formation. The semi-rural site at Boston Spa occupies around 60 acres of an ex-munitions factory and is well served by road links for easy distribution.

During the 1970s the range of services was expanded and made available to international customers and use of technology became a more integral part of the service. The use of Automated Requesting grew by about 40% in this time and the Lending Division often acted in collaboration with academic and scientific partners in early days of exploring the future of fax transmission and satellite communications.

In 1985, the title was changed to the BL Document Supply Centre to reflect the changing emphasis of document supply in which a greater proportion of requests were for copies of articles rather than loans. The stock has grown over the years and now contains over 260,000 journal titles, over 3 million books, almost 500,000 conference proceedings and almost 5 million reports, mostly of a scientific nature.

Current business from document supply totals about four million requests per year from 20,000 customers worldwide. In 2001 the 100 millionth request was received. Services are now provided not just to the traditional customer base of UK and international librarians and information professionals, but also to commercial and business users and individual researchers. Use of the Web has provided direct access to our collection information and supply services, and location is no longer an issue for distribution, as document supply moves increasingly to electronic delivery.

Other constituent organisations

Two institutions became part of the British Library in 1974: the British National Bibliography (BNB) and the Office of Scientific and Technical Information (OSTI).

Starting in 1950, BNB had been a run as a commercial company and its functions had been to produce and publish a weekly listing of all British publications and to develop a computer based system for storing and handling bibliographic information for the use of libraries and the book trade. OSTI was transferred from the Department of Education and Science to become the Library's Research and Development Department (in 1999 the functions of this were transferred from the British Library to the Library and Information Commission.

In 1982 the India Office Library and Records were transferred to the British Library from the Foreign and Commonwealth Office: these contained the entire archives of British India from the foundation of the East India Company in 1600 to independence. The following year (1983) the Library took over the British Institute of Recorded Sound, a unique institution which specialised in collecting sound recordings. Subsequently renamed the Sound Archive, this is now the largest sound archive in the world.

The British Library at St Pancras

The 1971 White Paper recognised that the constituent bodies of the proposed British Library (principally the British Museum Library) were seriously short of space and that rehousing the collections was a priority. However, legislation setting up the British Library made no reference to this nor to the geographical location of the new institution.

Shortage of storage space for the collections was not new. As early as the 1910s it was clear that the Museum's library was suffering from a lack of space as the ceaseless intake of books, periodicals and other materials continued without interruption. (By this time newspapers had been transferred from Bloomsbury to premises originally outside London, now the Newspaper Library at Colindale. The Museum building and collections sustained a number of direct hits by German bombers in the early 1940s which caused some of the original bookstacks to be rebuilt after 1945. By now lack of space was a major problem, and solution to this - leasing storage space in the Royal Arsenal at Woolwich in the early 1960s - was a short term expedient. In the

1960s the Museum considered extending its library premises in Bloomsbury, abandoned in 1967.

The initial plan at the time of the Library's formation was that lending activities would be concentrated at Boston Spa, and reference, research, and bibliographic services would be united and rehoused in a second complex, adjacent to the British Museum in London. The Library's first annual report for 1973-74 stated " A new building on the Bloomsbury site is the British Library's most urgent need ".

Colin St John Wilson, an architect who had previously worked on the 1960s scheme for extending the library of the British Museum, produced a plan for a new building adjacent to the Museum. However, in 1974, in response to local opposition to a building of that size being constructed in an historic area of central London, the Government abandoned the idea of housing the Library in Bloomsbury. The nearest vacant site to the environs of the Museum (where much of the Library's large collection of books and other material was kept) capable of housing so many items, staff and services was a derelict goods yard immediately to the west of St Pancras station.

The British Library was formally opened by HM The Queen in June 1998. Since then it has become firmly established as a major addition to London's library, intellectual and cultural scene.

Oriental Manuscripts

Oriental language manuscripts are viewed as valuable and rich collections in the British Museum and India Office Library and constitute probably the most comprehensive accumulation of Asian and African material in the world. With the complementary collections of the India Office Library, the combined department now holds about 65,000 oriental manuscripts (plus thousands more fragments in the Stein, Genizah and other collections), some 900,000 printed books in oriental languages and about 120,000 volumes of oriental periodicals and newspapers. Asian and North African language collections cover over 350 languages or language groups, ranging from Chinese, spoken by one-third of the world's population, to languages of the New Guinea group spoken by only a few hundred people.

The main language groups covered under the category of oriental disciplines are:

Arabic	Lao
Armenian	Malay
Bengali	Manchu
Burmese	Mongolian
Cambodian	Nepali
Chinese	Panjabi
Coptic	Persian
Ethiopic	Philippine
Georgian	Sanskrit
Gujarati	Syriac
Hebrew	Tamil
Hindi	Thai
Indonesian	Tibetan
Japanese	Turkic
Javanese	Urdu
Korean	Vietnamese

We have confined this survey to some selected languages and have neither included Asian and South East Asian Languages nor the languages of Non-Arab Africa.

Arabic Collection

The Library's collection of Arabic manuscripts is world-famous. It is one of the largest such collections in Europe or North America, comprising almost 14,000 manuscripts, representing nearly 20,000 works. It is renowned for the importance of many individual items, from some of the finest calligraphic and illuminated manuscripts of the Holy Qur'an to autograph and other high-quality copies of major legal, historical, literary and scientific works. The collection of Arabic printed books is among the largest in the UK and is made up of over 60,000 items, together with over 600 periodical titles. Current acquisitions policy aims to maintain a broad coverage of the humanities and social sciences by obtaining material from a number of Middle Eastern countries, focusing principally on Egypt, Lebanon, Syria, Jordan and the Palestinian Authority.

Some Arabic language books are held by the Science Technology and Business (STB) collections. These include specialised dictionaries, science publications, and some official publications. The Sound Archive holds an extensive collection of Arabic sound recordings.

Western language books about the Arab world are included in the main Humanities collections and the holdings of the Document Supply service in Yorkshire. The Document Supply Service holds many publications which are not held in London, particularly United States' social science publications, and Western-language serials relating to the Arab world. Some works in Western languages on the Arab world are among the holdings of the Oriental and India Office Collections. Most of these items are included in the Humanities on-line catalogues but a very small number are listed only in the Arabic printed catalogues. It is worth checking the printed catalogues if a particular Western language item cannot be found elsewhere. Newspapers in Arabic are held by the Oriental and India Office Collections, but English/ European-language newspapers from the Arab world are held by British Library Newspapers.

Persian Collections

The holdings, like most of those in oriental languages in Asia Pacific & Africa Collections (APAC), consist of three elements: material collected by the India Office Library prior to 1982; material collected by the British Museum Department of

Oriental Printed Books and Manuscripts prior to 1973; and subsequent acquisitions of the British Library era. Together they form a research collection recognised as being of world-ranking importance, especially strong in material from the Subcontinent.

The collection comprises well over 30,000 volumes of printed books and periodicals, approximately 12,000 manuscript texts in about 9,000 volumes of various types: archival materials (includes non-published and mixed material), maps (includes all types of cartographic material), music (only includes printed and manuscript music), newspapers (includes microfilm editions), official publications, and visual materials (includes photographs, prints, drawings, videos and films).

The manuscript collections originate from the whole of the Islamic world, in particular Iran, Central Asia and India, ranging in time from the 12th century to handwritten and typed texts of recent years, and are strong in most of the traditional fields of humanities and religious studies. Many of the Persian manuscripts are copies of rare texts, and the arts of the book are copiously represented at the highest level: illustrated volumes include some of the most famous miniature paintings of the Persian and Mogul schools.

Printed books and periodicals are from all parts of the Persian-speaking world and the Iranian diaspora, and ranging in date from early Iranian and Indian imprints to a selection of the latest publications. The collection includes numerous rarities from Iran, Afghanistan and India. Since the 1960s especially, a wider selection of subjects has been covered.

Catalogue Information

Catalogue of the Persian manuscripts in the British Museum. Rieu, C. London: British Museum, 1879-83. 3 vols. Reprinted 1966.

Supplement to the Catalogue of Persian manuscripts in the British Museum Rieu, C. London: British Museum, 1895. Reprinted 1966.

Handlist of Persian manuscripts, 1895-1966. Meredith-Owens, G. M. London: British Museum, 1968.

Catalogue of Persian manuscripts in the Library of the India Office. Ethe, H. Oxford, 1903-37. 2 vols. (vol. 2 revised and completed by E. Edwards). Reprinted London, 1980.

Hand-list of Islamic manuscripts acquired by the India Office Library, 1936-8. Arberry, A. J. Journal of the Royal Asiatic Society, 1939, part 3 (July), pp. [353]-396.

Notes on Islamic manuscripts recently acquired by the India Office Library. Arberry, A. J. Islamic Culture, vol. 13 (1939) , pp. 44-58.

Handlist of Islamic manuscripts acquired by the India Office Library 1938-85. Sims-Williams, U. London: India Office Library and Records, 1986.

Catalogue of two collections of Persian and Arabic manuscripts preserved in the India Office Library. Ross, E. Denison, and Browne, E. G. London, 1902.

A descriptive catalogue of miscellaneous Persian Mughal documents from Akbar to Bahadur Shah II. Shakeb, M. Z. A. London: India Office Library and Records, 1982.

A descriptive catalogue of Persian letters from Arcot and Baroda. Shakeb, M. Z. A. London: India Office Library and Records, 1982.

A descriptive catalogue of the Batala collection of Mughal documents, 1527-1757.

Shakeb, M. Z. A. London: British Library, 1990.

Supplementary handlist of Persian manuscripts, 1966-1998. Waley, M. I. London: British Library, 1999.

Catalogue of the Library of the India Office, Vol. II, Part VI: Persian books. Arberry, A. J. London: [India Office], 1937.

Catalogue of the Persian printed books in the British Museum. Edwards, E. London: British Museum, 1922.

Union catalogue of Persian serials & newspapers in British

libraries. Sims-Williams, U. London: Ithaca Press for the Middle East Libraries Committee, 1985.

Miniatures from Persian manuscripts: catalogue and subject index of paintings in the British Library and the British Museum. Titley, N. M. London: British Library, 1974.

Persian paintings in the India Office Library: a descriptive catalogue. Robinson, B. W. London; New York: Sotheby Parke Bernet, 1976.

North Indian Collections

Catalogues and Publications:

Assamese

Bengali

Gujarati

Hindi

Marathi

Oriya

Panjabi

Nepali and Newari

Collections

Manuscripts, Printed books (the printed books in oriental languages comprise not only works in oriental languages but also translations from an Oriental language into a European language) and Serials.

India: Rajasthan, Himachal Pradesh, Uttar Pradesh, Madhya Pradesh, Bihar, Bengal (Bangla), Tripura, Nagaland, Assam, Manipur, Orissa, Gujarat and Maharashtra.

Bangladesh

Nepal

Includes 8 major languages plus minor languages:

Major languages: Assamese; Bengali; Gujarati; Hindi; Marathi; Nepali; Oriya, and Panjabi.

Minor languages: Santhali; Konkani; Manipuri; Naga, et al.

Catalogues and Publications

Assamese

Catalogue of Bengali, Assamese and Oriya manuscripts, pp.34.

J. F. Blumhardt, Catalogue of the Marathi, Gujarati, Bengali, Assamese, Oriya, Pushtu and Sindhi manuscripts in the Library of the British Museum. London, 1905 (6 Assamese manuscripts).

J. F. Blumhardt, Catalogue of the Bengali and Assamese manuscripts in the India Office Library. London, 1924.

D. Ghosh, The handlists of Assamese, Bengali, Gujarati and Rajasthani mss. in the India Office Library. (4 Assamese items).

Proscribed Publications

Graham Shaw & Mary Lloyd (eds.), Publications proscribed by the Government of India: A catalogue of the collections in the India Office Library and Records and the Department of Oriental Manuscripts and Printed Books, British Library Reference Division. London, 1985. (About 5 books).

Bengali

There are about 41 manuscripts and 144 Bengal factory documents from the India Office Library and 37 manuscripts from the Oriental Collections of the British Museum / British Library. The manuscripts are on various topics, but, mainly religious poetry.

J. F. Blumhardt, Catalogue of the Marathi, Gujarati, Bengali, Assamese, Oriya, Pushtu and Sindhi manuscripts in the Library of the British Museum. London, 1905.

Classed Inventory of items acquired since 1906. Available for consultation in the OIOC Reading Room.

J. F. Blumhardt, Catalogue of the Bengali and Assamese manuscripts in the Library of the India Office. London, 1924.

Anisuzzaman, Factory correspondence and other Bengali documents in the India Office Library and Records: supplementary to J. F. Blumhardt. London, 1981.

Dipali Ghosh, A handlist of Bengali manuscripts in the India Office Library. London, 1993.

Gujarati

J. F. Blumhardt, Catalogue of the Marathi, Gujarati, Bengali, Assamese, Oriya, Pushtu and Sindhi manuscripts in the Library of the British Museum. London, 1905. (57 Gujarati items).

Classed Inventory. Includes 30 Gujarati items acquired since 1906.

J. F. Blumhardt, Catalogue of the Gujarati and Rajasthani manuscripts in the Library of the India Office. London, 1954. (19 Gujarati items).

Dipali Ghosh, The handlist of Assamese, Bengali, Gujarati and Rajasthani manuscripts in the Library of the India Office. London, 1993. (30 Gujarati items).

A. Gaur, Indian Charters of Copper Plates. London, 1975. (includes 2 Gujarati items).

Hindi/Urdu

There are about 286 manuscripts (139 from OC's collection and 147 items from IOL), ranging in date from the 17th to the 20th century and in subject-matter from history and poetry to medicine and divination.

J. F. Blumhardt, Catalogue of Hindi, Panjabi and Hindustani manuscripts in the Library of the British Museum. London, 1899.

D. Ghosh, A handlist of Hindi manuscripts in the Oriental Collections since Blumhardt's catalogue, 1899.

J. F. Blumhardt, A draft catalogue of Hindi manuscript of the IOL (Mss. Eur.D.500), unpublished.

A. Master, A short title catalogue of Hindi manuscripts of IOL.1954.

Dipali Ghosh, A handlist of all the Hindi IOL manuscripts. London, 1993.

Marathi

There are 258 Marathi manuscripts (OC: 81 and IOL: 177). They are either in Devnagari or in Modi scripts.

J. F. Blumhardt, Catalogue of the Marathi, Gujarati, Bengali, Assamese, Oriya, Pushtu, and Sindhi manuscripts in the Library of the British Museum. London, 1905.

Classed Inventory. Includes 7 Marathi ietms acquired since 1906 (74 items).

J. F. Blumhardt and Sadashiv Govind Kanhere, Catalogue of the Marathi manuscripts in the India Office Library. Oxford, 1950.

A handlist of the Marathi manuscripts in the India Office Collections, compiled by Dipali Ghosh. (175 items).

Oriya

J. F. Blumhardt, Catalogue of the Marathi, Gujarati, Bengali, Assamese, Oriya, Pushtu and Sindhi manuscripts in the Library of the British Museum. London, 1905. (10 Oriya items).

Classed Inventory (Includes 31 items, acquired since 1906). Available in the Oriental Reading Room.

J. F. Blumhardt, Catalogue of the Oriya manuscripts in the Library of the India Office. London, 1924. (50 items).

Punjabi

J. F. Blumhardt, Catalogue of Hindi and Punjabi manuscripts in the Library of the British Museum. London, 1899.

Classed Inventory. includes 19 items acquired since 1899.

C. Shackle, Catalogue of the Panjabi and Sindhi

manuscripts in the India Office Library. London, 1977.

Nepali and Newari

G. E. Marrison, Handlist of manuscripts in Nepali, Newari and Sanskrit in the Department of Oriental Manuscripts and Printed Books. Typescript, 1973.

Classed Inventory. Includes 16 Nepali and 11 Newari manuscripts in the OC's collections.

There is no printed catalogue for the Minor Languages, but blue slips and card catalogues are available in the Oriental Reading Room on request, recent books are on OPAC. There is no manuscript available in the collection.

Sanskrit Collections

The library holds about 10,800 Sanskrit and Prakrit manuscripts from the medieval and modern periods; and 1,700 Pali manuscripts. Over 3,500 Sanskrit and Gandhari manuscript fragments in brahmi and Kharosthi scripts respectively dating between the first and eleventh centuries AD. Early copperplate charters, rubbings and estampages represented in significant numbers.

The manuscript collections include the earliest known Buddhist manuscripts (the Gandhari birchbark scrolls, Or. 14915) and the earliest datable Sanskrit manuscript (Macartney and Godfrey, Or. 6403-04). The Stein, Hoernle, Kashgar and Gilgit manuscripts are rich in Buddhist sutra literature form the fourth to the tenth centuries, from Dunhuang, Khadalik and other Silk Road oases. Later Buddhist manuscripts, especially from Nepal, are numerous. Hindu manuscripts covering religion, literature, law, science, astrosciences and medicine, date from the tenth century or earlier (Or. 3568). Vedic manuscripts are well represented, numbering over 600, including accented texts and grhya and srauta ritual texts.

The collection is particularly strong in illustrated Himalayan manuscripts beginning with the Pala period; Jaina manuscripts; and western Indian manuscript illumination.

The printed book collections, especially monographs-in-series and "Vernacular Tracts" (but including Sanskrit), are especially strong in publications between 1867 and 1947 owing to the copyright legislation then in force. Pali texts both in manuscript (Nevill, Turnour collections) and printed in the scripts of Sri Lanka, Burma and Thailand, as well as Devanagari and Roman, form an important source for the study of Theravada Buddhism in all the countries where it was practised.

Printed Catalogues:

Catalogue of the Sanskrit manuscripts in the British Museum. Bendall, C. London, 1902.

Catalogue of Sanskrit and Prakrit manuscripts in the British Museum vol. II. Losty, J . Unpublished typescript. Classed inventory Manuscript register in 2 vols kept in OIOC Reading Room at Or Gen MSS 15

Catalogue of the Sanskrit and Prakrit manuscripts in the Library of the India Office.

Eggeling, J., Keith, AB, and Thomas, FW. London, 1887-1935. 2 vols.

Catalogue of two collections of Sanskrit manuscripts preserved in the India Office Library. Tawney, CH, and Thomas, FW. London, 1903.

Catalogue of the Nevill Collection. Nevill, H. Unpublished manuscript. 4 vols.

List of Pali, Sinhalese, Sanskrit and other manuscripts, formerly in the possession of Hugh Nevill sq. Barnett, L.D.

Unpublished manuscript.

Catalogue of the Hugh Nevill Collection of Sinhalese manuscripts in the British Library. Somadasa, K.D. London, 1987-95. 7 vols.

Catalogue of the Pali printed books in the India Office

Library. Raper, T.C.H., ed., and O'Keefe, M.J.C., rev. London, 1983 .

Ancient Buddhist Scrolls from Gandhara: the British Library Kharosthi fragments. Salomon, R. London/Seattle, 1999.

Preliminary list of manuscripts in languages of Central Asia and Sanskrit, from the collections ade by Sir Marc Aurel Stein, KCIE. Barnett, L.D.

Unpublished typescript (n,d,).

Indian charters on copper plates. Gaur, A. London, 1975.

Catalogue of Sanskrit, Pali and Prakrit Printed Books in the British Museum. Haas, E., Bendall, ., and Barnett, L.D. London, 1876-1928. 4 vols.

Catalogue of the Library of the India Office, vol. 2, part 1: Sanskrit books. Natha, P., Chaudhuri, J.B. and Napier, C.F. London, 1938-57. 4 vols.

Bibliography of South Asian periodicals: a union-list of periodicals in South Asian languages.

Shaw, G.W. and Quraishi, S. Brighton, 1982.

South Indian Collections

Tamil Collection

The South Indian Languages collection is made up of both the historic and modern collections of the British Library, and the India Office Library and Records. It includes materials in major and minor languages of South India.

The major languages in South India today are: Tamil, Telugu, Kannada and Malayalam. The minor languages are several and these are: Brahui, Gondi, Kui, Malto, Oraon (Kurukh), Toda, Tulu and Konkani (in Kannada script). Today, Tamil is the state language of Tamil Nadu, Telugu - the state language of Andhra Pradesh, Kannada - the state language of Karnataka, and Malayalam - the state language of Kerala. Of the minor languages, Tulu and Konkani are the only active languages and modern works continue to be published in these languages forming part of the literature of Karnataka State.

The collection comprises of manuscripts in both paper and palm leaves, copper plates, printed books and periodicals and newspapers, a small collection of South Indian classical music in audio casettes, and video casettes of interviews with eminent South Indian authors. It should noted that our collections in South Indian Languages contain a significant amount of literature centred around Sanskrit language and literature in our pre 1950's collections and hence, entries for classical works will also be found in our Sanskrit catalogues.

A number of South Indian Languages publications are listed in the catalogue by Graham Shaw and Mary Lloyd called the Publications proscribed by the Government of India: A catalogue of the collections in the India Office Library and Records and the Department of Oriental Manuscripts and Printed Books, British Library Reference Division. London, 1985.

Manuscripts have to ordered using manual tickets. Since quite a great number of South Indian Languages printed materials are stored in Woolwich items from the copy flow catalogues beginning with shelfmarks Tam, Tel, Kan, Mal etc., can be ordered on the reading room OPACs using the Direct Requesting option and selecting OIOC Printed Books and Serials. This also applies to South Indian Languages printed materials shelved in Basement 2 bearing shelfmarks beginning with 14— from the OC printed catalogues. In the same manner, periodicals can also be ordered on the Direct Requesting options.

Turkish and Turkic Collections

First of all there is the numerical and historical importance of the Turkic peoples, with a spread - in cultural terms - from Sarajevo to Kashghar. Most of the lands in between have at some time been under Turkish rule. The Seljuks, Mamluks, Timurids, Moghuls, Ottomans, and Qajars were all Turks. Secondly, the Turkic peoples have their own distinctive cultural forms, both within and outside the matrix of Islamic civilization. Modern research shows that the best of their literature, art, crafts and architecture bears comparison with the best of other Muslim peoples. Turkish rulers and patrons played a leading part in sustaining a form of Sunni Islam that prevailed for centuries. Thirdly there is the geopolitical importance of the Turkish world today, from the Republic of Turkey on the border of Europe and Asia, modernizing apace, to the newly independent states of Central Asia and northern Azerbaijan, the Tatars and other peoples within Russia's borders, and the Uighurs.

What, then, can the Library offer to those concerned with Turkish and Turkic studies? What are our collections like? Where are they? What has been done to augment and document them? It is hoped that the following pages will provide basic answers to these questions.

Tibetan Collections

The library holds ca.2700 blockprints and ca. 850 manuscripts the majority of which stem from the southern and central regions of Tibet. The collection also includes a number of official letters and documents from various Dalai and Panchen Lamas.

The Tibetan Buddhist canon in its various editions is particularly well represented. There are two copies of the sNar thang edition of the bka' 'gyur and bstan 'gyur. A manuscript bka' 'gyur from Shel dkar (related to the rGyal rtse Them spangs ma manuscript bka' 'gyur) also known as the 'London Kanjur'. Parts of the Peking edition of the bka' 'gyur. An illuminated late 18th century manuscript of the rNying ma rgyud 'bum from South Tibet.

The Tibetan part of the Stein Collection comprises ca. 3500 fragmentary paper documents (out of approximately 27,000) and 2350 wood slips.

As for modern printed books (Western and pothi style), there are Tibetan texts published in India, Tibetan language publications from the People's Republic of China (all subjects); reprints of sDe dge and Peking bka' 'gyur and bstan 'gyur. Bonpo canon: bstan 'gyur (Lhasa), and bka' 'gyur (Chengdu).

The collection also includes Microforms of Phug brag bka' 'gyur, dGa' ldan bstan 'gyur, Pelliot Tibétain.

Catalogue Information

Modern printed books from India and China are included in the British Library Public Catalogue. Transliteration scheme for modern printed books: Library of Congress.

Collection Printed Catalogues

Location List to the Texts in the Microfiche Edition of the Sel dkar (London) Manuscript bKa' 'gyur. Pagel, Ulrich and Gaffney, Sean. London: British Library, 1996.

Catalogue of Tibetan Manuscripts and Blockprints outside the Stein Collection in the India Office Library. Denwood, Phillip. 1975.

Unpublished typescript.

Catalogue of the Tibetan Manuscripts from Tun-huang in the India Office Library, Oxford. La Vallée Poussin, Louis de. 1962.

6
THE CHESTER BEATTY LIBRARY, DUBLIN

The Chester Beatty Library was founded by Sir Alfred Chester Beatty in 1950. It houses a large collection of Oriental and Western manuscripts and art. The Library is now located in a new extension to the old "Clock Tower" building in the grounds of Dublin Castle. It moved here in 1999, from its old home in a large house in Shrewsbury Road where it first opened its doors in 1954.

The Library is a treasure trove for anyone who is interested in the great religions and cultures of the world, and houses one of the very best collections of its kind. The artefacts and exhibits include ancient manuscripts, prints, miniature paintings, icons, early editions of printed books, and objets d'art from countries and Continents all around the world, such as Asia, the Middle East, Europe, and North Africa. More on these later, but first lets take a look at the man who was responsible for Ireland housing such a magnificent collection.

Alfred Chester Beatty was actually an American, born in New York City in 1875. Beatty was a respected mining engineer, who travelled the world on the various projects undertaken by his company. In 1911 he left America, and set up home in London, in 1912 buying a property, Baroda House, in Kensington Palace Gardens. Since his early childhood he had been an avid collector of all sorts of various objects of interest, including stamps, minerals, and such diverse things as Chinese snuff bottles. On his travels around the globe he began to collect more widely, buying, in particular, a wide selection of both European and Persian manuscripts.

In 1914, he visited Egypt, where he purchased some beautifully decorated copies of the Koran in the bazaars, and a visit to Asia in 1917 added Chinese and Japanese painting to his growing list of interests. He was primarily attracted to these manuscripts by their fine bindings and the rich illustrations, as well as the magnificent calligraphy, but he was also concerned to preserve the texts for posterity and for their historic value.

During the Second World War he was responsible for supplying the Allies with many strategic war materials, and he was later to receive a Knighthood from the British government in recognition of this valuable contribution to the war effort. He moved to Dublin in 1950, and built his library on Shrewsbury Road specifically to house his collection, and in recognition of this he became Ireland's first ever Honorary Citizen in 1957. Upon his death in 1968, he bequeathed his whole collection to the Irish people, and thanks to the generous and on-going support given by the Irish Government, it has since become one of the country's national institutions.

The Library

As stated earlier, in 1999 the Library moved to its new custom-built home in the precincts of Dublin Castle. Access is through the Castle's gardens, and there is a lovely glass-roofed entrance hall that links the new exhibition centre with the old 18th century Clock Tower.

On the ground floor there is a lecture theatre, small souvenir shop, and a restaurant, and here visitors can also avail themselves of a good audio-visual presentation on the life of Sir Chester Beatty and his great art collection.

The actual galleries and collection itself are situated on the first and second floors.

First Floor Gallery

As one enters the First Floor Gallery there is a display dedicated to Sir Chester Beatty and his collection, and a fine bust of the great man himself by the celebrated sculptor Carolyn Mulholland. This section contains many beautiful works of art from the Islamic, East Asian, and Western worlds. There is also a collection of fine miniature paintings from the old courts of the Mughal Emperors of India, illuminated Persian manuscripts, fine European printed books, bindings and drawings, and a whole range of exquisite calligraphy from all round the world.

Audio-visual presentations are available here to explain in more detail all the intricate techniques of print-making, paper-making, and book production.

Second Floor Gallery

The Second Floor Gallery is wholly dedicated to all the great religions of the world, including Christianity, Buddhism, Islam, and Hinduism. There are again audio-visual presentations exploring such topics as the history of the Muslim pilgrimage to Mecca, the lives of Buddha and Christ, and the rites of passage – birth, marriage and death – in the different belief systems.

One of the outstanding exhibits in this gallery is a collection of illuminated copies of the Koran, dating from as early as the 9th century, and going all the way to the 19th century.

There are ancient papyri from Egypt, including the famous Egyptian love poems from around 1100 BC, and also some of the very earliest Gospel and New Testament texts, dating back to 200 AD. These Christian texts are a fundamental source of information for all serious scholars of early Christianity, and the ancient texts of the Koran represent the very best expressions of Islam in terms of calligraphy and illumination.

There are also fine displays of fine scrolls and other religious artworks from Japan, China, Tibet, and South and Southeast Asia.

The collection of the Library contains early papyri, including some of the earliest texts of the Bible, in addition to other early Christian manuscripts, western prints and printed books. The Library also mounts special temporary exhibitions, (generally 2-3 per year).

The Library's collections are presented in two permanent exhibitions: "Sacred Traditions" and "Artistic Traditions". The "Sacred Traditions" Gallery exhibits sacred texts, illuminated manuscripts and miniature paintings from the Christian, Islamic and Buddhist traditions. The gallery also contains smaller displays on Confucianism, Daoism, Sikhism and Jainism. The "Artistic Traditions" gallery is devoted primarily to works of art on paper, techniques of print-making, binding and paper-making and the art of miniature painting. The display draws on manuscript holdings, rare printed books and decorative arts. The exhibition is introduced by a display dealing with the life and work of Sir Alfred Chester Beatty.

The Western collections

The Western collections contain the earliest items in the Library with examples of inscribed cuneiform clay tablets and a large collection of papyrus rolls and codices from ancient times.

The early Christian, Manichaean and Coptic papyri include many unique texts as well as some of the earliest examples of the Gospels.

The collections include medieval and Renaissance illuminated manuscripts from Western Europe and later calligraphic documents. The collections also include manuscripts from the Christian Orient - Byzantium, Syria, Armenia and Ethiopia. The illuminations and illustrations found in the manuscripts and printed books are augmented by a collection of over 33,000 Old Master prints.

Oriental Manuscripts

The systematic acquisition of Oriental manuscripts for the Bibliothèque du Roi, the royal library, began under Colbert, whose policy was directed towards the purchase of scholars' and collectors' material on the one hand, and the organization of expeditions to the East on the other. The Oriental collection in the Manuscripts department contains documents in more than one hundred different languages on a wide variety of media - papyrus, parchment, paper, leather, silk and ivory. They include 30,000 manuscript volumes and 280,000 printed volumes, mostly xylographs in Chinese, Japanese, Tibetan, Manchu and Mongolian, as well as a collection of rubbings obtained during archeological expeditions in Egypt, China, Cambodia and Nepal. Arab, Persian, Hebrew, Sanskrit and Indian manuscripts form the largest collections, but there is also a major collection of Chinese and Tibetan manuscripts brought back from Central Asia by the Pelliot expedition. Manuscripts from the western world Some 120,000 Western manuscripts dating from the fifth century A.D. to the present are organized into collections by linguistic group: French (the great majority), Latin, Greek and Modern Languages (from English to Romanian, from Italian to Scandinavian, among many others). These collections are encyclopedic in nature and contain material ranging from illuminated medieval manuscripts (some 10,000 of these form the world's largest museum of medieval painting) and historical items including medieval charters and chronicles in particular, to classical Greek and Latin literature including reference manuscripts for successive editions of the classics, Romance literature and modern and contemporary literature, together with manuscripts of the most famous French authors.

The present collections include mainly Persian, Turkish and Arabic manuscripts, most of which are adorned with illustrations, illuminations and fine bindings. They contains almost four thousand Arabic, Persian and Turkish manuscripts including many superb copies of the Qur'ân. The Islamic Collection is one of the finest in existence and is internationally renowned for the overall high quality and scope of its material. The Library houses examples of the earliest Islamic manuscripts, dated to the ninth and tenth centuries CE, through to those produced in the early years of the twentieth century.

The Islamic Collections are amongst the finest in existence and are internationally renowned for the overall high quality and scope of the material.

The manuscripts that comprise the collections range in date from the eighth century to the early years of the 20th century. They derive primarily - though not exclusively - from the Arab world, Iran, Turkey and India, and include some of the greatest documents of Islamic art and culture. Together they illustrate in exquisite form and detail the history and development of all aspects of the Islamic book: calligraphy, illumination, miniature painting, and bookbinding.

Pictured: Artistic Traditions Gallery: Islam

The Islamic Collections consist of five sub-collections. The Qur'an Collection includes more than 260 Qur'ans and Qur'an fragments and is one of the most important collections of Qur'ans outside the Middle East. The gem of the collection - and indeed one of the most treasured objects of the entire Library - is the splendid Qur'an copied in Baghdad in the year 1001 by Ibn al-Bawwab, one of the three greatest medieval Islamic calligraphers.

The Persian Collection consists mainly of copies of the works of the great Persian poets - Firdawsi, Nizami, Sa'di, Hafiz and Jami, to name but a few. Highlights of the approximately 330 manuscripts that make up the collection include illustrated folios from the so-called Great Mongol (Demotte) Shahnama, or Book of Kings, of about 1335, and a fragmentary copy of this same text made in the late 16th century for the Safavid ruler, Shah 'Abbas the Great. One of the most beautiful and most extensively illuminated manuscripts in the Library is a copy of the Gulistan of Sa'di, made in the 1420s for Baysunghur, one of history's greatest patrons of the book and a prince of the Timurid dynasty that ruled much of Iran throughout the 15th century.

The Library's Mughal-era Indian Collection comprises both illustrated manuscripts and a breathtaking array of almost one thousand individual paintings, produced in India during the period of Mughal rule for Islamic, Hindu and also European patrons. The collection is of especial renown and encompasses some of the finest examples of painting produced under the guidance of the emperors Akbar, Jahangir and Shah Jahan. Prominent amongst these are the illustrated folios from the Akbarnama, or History of Akbar, and the numerous portraits of the emperors themselves.

The Turkish Collection consists of just over 160 manuscripts, making it the smallest of the Islamic Collections. Nevertheless, it too is extremely important. Patronage of the arts, including the arts of the book, on behalf of the Ottoman sultans of Turkey peaked in the 16th century. The Turkish Collection includes some of the greatest manuscripts produced in this period, such as a rare, illustrated volume of the Life of the Prophet Muhammad and an illustrated History of Suleyman the Magnificent.

Most of the manuscripts of the Qur'an, Persian, Mughal and Turkish Collections have exquisite calligraphy and are magnificently illustrated and illuminated. In contrast to these manuscripts, however, is the approximately 2650 manuscripts of the Arabic Collection, few of which contain any decoration at all. These were collected by Chester Beatty for their texts, and many are in fact unique texts, preserved only in the Chester Beatty Library. They embrace a vast range of topics: religion, jurisprudence, history, geography, medicine, astronomy, mathematics and linguistics, to name but a few, as well as many early translations into Arabic of the works of the ancient Greeks.

The Islamic Collection consists of several sub-collections. Of these, the Qur'ân Collection, comprising some 250 manuscripts, is of special importance and is rivalled only by that of the Topkapi Sarayi in Istanbul, Turkey. Manuscripts of note are a Qur'ân of 972, the earliest dated Qur'ân copied on paper, and another copied some nine centuries later for the Ottoman Sultan cAbdulmecid, the binding and illuminations of which are exceptionally exquisite. However, the real gem of the collection

- and indeed one of the most treasured objects of the entire Library - is the splendid Qur'ân copied by the famed calligrapher Ibn al-Bawwâb in Baghdad in the year 1001.

The published manuscripts are in the following books:

1. A. J. Arberry, The Koran Illuminated: A Handlist Of The Korans In The Chester Beatty Library, 1967, Hodges Figgis & Co Ltd., Dublin.
2. David James, Qur'âns And Bindings From The Chester Beatty Library: A Facsimile Exhibition, 1980, World of Islam Festival Trust, London.

A. J. Arberry, The Chester Beatty Library: A Handlist Of The Arabic Manuscripts, 1955, Vols. 1-8, Emery Walker (Ireland) Ltd., St. Margaret's Donnybrook, Dublin.

The Islamic collections consist of five sub-collections.

* The Qur'an collection includes more than 260 Qur'ans and Qur'an fragments.
* The Persian Collection consists mainly of copies of the works of the great Persian poets - Firdawsi, Nizami, Sa'di, Hafiz and Jami.
* The Indian Collection consists of both illustrated manuscripts and an array of almost 1,000 individual paintings produced in India during the period of Mughal rule for Islamic, Hindu and European patrons.
* The Turkish Collection consists of just over 160 manuscripts, making it the smallest of the Islamic collections.
* The Arabic collection contains approximately 2,650 manuscripts, many of which are unique. The collection contains works on subjects like religion, history, jurisprudence, medicine, geography, astronomy, mathematics and linguistics. The collection also contains many early translations into Arabic of the works of the ancient Greeks.

The East Asian collections include manuscripts, paintings, printed material and decorative arts from Tibet, Mongolia, Nepal, India, Sri Lanka, Thailand, Burma and Indonesia.

The Chinese collection includes over 200 paintings and prints dating from the 17th to the 19th centuries, one of the world's largest collection of carved rhinoceros horn cups, a unique group of jade books, early Buddhist sutras from Dunhuang, three volumes of the Great Encyclopaedia of the Yongle Emperor and a small collection of silk dragon robes. The Japanese collection ontains paintings, handscrolls, wood prints and works of decorative art.

7
DHAKA UNIVERSITY LIBRARY, DHAKA

Bangladesh has a rich historical and cultural past, combining Dravidian, Indo-Aryan, Mongol/Mughul, Arab, Persian, Turkic, and West European cultures. Residents of Bangladesh, about 98% of whom are ethnic Bengali and speak Bangla, are called Bangladeshis. Urdu-speaking, non-Bengali Muslims of Indian origin, and various tribal groups, mostly in the Chittagong Hill Tracts, comprise the remainder. Most Bangladeshis (about 83%) are Muslims, but Hindus constitute a sizable (16%) minority. There are also a small number of Buddhists, Christians, and animists

When British India was partitioned and the independent dominions of India and Pakistan were created in 1947, the region of Bengal was divided along religious lines. The predominantly Muslim eastern half was designated East Pakistan-—and made part of the newly independent Pakistan—while the predominantly Hindu western part became the Indian state of West Bengal.

The University

The University of Dhaka was established in 1921 under the Govt. of India Act. XVIII of 1920 (Which was based on the recommendations of the Calcutta University Commission presided over by Sir Michael Sadler). It was founded as a unitary teaching and residential University with a constitution similar in many respects to those of the then contemporary English University. Following the creation in 1947 of the province of East Bengal as a part of Pakistan, the East Bengal Educational Ordinance, 1947, was promulgated, by which the University, without prejudice to its original character as a teaching and residential University was entrusted with sole authority to recognise and affiliate all educational institutions in East Bengal above Materict and High Madrasa standard. Accordingly, in 1947, the University of Dhaka affiliated 58 1st and 2nd grade colleges throughout the whole of East Bengal After independence the Government of the People's Republic of Bangladesh promulgated the adaptation of University Laws by the Bangladesh Ordinance No. 1 of 1972. Afterwards, in pursuance to the Constitution of the People's Republic of Bangladesh, the President Order No. 11 of 1973 which is called the "Dacca University Order, 1973 was Promulgated.

University Library

The library service is an integral part of the academic activities of both the faculty members and students. By the size of the collection (over 550,000 estimated), Dhaka University Library is the largest of all academic as well as other libraries of Bangladesh. But it is not the size, but the excellence of its collection, particularly in rare books, ancient manuscripts and collections developed out of special depositories, it is an academician's playground.

Apart from two major sites, the library also maintains the collections of a Seminar section in the main library and departmental libraries. The two major sites are known as the Main Library and the Science Library.

The Main Library is in the Arts Faculty Campus. It is housed on three floors. There are two distinct blocks or wings one of which was built in the '60s as the Central Public Library. After the Central Public Library was shifted to a new site, their building was annexed to the Dhaka University Library. Architecturally both the blocks blend together.

The main library houses reading materials including text books, reference materials, rare books, ancient manuscripts (over 30,000 manuscripts on various languages, viz., Sanskrit, Bengali,

Arabic, Urdu, Persian, Maithaly, etc.) special collections (including UN collection), current journals and periodicals, Abstracts and Indexes in the Humanities and Social Sciences, old journals and periodicals and many more of interest and requirements of the faculty members and students of the disciplines of arts, social sciences, business studies and law.

The faculties and departments of pure and applied sciences are located in a separate part of the university site. It is better known as the Curzon Hall site, where most of the science faculties are situated. The collection includes text books, reference materials, current journals and periodicals, abstracts and indexes in the pure and applied sciences.

The Science Library Collections contain text books, reference materials, journals and periodicals of interest to the faculty members and students of the pure and applied sciences. It subscribes to major abstracting and indexing journals of the world. Borrowing and photocopying facilities of reading materials for science students and teachers are available in that section of the library.

The library offers all services, including reading room, photocopy, readers' guidance. General text books can be borrowed for home reading by faculty members for a stipulated period. Students of the faculties and departments located in the main campus (known as the Arts campus) can borrow books for home reading from the Seminar section only. They are offered a full reading room use service for other holdings (books, journals, periodicals etc.). They all have access to photocopy services.

The current catalogue is maintained in card format and can be approached by author, title and subject. There are also an historical 'sheaf catalogue' for older materials.

Collections of Manuscripts

The Decca University Library ranks among the finest and the best libraries of the Indo-Pakistan sub-continent. Its collection of about 20,000 Arabic, Persian, Bengali, Urdu, Sanskrit, Hindi,

Maithili and Assames manuscripts give it the stature of a centre of research. This large collection is the result of planned and sustained efforts made on a long term and ambitious programmes of acquisitions upon the part of the University authority ever since its establishment in 1921.

Even in the planning stage as early as in 1912, the Decca University Committee recommended that the University Library should supply means for the promotion of advanced study and general culture. The avoid ideal of the university itself being " a model university of a type new to the presidency and to India", where it would not be possible to gain a degree by the mere memorizing of textbooks, the Library, in the fitness of things, claimed and received the necessary support though not always adequate or sustained.

The University of Decca employed agents at various places in the province and outside to seek and acquire old and rare manuscripts. The agents coaxed, cajoled and bribed the owners of manuscripts using many methods of high pressure salesmanship in order to acquire invaluable many manuscripts.

The annual report of the Decca University for the year 1925 records that "the University had since its inception a scheme of forming a good library of Sanskrit and Bengali manuscripts and set apart Rupees 5000/ for the purpose. The scheme however never materialized till the time when an honorary committee was formed for the collection of manuscripts". However, we first hear of Arabic and Persian manuscripts only in the annual report for the Decca University for 1928-29 when its report the generous donation of 790 volumes including 53 manuscripts by Khan Bahadur Kazimuddin Siddiqi, Zamindar of Baliadi, Decca. It was only from the year 1928-29 that a manuscript Committee for the Arabic, Persian, Urdu languages and the Punthis was constituted. The Committee consisted originally of seven members viz. the Head of the Committee, Department of Arabic and Islamic Studies; the Head of the Department of Urdu and Persian; two teachers, one each from the Department of Arabic and Islamic Studies and Urdu and Persian; one member of the Sanskrit Manuscript Committee; one other teacher and the Librarian. To start with the Committee resolved to advertise for MSS In different English and vernacular newspapers of wide circulation". As a result of these early endeavors two lots of manuscripts totaling 252 in number and covering a wide range of subjects viz. language and literature, history, religion, medicine, philosophy, astronomy etc. were acquired from the city of Decca itself in 1929-30, "particularly the first year of the existence of the Committee" which form the nucleolus of the collection. In 1929-30, the Committee reported with regret that it did not as yet got any Punthi manuscript.

Having extremely meager resources at their disposal, the committee, could not continue with their ambitious programme of acquisition, one restrictive clause in this regard being the apparently contradictory imposition that only such manuscripts could be purchased "as were considered of real importance and obtainable at very moderate price". Accordingly in 1930-31 only a small number of important works were added to Arabic, Persian and Urdu manuscripts collection in the Library.

As this time in consideration the often said physical states of the manuscripts acquired, the university sanctioned a grant of Rupees 150/ for their binding and repairing in some of the later years. In the next two years i. e. 1932-33 and 1933-34 the Committee had to depend on the rather paltry of previous years which further restricted its purchasing capacity and as a result, no substantial addition could be made to the Arabic, Persian and Urdu manuscripts sections. The total number of manuscripts in the collection stood at approximately 450 in the year 1933-34. The next three years were uneventful in as much as there was no addition to this section due to lack of funds.

It was only in1938-39 that a sum of Rupees one thousand was provided for the collection of Arabic, Persian manuscripts during the three following years but with the restrictive direction that the collection of manuscripts should principally be made by search of getting old manuscripts in the possession of private individuals in Bengal and Assam.

Gifts and donations have also gone a long way in building up the manuscripts collections. Notable among these are the generous gifts of 597 Punthis and 12 Persian and Arabic manuscripts donated by Maulvi Abdu Karim Sahitya Visharad of Chittagong in 1951-52 and of 90 manuscripts collected by Hakim Habibur Rehman of Decca donated by his heirs a few years later which were acquired through the strenuous efforts of Dr. W.H.A. Shadani. A collection of 26 manuscripts of the late Maulvi Ameenur Rehman of Bogra was donated his heirs in 1935-1936.

It was in the year 1938-39 that for the first time, there was a proposal for the preparation of the catlogue of Arabic, Persian, Urdu etc manuscripts in the possession of Decca University Library and it was held that "it is abosultely necessary to have a descriptive catalogue of the manuscripts prepared at an early date". The Committee under a director from the academic council decided that the descriptive catalogue should be prepared by an expert cataloguer after consultation with the authority on the subject. In 1941-42 a committee of expert consisting of Dr. M. Hasan, Dr. M. R. Borah, Dr. Mohammad Shahidullah and Mr. M.A. Taufiq was appointed to report as to the number of manuscripts "that are not already printed". It was decided that an expert cataloguer would be employed after this committee reported. This, however, did not materialize, and ultimately the elected secretary to the Arabic, Persian, etc. manuscripts committee himself undertook the work in the year 1945-46 but could not proceed far. There was another abortive effort subsequently in the academic session 1947-48.

The failure of all these attempt can justifiably be ascribed to the initially unrealistic estimates of the magnitudes of the work which required not only profound scholarship but also the possession of bibliographic expertise and entails of tremendous volumes of unremitting toil, industry and ample financial subsidies.

In subsequent years there was a lull in the efforts to compile a descriptive catalogue in the interim period, however the late Hakim Wahid Ali oriental cataloguer, Decca University Library, had been working own his own compiling a descriptive catalogue of the Arabic, Persian and Urdu manuscripts.

In June 1958 Rollet Andreano, Director of cultural relations, SEATO visited the Library and was greatly impressed by the nature and volume of work done by an oriental cataloguer and offered a financial grant on behalf of SEATO for the purpose of the publication of the manuscript catalogue. Originally SEATO granted $1500for a single volume catalogue consisting of 350 pages of demy size paper but subsequently raised the grant to $1850 to meet the estimated additional cost.

The library committee then suggested to the university that the work of revising and editing of the draft catalogue prepared by the oriental cataloguer ,should be entrusted to Dr. A.B.M. Habibullah, head of the department of Islamic history and culture.

Sometimes after taking the work in hand, Dr. Habibullah discovered that the catalogue prepared by the oriental Cataloguer of the Dacca University Library did not conform with the requirements f a systematic and accurate catalogue and, therefore, agreed to re-catalogue the manuscripts and prepare descriptive entries for each item afresh during his labour, it was realised that the publication was likely to exceed the originally planned volume in size. It was calculated that the work could only be completed in two volumes totaling 560 pages in all. To meet the additional expenditure involved, the University of Decca came forward with a grant of Rs. 9659.00. The work of cataloguing proceeded over five years through many difficulties, which tended to delay its progress. This was later completed and the description of 364 Persian manuscripts was issued as the first volume of catalogue of the Arabic, Persian and Urdu manuscripts to be completed in two volumes in order to constitute the first part of the Descriptive Catalogue of Oriental Manuscripts in the Decca University Library.

Important Manuscripts in the Collection

* Earliest recorded copy of the Mirat-I-Aftab Numa by Abdur Rehman Nawaz Khan, transcribed for the author during his life time in 1804 A.D.
* Shahjahan Nama, a rare history of Shahjahan's reign by Sahikh Mohammad Zahid, compiled in 1677.
* Futuhat-iUmar, a unique versified history of Umar, the secong caliph of Islam, in the author's own handwriting, by one Asaf written in 1211/1796 for presentation to Zaman shah, grandson of Ahmad Shah Abdali.
* Earliest recorded copy of Mirat-ul-Madari, a biography of the popular saint Shah Madarby Abdur Rehman Chishti, copied in 1718-19.
* Author's biography of hitherto unknown, Kitab-ul-Mazahik, a collection of witticismand humerous stories, by Mohammad Sa'ad Azimabadi, a writer of commentaries of Persian prose, poetry and grammatical textbooks who lived in late 17th century.
* Baghistan, an unrecorded commentary on the Bostan of Sa'adi Shirazi by the same Sa'ad Azimabadi.
* Maghazi-un-Nabi, a reare versified work in two parts on the Prophet's life written inimmitation of Nizami's Sikander nama and constituting the hitherto unrecorded fourth of the five Masnavis named Khamsa, by Shaikh Yakub Sarfi, the Sufi Poet of Kashmir in 1589 A,D.
* Earliest recorded manuscript of Kulliat-i-Qudsi, the poetic work of Mohammad Jan Qudsi who died in 1646.
* An unrecorded poetic version of the well-known Punjabi romance Heer Ranjha, by Azimuddin Azim, written at the desire of and, dedicated to Mir Fath Ali Talpur of Sindh in 1799.

* A complete copy of Adabul-Fuzala, one of the earliest Persian dictionaries written in India by Qazi Khan Badr Mahmud,Dharwal, in 1419.

8

GRAND AYATOLLAH MAR'ASHI NAJAFI PUBLIC LIBRARY, QOM

The written history of Iran begins with the early Achaemenids, some 2,500 years ago, but since then till the dawn of Islam in Iran, all that is available on the Iranian history has been written by the ancient Greeks, who were then Iran's greatest enemies. So, the pre-Islamic historical sources are not completely reliable although there are indications that Greek historians often faithfully recorded the facts.

Iranians are said to be Aryans and this is in part true. Though predominantly Aryan, they are in fact a mixture of many nations and races: the Old Asian people who lived on the Iranian plateau before the arrival of the Aryans; the Aryans who moved to the plateau mostly in the first millennium BC; and finally the descendants of the later conquerors: Arabs, Turks, and Mongols.

At any rate Persians became Moslems and retained Islam even when they had regained their independence and developed their new language. Just about I 00 years after Persia had become a pad of the Moslem world, an Iranian by the name of Abu Muslim led an uprising in Khorassan against the Omayyad rulers and in favor of Abdollah Saffah, a descendant of Abbas, one of the cousins of the holy Prophet Mohammad. In 750 AD the Omayyads were overthrown and Abdollah Saffah became caliph, the first in line of the Abbasid dynasty. From then on Iranians penetrated further and further into the Arab society and the Moslem world, and contributed greatly to Moslem civilization, art, literature and sciences. Meanwhile, Iranians with a fighting spirits sprang up here and there in the empire, struggling for independence from the Arab yoke.

From early 11th century there ruled in various parts of Iran, Turkish kings who were more Moslems than Turks, and became increasingly more absorbed into the Islamic and Iranian cultures. One of their greatest plea sures was listening to recitations from the Shahnameh, the legendary epic of ancient Persia's heroes. Thus Iran was divided into a number of kingdoms, mostly with Turkish monarchs, who ruled on the advice and guidance of their Iranian viziers, or prime ministers.

In 1220 AD, however, the history of Iran began to take yet another turn, more bloody, more tragic, and sadder than any before or since. There was a man approaching Iran on his horse who eventually became a nightmare to the whole world: Chengiz Khan. In 1405 Teymoor died and his son Shahrokh acceded to his throne. Shahrokh, though a warrior, was mild and generous. He loved the Persian language and poetry and was deeply interested in arts and sciences which he encouraged and supported. Once again the Invader became assimilated into the way of life of the conquered Iranian; Shahrokh and his descendants came to think of themselves more and more as Iranians than Tatars.

From those prime centuries, a lot of literates, narrators and Islamic learned men began the editing of Islamic sciences and wrote essays, books and worthy collections in different fields; through this way, there were built thousands of libraries. They were established libraries in mosques, schools, hospitals and shrines of Islamic nobles, then due to the holy work being of books authorization, authoring books and basing libraries was done so rapidly.

Book authoring and library establishing never stopped even facing with so many wars in the early centuries of Islam and developed rapidly up to the late of six century. But, by the seven century with the Mongols' destructive attacks to the Islamic libraries that had been damaged a little before due to crusades, they damaged badly. Irrecoverable damages abolished a lot of scientific and cultural works of these worthy libraries, so there is only their name that stays nowadays.

Strict identifying of the Islamic antique libraries, which were the kernels of civilization and culture of mankind, helps us to re-know the Islamic culture and civilization. Besides, it makes the Moslems more familiar with their bright history and makes the way to future easy for them. Also, other nations and culture will become familiar with the Islamic worthy culture and civilization.

The Library

The historical foundation of this Library goes back to the time when Grand Ayatollah Mar'ashi Najafi was studying in the Islamic Seminary of Najaf. That was a time when the importance and value of old manuscripts - Islamic educational and cultural heritage - were not realized. Through great efforts of warding off hunger (after cutting back on food), and working hard in a rice-cleaning factory in Najaf, Ayatollah Mar'ashi saved money to buy old manuscripts and rare books. After coming to Iran, he continued this effort to gather up the precious books, till he had collected an abundant amount of manuscripts and rare books. Thereupon, he founded a small library in a seminary school that he established - The Mar'ashiyyah Seminary School. Later he bought the present building of the library and transferred the books to the newly established library. His great efforts led to the formation of the well-known and precious library of Mar'ashi Najafi.

The founder of this library Ayat Allah Sayid Shahab Al-Din Marashi Najafi (p. b. u. h.) was born on 21st Jul. 1897 in holy Najaf city in Iraq, in a very well known learned and religious family. He learnt the first steps of science by his father, Ayat Allah Sayid Shams Al-Din Mahmoud Hosseini Marashi Najafi (deceased on 1920) who was one of the greatest religious authorities of that era, and also by Sheik Mortaza Taleqani , Sheik Mohammad Hossein Isfahani, his grandmother Hajji Bibi Shams Sharafbeigom Tabatabaei. He learned science of Holy Koran reciting, tajwid and commentary by his father and Mirza Aboll Hassan Meshkini, Sheik Mohammad Hossein Shirazi, Sayid Hab Al-Din Shahrestani and Sayid Ebrahim Shafei Rafaei Baghdadi. Science of Genealogy by his father and Sayid Reza Mousavi Ghoraifi Saegh Bahrani and his brother Sayid Mahdi Ghoraifi, Science of Religious Jurisprudence and Principles by his father, Sheik Mortaza Taleqani, Sayid Mahammad Reza Rafsanjani, Sheik Gholam Ali Qomi, Mirza Abol Hassan Meshkini, Sayid Aqa Shoushtari, Nirza Mohammad Ali Kazemini, Sheik Abdol Hossain Rashti, Mirza Aqa Estahbanati, Sheik Mousa Kermanshahi, Sheik Nemat Allah Larijani and Sayid Ali Tabatabaei, Mathematics and Astronomy by Sheik Abdol Karim Boushehri, Sayid Abol Qasem Mousavi Khansari, Dr. Andalibzadeh, Mirza Mahmoud Ahari, Aqa Mohammad Mahallati, Sheik Abdol Hamid Dashti, Mirza Ahmad Monajem and Sayid Kazem Asaar, Medicine by his father and Mohammad Ali Khan Moaied Al Atteba, Science of Rejal, Derayeh and Hadis by his father and Sayid Abou Torab Khansari, Mirza Mohammad Tehrani, Sheik Abdollah Mamqani and Mirza Abolhoda Karbasi, Religious Jurisprudence and Logical Principles by Sheik Zia Al-Din Araqi the greatest teacher of principles in Holy Najaf, Sayid Ahmad Behbahani, Sheik Ahmad Kashef Algheta, Sheik Ali Asghar Khataei Tabrizi and Sheik Mohammad Reza Masjed Shahi. He spent three years in Samera and Kazemein to learn the complementary scince of Religious Jurisprudence, Hadis and Rejal by Sayid Hassan Sadr, and learned Principles by Sheik Mahdi Khalesi. Then after he returned again to Najaf and learned Science of Speech by his father, Sheik Mohammad Javad Bolaghi, Sheik Mohammad Esmaeil Mahallati and Sayid Hab Al-Din Shahrestani.

Aside from gathering books, films, microfiches, and photos of old and rare books, the library is a study center for many university and theology students, both Iranian and foreigner. The number of both male and female students taking advantage of the library's facilities is increasing every day.

The library is made up of different departments:

1. Department for obtaining important books & manuscripts, and distribution.
2. Department for book indexing.
3. Department of book restoration and preservation.
4. Department for bookbinding.
5. Department for compiling an encyclopedia of outstanding Libraries around the world (especially those having Islamic manuscripts).

Collections of the Library

By establishing such a great library and collecting Islamic reserves for the usage of the researchers, the founder of the Library sought some goals titled below:

1. Establishing a great international Islamic cultural center that shows the development periods of the Islamic scientists among the 12th century
2. Developing the mind of researching in the society, which was essentially needed more than any other past periods
3. Informing other researches about the written sources that have been collected in a great center, as well as their acquaintance about the Islamic heritage which has been written in several sciences but they have not listed in the current sources, by authoring and publishing their lists
4. Collecting Islamic unique and valuable handwritten books in a great center to prevent the sacking of this national wealth that were being continuously exited of the Islamic countries by the international smugglers
5. Giving priority to collecting the old handwritten books or the original books by their authors handwriting which are mostly honored, and focusing them in a center for the usage of the researchers
6. Preparing and collecting photos and microfilms and

archiving the honored Islamic handwritten books that have been sending out of Iran and or Islamic countries before, and are in the other nations libraries as well as focusing them for the usage of the researchers

7. Presenting this great human treasure to the next coming generations to be known about the wealthy civilization of their ancestors and be able to write the history of science using it, which is the only key to find it

8. Keeping and protecting of the Islamic written reserves that have arrived us within the layers of history (such as fire accidents, carelessness to the written heritage by the unworthy and unti-science governers, raising and aggravating of religious disagreements among the ages, inundation and earth quick) besides renovation, fixing and making microfilms of them to prevent the more erosion of this mankind's heritage

The library is one of the most important and rich sources of manuscripts in Iran and in terms of the number of the volumes, is considered the first largest in Iran and the third in the world, after the libraries of Suleimaniyeh in Turkey and Dar ol-Kotob in Cairo, Egypt. The library is a labor of love by a man whose cultural activities are eclipsed by his religious work, making him more famous as a top cleric rather than a guardian of the national heritage of the past.

In a time when the importance of cultural heritage was not known to the society, following his personal interest, Ayatollah Marashi purchased and gathered manuscripts by selling personal stuff and bearing hardship, preventing the export of the manuscripts from the country. To show his humbleness to pursuers of science, he asked in his will to be buried in the entrance hallway of the library under the footsteps of incoming students.

The library, a treasury of great ancient cultural works, is now being managed by Dr. Seyed Mahmoud Marashi, son of

Ayatollah Marashi, who himself is one of the noted experts of manuscripts in the world and during these years has carried out various efforts to improve and extend the library, to provide more facilities to Iranian and foreign researchers, making contacts with other libraries and cultural-scientific centers all around the world, and furnishing microfilms of the manuscripts.

At the moment, recent renovations on the library have been completed. The substructure of the library is 21000 square meters stretching across two separate buildings. One of the buildings is a five floor complex, and the other is a seven floor building.

The library has the capacity to hold more than 3,000,000 books and 120,000 manuscripts; currently is has over 500,000 published books and about 30,000 manuscripts under more than 60,000 various titles. The books in the library are written in different languages such as Persian, Arabic, Turkish, Urdu, Sanskrit, Ethiopic, French, German, English, Russian, Italian, and more.

The number of published books in - thirty different - European languages is over 30,000 volumes. The number of published books in Arabic, Turkish, Urdu, and Persian exceeds 450,000 volumes. The library is currently holding more than 30,000 rare books, some of them being published 400 years ago and others dating back to Islam's appearance. At present, the library also has more than 3000 books on microfiche.

Today, the Najafi Mar'ashi Library is in direct contact with more than 400 scientific research centers, cultural institutions, universities, and great libraries around the world. The newly installed computer equipment in the library has made considerable improvement its' organizing and transferring of information. New technology has also made it possible to connect the library to the Internet. The documents and scripts of various historical eras owned by the libraries as well as cultural and scientific centers of Iran and Uzbekistan are constantly being exchanged. "Rare versions of historical scripts are currently examined by experts in the Irano-Uzbek libraries to present a copy of any particular version to the other nation if necessary." The xample of such act are the versions of Imam Bokhari's scripts on Islamic jurisprudence belonging to Marashi Najafi's library and Abu Reyhan Birouni's orienthology research institute in Tashkent and the current exchange of information and expertise on the fundamental ways of preserving and restoring handwritten books between Abu Reyhan Birouni library in Tashkent and Ayatollah Marashi Najafi library in Qom.

9
GOVERNMENT ORIENTAL MANUSCRIPTS LIBRARY, CHENNAI

The Governemnt Oriental Library Madras is located in the Western Wing of the first floor of the Madras University Library. It is unique in respect of its precious holdings and one of the oldest oriental libraries of the country. The Library possess invaluable printed books and manuscripts of many languages in different scripts specially, Tamil, Telugu, Kannada, Marathi, Malayalam and Persian which provided immense knowledge on the history of South India.

The Library was established out of the efforts of Colonel Mackenzie, an Englishman and an engineer by profession. He studied and collected materials on Indian Mathematics and Logarithm as per the instruction of Lord Makinston. He collected a number of documentary sources including manuscripts, coins etc. from 1782 to 1820. After his death, these materials were sold by his wife to the Governor General Marquis Hastings which was went in possession of the East India company and was later sent to Madras and Kolkatta for the Asiatic society.

The collection of the Library increased with the passage of time and the Britishers were the main promoters for it. The Collections of colonel Mackenzie (1754-1821), Dr. Leyden and Mr. C. P. Brown constitute the nucleus of the vast collection of manuscripts preserved in Government Oriental Manuscripts Library, Madras, which consists of manuscripts of works in literature, history, philosophy and science, written in South Indian and Oriental Languages, and of Kaifiyats and inscriptions found in many places belonging to different periods.

The work of preparing catalogues of the manuscripts started in 1873 and since then many volumes have come out. Grants were allocated for the purpose both by the Central as well as State governments. The curator Mr. T. Chandrashekhar played a very active role in bringing out the catalogues of the manuscripts of historical value.

There was a committee of experts called the Editorial Board of the Library, which was responsible for identification of the manuscripts of historical value before they were printed in book form. In addition the committee was responsible for selection of books as well as editors. Books were published in series and the two famous series were Madras Government Oriental series and Government Oriental Manuscripts series. The Library has provision of copying of manuscripts through its qualified staff specially appointed for the purpose. It also has a bindery.

The holding of the Library have been divided into collection and these various collections as described below:

Mackenzie's Collection

Colonel Colin Mackenzie who came to India in 1783 as a Cadet of Engineers on the Madras Establishment of the East India Company took a keen interest in the study of ancient mathematics and, of Logarithm in particular, and in Oriental languages. He collected a large number of manuscripts, coins, inscriptions, maps etc., bearing on the liberature, religion, history, manners and customs of the people not only from different parts of India but also from Ceylon and Java.

On his appointment as Surveyor-General of India in 1818, Colonel Mackenzie took his valuable collections with him to Calcutta and went on adding to them till his death in 1821.

This collection was bought from Mrs. Mackenzie for 10,000 pounds by the East India Company in 1821 and divided into three parts. While one part was retained in London, the other parts were sent to Calcutta and Madras.

Leyden's Collection

In 1837, C.P.Brown noticed a collection of manuscripts in Tamil, Telugu and Kannada characters in the India Office Library, London. This invaluable collection belonged to Dr. Leyden, a remarkable linguist and traveller who was in India during 1803-1811. After his death, the East India Company purchased it and lodged at the India House, London. Thanks to the efforts of C.P.Brown, who had joined Indian Civil Service, it was subsequently brought to India.

Brown's Collection

Brown (1798-1184) himself presented to the East India Company his own valuable collections of paper manuscripts of Sanskrit and Telugu works. This collection was brought to India in 1855.

Growth of the Collection

Full fledged library in the true sense was started in 1869. Three collections i.e. the Mackenzie Collection and Brown Collection were transferred to Presidency College, Madras in 1870 and Mr. Pickford who was Professor of Sanskrit in Presidency College, was directed to prepare a Catalogue for them.

He was then called upon to prepare a scheme for publication of important literary and historical manuscripts. In 1876 he was requested to explore for new manuscripts and to purchase or acquire them by transcription.

Accordingly, many manuscripts were acquired from time to time and added to the Library collection.

From such small beginnings, GOML, MADRAS, has grown to its present dimensions and it possesses 71180 manuscripts in the following languages:

Telugu	2150
Sanskrit	48884
Tamil	16398

Kannada	250
Marathi	956
Urdu	184
Arabic	407
Persian	1390
Other Oriental languages	127
Local Records	434
	71180

Consequent on the formation of linguistic States in our country about 7,000 manluscripts in Telugu, Kannada and Malayalam were transferred to Andhra Pradesh, Karnataka and Kerala respectively. Apart from this 22,887 printed books are available for reference in the Library.

Functions

The main functions of GOML are as follows:

1. Acquisition and preservation of manuscripts.
2. Classification and Cataloguing of manuscripts.
3. Publication of rare manuscripts and Library Catalogues.
4. Purchase of books and periodicalsl for reference, and
5. Supply of information of manuscripts to the scholars.

Preservation

The rare and valuable palm-leaf manuscripts are carefully preserved by adopting manual and chemical methods. The injured and damaged paper manuscripts are preserved by being mended with Chiffon cloth.

Publications

GOML has brought out so far 350 publications including Descriptive and Triennial Catalogues of its manuscripts in various languages. The publication have been broughtl under two series. GOVERNMENT ORIENTAL MANUSCRIPTS SERIES and

GOVERNMENT ORIENTAL SERIES, those in the latter being edited by the Curator and the staffr of the Library.

Bulletin

Multilingual Bulletin published annually by GOML contains in-print, rare and unpublished manuscripts in various languages. Twenty one volumes have been published so far.

Participation in Exhibition

The rare and valuable manuscripts of GOML were displayed in the manuscript exhibitions on the following occasions:

1. 1964 - The Twenty Sixth International Congress of Orientalists in New Delhi.
2. 1964 - The Third All India Agama Silpa Bharata Forklore Conference in Kancheepuram.
3. 1965 - The World Telugu Conference in Hyderabad
4. 1968 - The Second World Tamil Conference in Madras.
5. 1968 - The Lord Mahaveera's 25th Parinirvana Centenary Celebrations in Madras
6. 1980 - The Silver Jubilee Celebrations of the Sanskrit Department Vevekananda College in Madras
7. 1980 - The Chitirai Festival in Madurai
8. 1981 - The Fifth World Tamil Conference in Madurai
9. 1982 - Seminar on Sanskrit Literature at Vivekananda College in Madras

GOML is a government institution headed by the Curator under the control ofl the Director of Archaeology, Government of Tamilnadu.

Service

Manuscripts and books are issued to visitors for study or consultation on request. Permission is accorded to research scholars for studying, copying and comparing the manuscripts.

10

INDIA OFFICE LIBRARY, LONDON

The East India Company was established in 1600 by English merchants who received, by a series of charters, exclusive rights to trade to the 'Indies'. The 'Indies' were defined as the lands lying between the Cape of Good Hope and the Straits of Magellan, and the Company soon established a network of warehouses or 'factories' throughout south and east Asia. Over a period of 250 years the Company underwent several substantial changes in its basic character and functions.

With the India Act of 1858 the Company and the Board of Control were replaced by a single new department of state, the India Office, which functioned, under the Secretary of State for India, as an executive office of United Kingdom government alongside the Foreign Office, Colonial Office, Home Office and War Office. The Secretary of State was assisted by a statutory body of advisers, the Council of India, and headed a staff of civil servants organised into a system of departments largely taken over from the East India Company and Board of Control establishments, and housed in a new India Office building in Whitehall.

The Library

The Company established a library in East India House in 1801 as a public repository for the safe custody of books, manuscripts and works of art placed in its care by its servants in India and by others. The East India Company's Library was systematically developed by the Company and the India Office as a reference library for official administration and as a learned library for scholars, and it served, from 1867, the archival function as the place of legal deposit in Britain for works published in

British India. The collection and preservation of the private papers of individuals and organisations connected with India had been carried on by the East India Company and the India Office since early in the nineteenth century, and this activity continues in the Private Papers section of the India Office Records.

Both the East India Company and the Board of Control made provision for the care and custody of their records, the Company mainly through the office of Registrar and Keeper of the Indian Books (from 1771), and the Board through the Librarian and Keeper of the Papers (from 1811). In 1860 the India Office surveyed its predecessors' records, and destroyed a large amount of material, particularly commercial records, considered to be ephemeral, while retaining what were judged to be the important historical records. The preservation of the pre-1858 records and of the newly-accumulating records of the India Office was assigned to a central Record Department in 1884.

After the independence of India, Pakistan and Burma in 1947 and 1948 the Indian Records Section (later the India Office Records) and the India Office Library were administered by the Commonwealth Relations Office, later the Commonwealth Office, and (from 1968) by the Foreign and Commonwealth Office. In 1982 the India Office Library and Records were placed on deposit with the British Library Board, and the India Office Records have since been administered, as Public Records, in the British Library Asia Pacific & Africa Collections (formerly Oriental and India Office Collections).

The India Office Library holds the documentary archives of the administration in London of the pre-1947 government of India. The 14 kilometres of shelves of volumes, files and boxes of papers, together with 70,000 volumes of official publications and 105,000 manuscript and printed maps, comprise the archives of the East India Company (1600-1858), of the Board of Control or Board of Commissioners for the Affairs of India (1784-1858), of the India Office (1858-1947), of the Burma Office (1937-1948), and of a number of British agencies overseas which were officially linked with one or other of the four main bodies. The India Office Records are part of the Public Records of the United Kingdom, and are open for public consultation under the provisions of the Public Record Acts and in accordance with regulations established by the Lord Chancellor.

The central focus of the India Office Records is in the territories now included in India, Pakistan, Burma and Bangladesh, and the major part of the records concern their administration before 1947. As a result of the widespread commercial activities of the East India Company, and of India Office involvement in the external relations and defence policy of pre-1947 India, the Records also include a substantial body of historical source materials for neighbouring or connected areas at different times. Among the most significant of these are:

St Helena (to 1834);

Cape of Good Hope (to 1836);

Zanzibar, Somalia and Ethiopia (mainly nineteenth century);

Red Sea, Arabian Peninsula, Gulf States, Iraq and Iran (c1600-1947);

Afghanistan, Russian and Chinese Central Asia, Tibet, Nepal, Bhutan and Sikkim (late eighteenth century to 1947);

Sri Lanka (c1750-1802);

Malaysia and South-East Asia (to c1867);

Indonesia (to c1825);

China (early seventeenth century to 1947); and

Japan (seventeenth century).

Other groups of documents have resulted from India Office interest in the status of Indian emigrants to the West Indies, south and east Africa, and Fiji.

The original documentary archives which form the India Office Records are mainly arranged in the regular administrative series in which they were used in the East India Company and the India Office, for example, series of original letters received, drafts or copies of letters sent, registered files of correspondence, minutes and proceedings of committees and other corporate bodies, lists of personnel and nominal returns, title deeds and other legal documents, books of account, reports, memoranda, ships' journals, etc. Embedded in these documentary archives are extensive collections of official publications and maps, assembled by the India Office and its predecessors chiefly from materials received in the official correspondence. The practice by which the councils and committees in factories, settlements and centres of government routinely sent copies of their own proceedings and minutes to London for reference contributed significantly to the comprehensiveness of the archives of the East India Company and the India Office from the earliest years.

Manuscript Collections

The manuscript collections of the Library form part of the national repository of manuscripts, private papers and archives. They contain material of outstanding research importance for all periods, countries and disciplines.

Manuscript Catalogues

Much of the work of the Department is devoted to the arrangement, description and indexing of the collections. This page details the main online catalogues to the collections and outlines some of the other catalogues and search aids.

Manuscripts Online Catalogue

The Manuscripts Online Catalogue is based on the traditional cataloguing of the Department of Manuscripts and aims to cover all accessions from 1753 to date.

* The British Library's catalogues of manuscripts are traditionally constructed in two parts, descriptions and indexes. The Online Catalogue allows searching of both elements:
    * Each numbered volume or entity has a narrative

description recording such information as content, date, language, bibliography, provenance and physical details.

* Indexes provide access based on personal and place names, with some corporate names and subject terms. An entry may refer to a multi-volume collection, a volume or group of volumes, a span of leaves or one side of a single leaf. Indexes are compiled from the manuscripts, not from the descriptions, and will often contain additional information.
* Much of the Online Catalogue is derived from digital scans of printed catalogues. Some indexes and descriptions have so far proved resistant to such techniques and have not yet been converted. These include the following:
    * Burney manuscripts descriptions.
    * Harley manuscripts descriptions & indexes.
    * 1783-1835 accessions index.
    * King's manuscripts index.
    * Lansdowne manuscripts index.
    * Royal manuscripts index.
    * Index Locorum of Charters and Rolls.
    * Other non-published handlists and card indexes available only in the Manuscripts Reading Room.

Digital Catalogue of Illuminated Manuscripts

The pilot Digital Catalogue of Illuminated Manuscripts allows in-depth exploration of the British Library's unrivalled collection of medieval and Renaissance manuscripts. You can view detailed descriptions with images and also take tours of the Library's illuminated manuscript holdings.

Other catalogues

Published catalogues exist for a large proportion of the named Manuscript Collections - they usually include both descriptions of and indexes to the manuscripts in particular collections. In addition, many of these separate indexes have been brought together in an amalgamated index known as the *Index of Manuscripts*, 10 vols. (Cambridge, 1984-1986).

An unpublished subject index and a 19th-century 'Class Catalogue' provide further means of accessing the collections in the Manuscripts Reading Room. There is also a wealth of published material available, providing summaries, descriptions and indexes to manuscripts arranged chronologically, by language, or by subject matter. Many of these books are available on the open access shelves of the Manuscripts Reading Room.

11

INDIRA GANDHI NATIONAL CENTRE FOR THE ARTS LIBRARY, NEW DELHI

The Indira Gandhi National Centre for the Arts was established in the memory of Smt. Indira Gandhi, the prime minster of India. It is visualized as a centre encompassing the study and experience of all the arts — each form with its own integrity, yet within a dimension of mutual interdependence, interrelated with nature, social structure and cosmology.

This view of the arts, integrated with, and essential to the larger matrix of human culture, is predicated upon Smt. Gandhi's recognition of the role of the arts as essential to the integral quality of person, at home with himself and society. It partakes of the holistic worldview so powerfully articulated throughout Indian tradition, and emphasized by modern Indian leaders from Mahatma Gandhi to Rabindranath Tagore.

The arts are here understood to comprise the fields of creative and critical literature, written and oral; the visual arts, ranging from architecture, sculpture, painting and graphics to general material culture, photography and film; the performing arts of music, dance and theatre in their broadest connotation; and all else in fairs, festivals and lifestyle that has an artistic dimension. In its initial stages the Centre will focus attention on India; it will later expand its horizons to other civilizations and cultures. Through diverse programmes of research, publication, training, creative activities and performance, the IGNCA seeks to place the arts within the context of the natural and human environment. The fundamental approach of the Centre is all its work will be both multidisciplinary and interdisciplinary.

Recognizing the need to encompass and preserve the distributed fragments of Indian art and culture, a pioneering attempt has been made by Indira Gandhi National Centre for the Arts (IGNCA) to serve as a major resource centre for the arts, especially written, oral and visual materials. One of the programmes of this centre, in collaboration with UNDP, is to utilize multimedia computer technology to create a wide variety of software packages that communicate cultural information. Multimedia technology allows the user to interact and explore the subject in a non-linear mode by combining audio, text, graphics, animation and video on a computer.

Collections

The IGNCA is a National Information System and a Data Bank of the arts, humanities, cultural heritage with a fully supported reference library of multimedia collections. This information System and Data Bank will serve as a major resource centre for research in humanities, in the arts, in the disciplines of Archaeology, Anthropology, History, Philosophy, Literature, Language, Arts , Crafts etc. It is proposed to have very large library of microfilms / microfisches along with the printed material on Greater India, South Asia, Southeast, Asia and West Asia. Language won't be a barrier in its collection development policy. It is also proposed to have a collection of about half a million works during the next few years.

The reference library of IGNCA has a large collection of primary and secondary material in the broad areas of humanities and the arts. It constitutes books, reprographics of several folios of unpublished Sanskrit, Pali, Persian and Arabic manuscripts in microfilm and microfische, Photographs and slides. The Collection includes books on archaeology, philosophy, religion and ritual studies, history and anthropology, art and literature as well as folk, pastoral and community studies. The library is enriched by many rare collections of illustrious scholars who have made path-breaking contributions in fields related to arts.

The library concentrates on encyclopaedias, dictionaries, bibliographies, atlases and catalogues of unpublished manuscripts of Indian and Asian origin. Its holdings and expertize are complemented by those of the other divisions of the Centre.

Rare Books

Acquisition of rare books is a special feature of the Library. It has acquired books published in 18th and 19th centuries such as: The Travels of Sir John Charlin (1688). The Ceremonies and Religious Customs of various Nations of the known world together with historical annotations/Bernard Picard (1733-37); The works of Sir William Jones,(1759-1801); Considerations of Indian Affairs/William Botts.(1772); Journal of a route to Nagpore (1790); Narrative of the Compaign in India/Dirom (1793); Oriental Repertory (1793-94);A Journey from Bengal to England through the northern part of India Kashmire, Afghanistan/George Forester (1797);Oriental Memories/James Forbes (1831); A Sketch of the History of the East India Company from its first formation to the passing/Robert Grant, (1813); Letters Written in a Mahratta Camp/Thomas Duer Broughton (1815); Views in the Himalayan Mountains /James Baille Fraser (1820); The History of Jawa/T.S. Raffles (1817); An Account of the fishes found in river Ganges/Francis hamilton (1822); Historical Fragments of the Moghul Empire of the Mora-Hoes and of the English Concerns in Hindustan from the year/ Robert Orme (1825); The History of British India/James Mills(1826);

Personal Collections

A Unique feature of the library is the Personal Collection of eminent scholars and artists. Already major Collection have been gifted to the library. These Include:

Dr. Suniti Kumar Chatterjee Collection - Suniti Kumar Chatterjee (1890-1977) belonged to a generation of intellectuals who gave Indian thought a new direction. A multidisciplinary scholar, philologist and connoisseur of art, Chatterjee was professor of linguistics and languages at the University of Calcutta for thirty years.

Dr. Thakur Jaideva Singh Collection - Thakur Jaideva Singh (1893-1986) was a versatile genius and a rare combination of a philosopher, Sanskritist and musicologist and leading expert on Kashmir Saivaism.

Krishna Kriplani Collection - Krishna Kriplani was a close associate of Gurudev Rabindranath Tagore and later secretary to Maulana Azad.

Acharya Hazari Prasad Dwivedi Collection - Acharya Hazari Prasad Dwivedi (1907-1979) was a man off phenomenal reading and an encyclopaedic mind. He was a doyen among teachers and a well-known Hindi scholar.

Heeramaneck Collection - The rich collection of Nasi Heeramaneck, comprising about 2,500 books, was donated by his wife Alice Heeramanech. The collection contains several books on Asian arts. The rich collection of Nasi Heeramaneck, comprising about 2,500 books, was donated by his wife Alice Heeramanech. The collection contains several books on Asian arts. The rich collection of Nasi Heeramaneck, comprising about 2,500 books, was donated by his wife Alice Heeramanech. The collection contains several books on Asian arts.

Lance Dane Collection - A significant contribution of about 5,000 rare books, covering Indian art and architecture, has been made by this renowned photographer.

Chaturvedi Dwarka Prasad Collection - More than 12,000 books and 2,500 periodicals from the library of Chaturvedi Dwarka Prasad Sharma have been acquired through his grandson Shail Nath Chaturvedi. The illustrious scholar was an authority on modern Indian history.

Area Collections

Research and exchange programmes with South-East Asia, East Asia and Eurasia have brought in cultural material and acquisitions, covering a wide range of disciplines, enriching the core collections on the region

Series and Catalogue

The library is concentrating on building a complete corpus of printed material on Catalogue of manuscripts of indic and Asian origin published in all parts of the world. So for besides the Catalogues Catalogrum, it has acquired catalogues of major Sanskrit, Persian, Arabic manuscripts from libraries/research institutions of India, UK, USA, FRG, GDR, France, Italy and Japan.The series acquisition programme includes the LD series; Ecolede France; Institute of Indian Studies, Pondicherry Series; K. P. Jayaswal Research Institute, Patna; Satapitaka series, Bibliotheca Indica, Chowkhambha Series; Gaekwad Oriental Series, Barodal ; Pali Text Society Series; Rajasthan Puratana Granthmala; Sampurnanand Sanskrit Vishvavidyalaya Granthmala; Sri Ananthacharya Indological Research Institute Series; Woolner Indological Series, and many others.

Journals

The library subscribes to over 400 journals relating to arts. It is also building a serial collection of back volumes of periodicals. Among the journals obtained are Central Asian Survey, Asian Theatre Journal, Asian Music, Dance Chronicle,Australian Aboriginal Studies, SPAFA Journal, South East Asian Review, Russian Studies in History, Journal of the Oriental Institute, Praehistorische Zietschouft, MankindQuarterly, Journal of American Oriental Sociology, Journal of Ritual Studies, Leonardo, Visual Computer, Visual Anthropology, Journal of the History of Ideas, Revive de L'Art,Artibus Asiae, and Journal of American Oriental Society.

Microfilms/Microfische

A unique feature of the IGNCA library is the reprographic compilation of unpublished manuscripts in Indian and foreign collections from private and public libraries. A pioneering attempt has been made to bring under one roof primary sources of the Indian tradition lying scattered, fragmented, inaccessible or worse, in danger of extinction. At present the library contains about ten million folios of unpublished Sanskrit, Pali, Persian and Arabic manuscripts.

Reprographic material of various primary and secondary texts has been obtained from many foreign institutions including Bibliotheque Nationale (Paris), Cambridge University Library (Cambridge, UK), Staatsbibliothek (Berlin), INION (Russia), Wellcome Institute for the History of Medicine (London), and Oriental & India Office Collection, British Library (London).

Manuscripts are acquired in the form of micrographic records from major institutions across the country, like Khuda Baksh Oriental Public Library (Patna), Bhandarkar Oriental Research Institute (Pune), Asiatic Society (Calcutta), Manipur State Kala Academy (Imphal), Atombapu Research Centre (Imphal), Vaidika Samsodhana Mandala (Pune), Saraswati Bhawan Library (Varanasi), Government Oriental MSS Library (Madras), Oriental Research Institute and MSS Library (Trivandrum), Shri Ram Verma Government Sanskrit College (Tripunithura), Tanjavur Maharaja Serfoji's Saraswati Mahal Library (Tanjavur), and Shri Ranbir Sanskrit Research Institute (Jammu).

Manuscripts Collection

A National Mission has been launched to locate, enumerate, preserve and catalogue Indian manuscripts within the country and abroad with a view to enhancing their access and conserving them for posterity.

A National Manuscripts Library is to be set up in Indira Gandhi National Centre for the Arts, New Delhi as a part of the Mission's activities. The LPibrary is to be the central repository for original and microfilmed copies of all Indian manuscripts.

Under the National Mission, manuscripts will be documented and preserved by adopting a multi-pronged strategy which include spreading public awareness, surveys on extending need-based infrastructural support to the major custodial institutions, conservation, micro-filming, digitisation and cataloguing. A National Empowered Committee under the chairmanship of the Minister-in-charge of Culture and the Executive Committee under the chairmanship of Secretary (Culture) have been constituted to provide policy advice, guidance, prepare action plans and evolve procedures for implementation of the objectives of the National Mission for Manuscripts.

Prior to Independence, a large number of cultural objects including manuscripts had moved from the Indian sub-continent to different parts of the world. These objects are scattered among innumerable museums and private collections. There was no international covenant for the restitution of such objects.

The Antiquities (Export Control) Act was promulgated in 1947. It was succeeded by the enactment of the Antiquities and Art Treasures Act, 1972. Under this Act, illegal export of manuscripts is a crime. Moreover, registration of manuscripts is mandatory under this Act. In respect of the countries, which are signatories to the UNESCO Convention on "Means of Prohibiting and Preventing the Illicit Imports, Exports and Transfer of Ownership of Cultural Property", action can be initiated as per the provisions of the Convention. India is a signatory to this Convention. The Archaeological Survey of India has been taking action wherever instances of objects taken illegally out of the country have come to its notice.

National Mission for Manuscripts

Survey to identify manuscripts, acquiring or copying and preserving them would form the most immediate tasks of the National Mission for Manuscripts, expected to be launched by early October. According to the Mission Document finalised by the Department of Culture, there is no accurate account of the number of manuscripts available in the country. Various sources place the estimates differently. Hence, it becomes imperative to identify the manuscripts available, as they are with custodians ranging from institutions to individuals.

The manuscripts once identified have to be acquired or copied so that they can be preserved at least in the state they are in. It is this urgency that Secretary Culture, Shri N. Gopalaswami, underlined while inaugurating a one-day seminar, where the Discussion paper for the Mission Document was circulated. Quoting the words of Whiltey Stokes, Secretary to the Council of Governor General in 1868, the Secretary Culture said what was said about manuscripts in India 134 years ago was still relevant.

Mr. Stokes then writing on the state of the manuscripts had said that 'no time should be lost in taking measures to save the manuscripts which are degenerating because of the climate, white ants and declining interest.' Experts, subject scholars, government representatives and the implementing agencies participated in the seminar to consider the proposals in the Discussion Paper.

According to the Discussion Paper only a small percentage of the manuscripts has been surveyed and catalogued and their number may not be more than 20-25 per cent of the estimated total. The most daunting task for the Mission arises from the fact that the custodians of the manuscripts are dispersed and unidentified. Manuscripts are in the possession of various institutions - libraries, museums and archives, religious bodies, private collectors as also individuals. According to a conservative estimate there are over five million manuscripts in India in various forms and scripts, 60,000 in European countries and 1.5 million in South Asia and Asian countries. Sanskrit manuscripts form 67 per cent of the total number. Some of the practical difficulties anticipated are in preserving the manuscripts once they are identified. Since the manuscripts are in different forms and materials like birch bark, leather, palm leaf, paper etc. it is necessary to train the owners of the manuscripts in their preservation.

The Mission has designated IGNCA as the Nodal Agency for implementing the Mission. The Mission has an estimated outlay of Rs. 250 million for 5 years. The implementation period will coincide with the 10th Five-Year Plan. The Directorate of the Mission will be located at the Centre and IGNCA will also set up a National Manuscripts Library.

The IGNCA Trust will constitute the National Empowered Committee for the implementation of the Mission, chaired by the President of the IGNCA Executive Committee. The Empowered Committee shall have as members the member Secretary. IGNCA, Secretary Culture, The Director General of the National Archives and 10 - 15 others nominated by IGNCA.

Opening discussions at the seminar, Prof. N.R.Shetty, Member Secretary, IGNCA, gave a short background on the work the Centre has done with regard to documenting, preserving and dissemination of the manuscript wealth of the country. He also emphasized on the need to create a National Register of manuscripts as one of the first steps in the implementation of the Mission.

A substantial number of Indian manuscripts have been taken outside the country. It will be part of the Mission's efforts to get copies of these manuscripts, for which budgetary provision has been made. The Mission will also extend financial help to institutions, universities and other sources that have considerable number of manuscripts to improve their storage facility. Some of the States where major wealth of manuscripts are available are Tamil Nadu, Uttar Pradesh, Andhra Pradesh, Rajasthan and Orissa. (See list for major State administered institutions with huge collection of manuscripts)

The Mission Document states that the objectives of the Mission are: (1) To enhance the access to the manuscripts, improve awareness about cultural inheritance and encourage the use of manuscripts for educational and research purpose and lifelong learning; (2) to facilitate conservation and preservation of manuscripts through training, awareness and financial support; (3) to document and catalogue Indian manuscripts, wherever they may be, maintain accurate and up-to-date information about them and the conditions under which they may be consulted; (4) to promote ready access to these manuscripts through publication, both in book form as well as machine readable form; (5) to boost scholarship and research in the study of Indian languages and manuscriptology; (6) to build up a National Manuscripts Library at IGNCA.

Availability of Manuscripts in some primier institutions of the country is shown in the table below:

S.No.	Organisation	Number of Manuscripts
1.	Sampurnanand Sanskrit University, Varanasi	1,20,000
2.	Government Oriental Manuscript Library, Chennai	66,077
3.	Oriental Institute and Manuscript Library, Tiruananthapuram	56,000
4.	Saraswati Mahal Library, Thanjavur	47,000
5.	Adayar Library and Research Centre, Chennai	40,000
6.	Orissa State Museum, Bhuvaneshwar	25,000
7.	Andhra Pradesh Oriental Manuscript Library & Research Institute, Hyderabad	21,136
8.	State-Central Library, Hyderabad	17,000
9.	Rajasthan State Archives, Jaipur	14,000
10.	Rajasthan Oriental Research Institute, Jodhpur	12,262
11.	Government Manuscript Library, Allahabad	11,000

12

INSTITUTE OF ASIAN STUDIES LIBRARY, CHENNAI

The Institute of Asian Studies in Chennai is a joint venture launched by a few scholars from India and Japan and its main aim is to promote academic research on the cultural facets of Asian countries. One of its main objectives is the quest for perception of Asian literature and culture as a unified and composite whole, transcending geographical, linguistic, and cultural barriers.

Many eminent scholars from Western Europe, the former Soviet states, and the United States have made invaluable contributions to Oriental culture. Similarly, laden with emotional as well as intellectual involvement, few Asian scholars have also devoted themselves hear and soul to Asian Studies. Yet, the area of studies covered so far is not considerable and much more remains to be done. This is brought home to us by the ignorance that prevails in the world of scholarship about the similarities and diversities that exist among the Asian cultures. Only a few Asian works are available in translations in the various languages of the people of Asia. The paucity of reference material is another limitation to scholars who pursue Asiatic researches. Moreover, there are only a few centres of study, which are devoted to the study of Asian cultures in depth. The Institute of Asian Studies in Chennai has been established with a view to overcoming the existing limitations and to pooling together the scattered resource persons and materials available in various countries so as to enable our academics to carry out research on various aspects of the cultural heritage of the people of Asia in a very systematic way.

The Institute proposes to introduce the teaching of all important Asian languages and literatures sequentially. Translations of great works (literary, philosophical, theological and so forth) will also be undertaken by this Institute. Promoting comparative studies in Asian literature and of the philosophical works of Asian countries will be one of the important activities of the Institute. It is proposed to establish a strong faculty of archaeology which should engage in undertaking the much needed explorations in various parts of Asia and also serve as an up-to-date information centre of all archaeological works in Asia.

One of the main faculties of the Institute, namely the faculty of manuscriptology, is designed in such a way that its programmes include collections of all unpublished materials available on palm-leaf and other manuscripts and preserving them from further decay and disintegration. This vital part of the Institute will be engaged in protecting the cultural treasures of the people of Asia from decay and deterioration and publishing them with detailed editorial notes and critical commentaries.

This non-profit research centre was registered as an autonomous Society in 1982 and it is governed by a team of members in the capacity of the Board of Governors. Eminent personalities from various walk of life - judiciary, education, government, culture -who evince a keen interest in Asian culture, language, and literature form the Board of Governors which is headed by Justice V.R. Krishna Iyer.

Translation being an important mode of cultural transmission, the Institute has a number of programmes which are designed to translate Asian classics from one language into another to enable a mutual flow of ideas from one linguistic community into another. During the initial stages literary classics with a universal perspective and relevance in the important languages in Asia are being accepted for translation.

To begin with, the reference works prepared by the Institute will be in English and the materials include encyclopedias for literatures, arts, cultures, folklore and so on of the Asian countries, multi-lingual dictionaries, descriptive catalogues of manuscripts, an archaeological atlas, descriptive surveys of folk culture, encyclopedias of place names. Such works prepared with a wider Asian perspective will form basic source material not only for cross-cultural studies but also for the students of comparative studies and researchers in the respective individual languages.

The following nine departments have been founded so far. With the shifting of the Institute to its permanent premises in March 1996, eight more departments will be opened so that its activities will be expanded to more areas. Moreover, collaboration with a few Japanese, American, and german universities will start in the next academic year. the departments are:

Tamil Studies; Kannada Studies; Telugu Studies; Buddhism; Manuscriptology; Japanese Studies, Translation; and a Publications Division.

Department of Manuscriptology Library

The department of manuscriptology is one of the most important components of this Institute. It is engaged in the collection preservation and publication of rare texts which are available on fragile palm-leaf and other manuscripts. A tentative survey made by this department pertaining to the palm-leaf manuscripts available in the Tamil language shows that 21% of manuscripts have been published and 79% of them still remain unpublished. These unpublished materials, which are written in a fragile, organic, medium namely palm-leaf, are disintegrating due to human negligence and natural calamities. The department of manuscriptology is engaged in launching projects, which are aimed at preserving the cultural treasures of the people of the southern part of India from decay and disintegration. The academic programmes of this department will gradually be expanded to the rare manuscripts available in other parts of Asia. There is a good palm-leaf manuscripts library at the department with large numbers of rare, unpublished work which the Institute is planning to publish one by one with English translation.

This department is also launching a project on the works available in manuscripts dealing with traditional science. One of the main projects of this department is the preparation of a detailed Descriptive Catalogue of Palm-leaf Manuscripts in Tamil in about 25 volumes each consisting of two parts. The first four volumes in eight parts have already been published. The department has also conducted a seminar on the palm-leaf manuscripts available in various Indian languages. The proceedings of this seminar will be published.

The department periodically conducts workshops with a view to imparting training for young scholars in reading and editing the manuscripts.

The Department of Manuscriptology came into being in 1985 thriugh the efforts of Dr (Mrs) Kapila Vatsyayan and Justice V.R. Krishna Iyer.

The objectives of the Department of Manuscriptology are:

1. To host professional seminars and workshops on manuscriptology as well as post-graduate studies and fieldwork in manuscriptology;
2. To preserve palm-leaf manuscripts in which lie embodied ancient knowledge and cultural memories;
3. To collect palm-leaf manuscripts;
4. To establish and maintain a library of palm-leaf manuscripts;
5. To translate palm-leaf manuscripts into English;
6. To store the information derived from palm-leaf manuscripts on a ditigally searchable database (For details: enquire by e- mail)
7. To compile and publish a comprehensive index of palm-leaf manuscripts in 25 volumes;
8. To depute scholars to training programmes on preservation of palm- leaf manuscripts;

9. To record palm-leaf manuscripts on micro-film and other media;
10. To conduct research on traditional sciences;

The IAS Index of Palm-leaf Manuscripts

The Institute is aware of the shortage of reference books on manuscriptology to pursue comparative studies in the field and has taken steps to remedy the situation. Along the lines of the Tamil Department which has begun publishing an Encyclopaedia of Tamil Literature, the Department of Manuscriptology has an ambitious plan of bringing out an Index of palm-leaf manuscripts available on subjects as varied as the history of the Tamil language and literature, Tamil culture, fine arts, logic, astrology, folklore, medicine and magic with a typical Tamil bias. This will be an ideal reference book for scholars engaged in research in their respective fields.

The oldest and perhaps the biggest library of manuscripts, the Government Library of Oriental Manuscripts (Chennai), the U.V. Swaminathaiyar Library, the Saraswathi Mahal Library (Tañjavur) and the Tamil University Library have also brought out indexes to the palm-leaf manuscripts available in the country. But the information containe d in these catalogues is not exhaustive enough to enable a student of research to make use of it effectively. But the database listing of palm-leaf manuscripts prepared by the Institute of Asian Studies contain all relevant information classified under four categories:

1. In the first category, material description of the manuscript includes the number of leaves it contains, the present condition of the manuscript, the name of the author and the commentator as well as the name of the copyist.
2. The second section can be broadly described as bibliographical description. The date of the publication of the manuscript and the number of editions are given for those that have been printed in book form. In the case of manuscripts, which have not been printed, details regarding

the use of the information in other printed works, if any, hav e been provided.

3. The third section is devoted to the contents of the manuscript. This may be called subject description. Besides the contents, the genre to which the text belongs, its relevance to the social life of the day, its style and historical associations if any, are detailed. The beginning and ending lines of all the manuscripts are given.
4. The fourth section highlights the uniqueness of the manuscript, its relationship to similar manuscripts, the views of the scholars and also the impact of the manuscript on the writings of others.

Indeed, the Institute of Asian Studies is undertaking a very ambitious project of assembling indices for all the Tamil palm-leaf manuscripts available in the world in 25 volumes, each volume containing two distinct parts. With the co- operation of the Government of India, the Government of Tamil Nadu and the Indira Gandhi Centre for the Development of National Culture, efforts are underway to collect details of palm- leaf manuscripts.

The extent of indexing work to date may be seen in the following table:

Indices of palm-leaf manuscripts	**Library Indexed Manuscripts**
Dr U.V. Swaminathaiyar Library	2398
TiruvAvaTutuRai aTINam	1266
Central Research Institute of Siddha Medicine (Chennai)	2149
Madurai Tamil Cankam (Madurai)	389
Tarumapuram aTINam	481
Kalaimakal Kalvi Nilayam (Erode)	133
Theosophical Seminary (Madurai)	159
KumAratEvar maTam (Viruddachalam)	185

Tamil Nadu Siddha Hospital Library (Chennai)	1526
Institute of Asian Studies (Chennai)	1285

Descriptive Catalogues

To date four descriptive catalogues have been published by the IAS:

Descriptive Catalogue Vol I-II

These two volumes contain the list of palm-leaf manuscripts available in the U.V. Swaminathaiyar Library. The spade work was done by M.K. Raman and later it was exhaustively edited by M. Shanmugam Pillai. The first two volumes containing four parts have been published. These two volumes contain commentary for 2,398 manuscripts.

Descriptive Catalogue Vol III

This lists with commentary the palm-leaf manuscripts available at the TiruvAvaTuturai aTINam Library and is published in two parts. A total of 1266 manuscripts figure in the list. (Part - I. 603 + Part - II. 663 = 1266).

Descriptive Catalogue Vol IV

This Volume covers 815 manuscripts available in the Institute of Asian Studies (part I 438 + part II 377). Most of them have a bearing on the South, to be more precise, most of them belong to Kumari and Nellai Districts.

Descriptive Catalogue Vol V

Vol V Part I contains descriptions of 470 manuscripts available in the Institute of Asian Studies and Vol V part II contains manuscripts available in CRIS, Chennai.

Published Manuscripts in Tamil with English translation

Among the palm-leaf manuscripts preserved in the Institute, fifty are on magic and medicine. More than a hundred are on folklore. Out of this, seventy are ballads. Some of the ballads are being brought out in book form by the Institute. It is proposed to publish many of these manuscripts in book form in the near future.

In the Kerala University Library of Manuscriptology, containing a large number of manuscripts, most of the manuscripts are in the form of ballads collected from the districts of the deep South. Similarly, the manuscripts available in the Institute of Asian Studies also have their origin in the same area. In fact, next to the Kerala University Library of Manuscriptology, the Institute of Asian Studies has the greatest number of manuscripts on folklore. These have largely for their subject matter the glorification of minor deities and their worship. Some fifty manuscripts deal with astrology, yoga, mantra, etc. About twenty manuscripts have bearing on grammar, literature, drama and purANas. There are some manuscripts in the *grantha* script carrying the titles PushpAñcali, Vakai, KalacApishEkappiracitti, TaNañcaya nikaNTu and yOjANAppiramANam. Their number is about fifty. The descriptive catalogue (Vol IV Part I & II and Vol V Part I) carries the full list.

1. The Wandering Voice
2. The Art of Drumming
3. The Dateless Muse - The Story of Venkala RAjan
4. The Unsung Melodies
5. Elder Brother's Story *ANNanmAr katai* Part I & II
6. The Divine Pilgrimage
7. A Tale of Romance - *Sakuntalai VilAcam*
8. *Varma CUttiram*
9. NiIli yaTcakAnam
10. The Valorous Virgins *(PeNNaraciyar Katai)*
11. The Epic Eternal *(IrAmar katai)* Part I & II
12. The Vows Fulfilled *(AmaiyAr ammAnai)*
13. Destiny and Divinity *(VarAnkata maharAjan katai)*
14. A Tale of Betrayal *(CArankataran yaTcakAn\am)*

15. Poetic Petal in the Interior Landscape *(UttaNTan kOvai)*
16. MEriI KaruttammaL ammANai
17. Where Justice Chimes(TErUrnta cOLan yaTcakANam)

Works in progress

Other than the seventeen manuscripts that have been published in book form, the Institute has plans to release another seven books in 1997 on the following titles from YaTcakANam, AmmANai, and Jain literature:

1. TinkaLur MAmalaiyAn noNTinATakam

This work, written by the poet AvinAci, falls under the genre *noNTinATakam,* one of the kinds of minor literature. It extols the greatness of Lord Murukan, residing in TinkaLUr near Erode. The work that depicts many histrical characters and events is being edited by M. Maruthamuthu.

2. Tirukkalampakam

This text, which belongs to the *kalampakam* genre of minor literature, glorifies the greatness of the Jaina god, Aruka tEvar and Jain philosophy. The author of this text is UtIcittEvar. The manuscript is being edited by M. Parimanan.

3. KOlavarittuyilarankan caritam

This manuscript which glorifies the God residing in Cinkapuram, near Ceñci, is being edited by Dr P. Subramaniam and M. Satiyabama.

4. VaikuNTa mmANai

This manuscript which is a sequel to the epic Mahabharatam, depicts the voyage of PANTavas to heaven in AmmAnai form. Editing this manuscript is entrusted with Dr K. Jaya Kumar.

5. TaTciNAmUrtti ValaivAkaTam

Dr P. Subramaniam and Pirasanna have colloborated in editing this medical manuscript available in Anna Hospital.

6. MataNa kAmEcuram

This is another medical manuscript preserved at Anna Hospital. Dr K. Jayakumar and ALakapparAcu are collobarated in editing this manuscript.

Time was when Tamilians recorded their ideas in palm-leaf manuscripts. Thanks to the printing press, this method of preserving knowledge for posterity fell into obsolesence. Still today, surviving palm-leaf manuscripts are store-houses of age-old knowledge and wisdom.

If these palm-leaf manuscripts are to be saved and recorded, it will demand the time of many trained scholars. And yet, there are very few people who know the intricacies of palm-leaf writing and can decipher them. So the urgency to train people to read the manuscripts cannot be minimised. The Institute of Asian Studies has sought the help of the Government of India to run workshops on manuscript reading. Earlier the workshops were held once in two years; now it has become an annual affair.

1. First Workshop on Palm-leaf Manuscript Deciphering

The first workshop was held on 21.3.90 in the presence of the Chairman of the Governing body, Justice V.R. Krishna Iyer. Prof. M. Shanmugam Pillai was the project head. Twenty-five participants were trained over a period of 21 days.

2. Second Workshop on Palm-leaf Manuscript Deciphering

The second workshop was held from 17.2.92 to 9.3.92 and was conducted by Prof. M. Shanmugam Pillai. Most of the people who underwent training were practitioners of the Siddha school of medicine.

3. Third Workshop on Palm-leaf Manuscript Deciphering

This was held from 14.02.94 to 07.03.94. Dr A. Thasarathan was in charge. Mutual exchange of ideas and the work to be done in future were the subjects on the agenda.

4. Fourth Workshop on Palm-leaf Manuscript Deciphering

A fourth workshop was held between 1.3.95 and 21.3.95. Dr P. Subramaniam and Dr K. Jayakumar were in charge of this workshop.

5. Fifth Workshop on Palm-leaf Manuscript Deciphering

The fifth workshop was held between 3.2.97 and 27.2.97 at the new IAS campus. This was conducted by Dr P. Subramaniam and Dr K. Jaya Kumar.

The Department was started with the idea of examining Tamil palm-leaf manuscripts only, but its range of operation has grown to include other languages as well. This has added to its stature as a regional center of manuscriptology where palm-leaf manuscripts of a diverse nature written in different languages are studied and published authoritative ly. Under the guidance of IAS Director for Research Programmes Dr G. John Samuel, the Department has evolved an ambitious programme to study the scientific truths lying embedded in old palm-leaf manuscripts dealing with diverse subjects like astrology, medicine, architecture, astronomy and geology, among other fields.

UNESCO and the Memory of the World

The United Nations Educational Scientific and Cultural Organisation (UNESCO) has recognised the ongoing contribution of the IAS to the preservation of the world's cultural heritage. In its Memory of the World programme covering all the cultural relics available in the world, UNESCO has commended the substantial achievements of the Institute of Asian Studies.

The Institute's Director Dr G. John Samuel has been serving on the World Expert Committee of the UNESCO appointed to identify the world's treasure- stores of knowledge since 1993. As India's expert on the World Expert Committee, Dr Samuel has underscored India's unexplored contribution to the world's body of knowledge.

The first meeting of the World Expert Committee was held in Warsaw during 12-14 Sept 1993. At the first meeting, discussion centerd around the memorable relics of the world and various recommendations were made to the General Conference. The memorable relics included rare manuscripts, palm- leaf manuscripts, oral traditions and the knowledge of tho se whose language lacked a script, inventions, unexplored arts and religious practices, beliefs and mores. The need to record and catalogue all the above items was unanimously agreed upon. Subsequent to the Committee meeting in Warsaw, Dr Samuel also participated by invitation in the meeting of the Advisory Committee when it met in Oslo on 1-8 Jun e 1996.

Following the recognition of palm-leaf manuscripts as memorable relics of the world, the Institute of Asian Studies drew up a programme to assess and study the Tamil manuscripts available in the world. It was decided to hold an international seminar to underline the urgency. As a first step, a national seminar on palm-leaf manuscripts was jointly organised by the Institute of Asian Studies and Pondicherry Central University.

Dr A. Pandurangan organised the seminar, which was presided over by Dr Gnanam with keynote address delivered by the Director of the Institute of French Culture, Pondicherry, Dr. Francois Gros. Information regarding palm- leaf manuscripts in Assamese, Oriya, Gujarathi, Sanskrit, Punjabi, Pali, Bengali and Marathi was exchanged. Scholarly papers on palm-leaf manuscripts available in the South Indian languages, namely Kannada, Tamil, Telugu, Tulu and Malayalam were presented.

The Sanskrit manuscripts were discussed separately under two heads: Sanskrit manuscripts available in India those available outside India. The discussion also centred on the denominators of various scripts employed in the palm-leaf manuscripts such as Bengali, Moti and CAratA. There was a presentation concerning palm-leaf manuscripts found in the Raghunath temple in Jammu. Three articles were presented on the collection and preservation of palm-leaf manuscripts. The conference brought to light the places where Tamil manuscripts had been found and highlighted the location of manuscripts in other languages. The proceedings of the seminar were published under the title Palm-leaf and other Manuscripts in Indian Languages in August 1996.

The collecting and preserving of palm-leaf manuscripts

Director of the Institute of Asian Studies Dr G. John Samuel has pioneered the collecting and documenting of palm-leaf manuscripts from diverse sources. Many others like Dr A. Thasarathan, Dr N.Ramachandran, Dr Govindasami, D. Boominaganathan and Pulavar B. Kannaiyan followed his example, collecting many invaluable manuscripts.

Most of the manuscripts that have been collected are from the Southern part of the PaNTyanATu. Thus far, palm-leaf manuscripts have been obtained from the following localities:

13
INSTITUTE OF MANUSCRIPTS, BAKU

Baku is a major city and the capiral of Azerbaijan, a country lying at the crossroads between Europe, Asia, and the Middle East. It borders Russia and Georgia to the north, Iran and Turkey to the south, Armenia to the west, and the Caspian Sea to the east. The original Republic of Azerbaijan was formed in 1918 in the wake of World War I and was the first nation in the Caucasus to establish an independent, secular, and democratic government. Not long after, the newly formed state of Azerbaijan became a part of the Soviet Union and continued until December 3,1991, when a new independent Republic of Azerbaijan was formed after more than seventy years of Soviet rule. The 7.9 million people of Azerbaijan live on 86,600 square kilometers, while 20 percent of the territory is occupied by Armenians as a result of the Nagorno-Karabakh conflict. Armenians and Azerbaijanis went to war in the late 1980s over Nagorno Karabakh—a part of Azerbaijani territory inside Azerbaijan's borders mainly populated by Armenians. More than thirty-five thousand people were killed and one million Azerbaijani refugees were created in the process of war. Both sides have generally observed a Russian-mediated cease-fire in place since May 1994, and support the Organization for Cooperation and Security (OCSE) - mediated peace process, now entering its fifth year.

Besides the capital of Azerbaijan Baku, other principal cities are Gyandzha, Sumgayut and Mingyazevir. The natural resources of the country are petroleum, natural gas, iron ore, nonferrous metals and aluminum. The tremendous energy resources of Azerbaijan serve as a long-term alternative for the Western countries to lessen dependence on the vulnerable supplies of Persian Gulf oil. With potential reserves of two hundred billion barrels of oil, the Caspian region will become the most important new player in world oil markets over the next decade.

Libraries in Azerbaijan

The earliest library in Azerbaijan appeared in the thirteenth century and belonged to the Maruha Observatory. This observatory was created in the second half of the thirteenth century in the city of Meraga of Eastern Azerbaijan in Iran. The library of more than 400,000 volumes was founded by Nasiruddin Tusi — a great scientist, thinker and statesman of that period. In the sixteenth century the biggest library of that time existed at the palace of the Shah Ismail Khatai — a founder of the Safavid dynasty and a famous poet. In the nineteenth century most libraries were private collections. The biggest ones were the personal libraries of Abaskuli bek Bakikhanov and Mirza Fatali Akhundov. Bakikhanov was a prominent Azerbaijani scientist and writer. He is the author of number of works on history, education, philosophy, astronomy and geography. Akhundov was a great Azerbaijani playwright, educator and philosopher. He is considered a founder of Azerbaijani dramatic art and contributed to the development of literary and social thought of the whole Middle East. The first public library was opened in Azerbaijan in 1894.

The most ancient manuscripts of the Azerbaijani language go back to the fourteenth (Divans of Gazi Burkhanaddin and Nasimi) and fifteenth centuries (manuscript of the epic Dede Gorgut). The epic itself was written in the twelfth-thirteenth centuries. All the manuscripts in the Azerbaijani language created before the middle of the nineteenth century are kept in the Manuscripts Institute of Azerbaijan.

Azerbaijani books published in the eighteenth and nineteenth centuries form part of the Turkic collections of many libraries of the former Soviet Union. The Azerbaijani collection

(1845-1931), part of a Turkic collection of the St. Petersburg branch of the Institute of the Asian Nations by number of volumes, occupies the second place among all their collections. These materials mainly cover a period before the 1917 Revolution and are marked by a prevalence of literature on history, art, and folklore. Good examples from this collection include the early works by M. Akhundov (Hikayat Mulla Ibrahim Xalil Kimiyakira, Tiflis, 1859), by N. Narimanov (Shakh- Nadir, Baku, 1899 and Shamdan bek, Baku, 1913), by Fizuli (Leyla and Medznun, Baku, 1915), by Molla Nasreddin (Post Box, Tiflis, 1912). Early translations of Russian and foreign literature into Azerbaijani are also represented in the collection; for example Tolstoy's What Men Line By and A Captive in the Caucasus (Baku, 1912), Karamzin's Poor Lisa (Baku, 1912), Gorky's The Children of the Sun, Shakespeare's Othello (Baku, 1893) and also many textbooks and recreational reading. Copies of the following journals, published before the Revolution, are also pan of a collection: Molla Nasreddin (Tiflis, 1906-1930), Sedai Kafkaz (Baku, 1915-1916), Mertep (Baku, 1911-1916).

As a result of the Nagorno Karabakh conflict with Armenians, almost two thousand libraries with millions of volumes in their collections located in Nagorno Karabakh and near the Azerbaijani-Armenian border were destroyed and burned by Armenians. The collections contained rare books as well as material on Azerbaijani history, literature and culture. That was a big cultural loss for Azerbaijan.

A former school is now used to house the Institute of Manuscripts and its collection of rare medieval Eastern texts. Taghiyev would have been proud, although he wouldn't have been able to read the books kept there. The sad truth is that neither can most Azerbaijanis in the Republic today, as the Azeri alphabet has changed three times since Arabic was the state. The Arabic script was banned by the Soviets in 1939 in an effort to eradicate Islam.

Farid Alakbarov, medical historian at the Manuscripts

Institute, is one of the few younger people in the Republic who is able to read the medieval Azeri Arabic texts. He has devoted his academic career to studying early handwritten medical manuscripts, hoping to restore some of the medical knowledge that has been forgotten. Here Farid identifies some of the highlights from the Institute's unique collection.

Collection of Manuscripts

The Institute of Manuscripts of the Azerbaijan Academy of Sciences is a center for collecting, systematizing, storing and publishing Eastern medieval manuscripts. It currently includes about 40,000 works, in languages that include Azeri, Turkish, Uzbek, Persian and Arabic. These texts help us understand what Azerbaijanis from the Middle Ages thought about medicine, astronomy, mathematics, poetry, philosophy, law, history and geography.

The basis for the Institute was laid in 1924, when the first all-Azerbaijan Regional Congress was held in Baku. The Congress decided to organize a scientific library with a special department dedicated to ancient manuscripts and rare books. At first, this library was part of the Investigation Society of Azerbaijan; then it became attached to the Nizami Institute of Literature. In 1950 the Manuscript Department became the Independent Center of Scientific Research. In 1986, its name was changed to the Institute of Manuscripts.

Many of the ancient manuscripts found at the Institute came from the private collections of Azerbaijan's most prominent 19th- and early 20th-century thinkers, including Abbasgulu agha Bakikhanov, Mirza Fatali Akhundov, Abdulgani Afandi Khalisagarizada, Husein Afandi Gaibov, Bahman Mirza Gajar and Mir Mohsun Navvab. It continues to collect manuscripts, rare books and historical documents from all over Azerbaijan.

The Institute is located in the former Alexandrian Russian Muslim Female Boarding School, which was built by Haji Zeynalabdin Taghiyev between 1898 and 1901. This was the first girl's school in the Muslim East. The building was designed by Polish architect Joseph V. Goslavski (1865-1904), who also designed Baku's City Hall and Taghiyev's private residence, which now serves as the Taghiyev Museum housing the National History Museum collection.

In 1918, when Azerbaijan became independent, Taghiyev gave the building to the government of Azerbaijan to be used for ministers' offices. In 1920, after the Red Army invaded Azerbaijan, the Bolsheviks turned the building into the headquarters for the Worker, Peasant and Soldier Deputies. After that, it housed the Presidium of the Supreme Soviet of the Azerbaijan Republic (the governing body of Parliament). Since 1950, the building has housed what is now called the Institute of Manuscripts.

One of the Institute's greatest treasures is a complete manuscript of "Khamsa", a collection of poems by the 12th-century Azerbaijani writer Nizami Ganjavi, who is often referred to as Nizami. The manuscript was copied in 1636 by Dust Muhammed ibn Darvish Muhammed Darakhtichi. This version is unique in that the copyist, after finishing his work with the manuscript, borrowed the oldest "Khamsa" manuscript available and used it to write exhaustive margin notes in his own copy of the manuscript. The text is written in the nastalik script, a popular style of handwriting that was developed in the 15th century.

The earliest-known miniatures for Nizami's "Khamsa" appear in 15th-century manuscripts. In this period, Nizami's stories were illustrated by artists from the miniature schools of Shiraz and Herat. In the 16th century, Azerbaijani miniatures laid the foundation for the Tabriz miniature school. Important artists included Sultan Mohammad Tabrizi, Agha Mirak, Mirza Ali, Muzaffar Ali and Mir Seyid Ali.

The Institute of Manuscripts has many other ancient books that are decorated with miniatures, including: "The Garden of Truth" by Sana'i (painted in 1625), "The Eight Paradises" by

Amir Khosrov Dehlavi (1579), "The Seven Beauties" by Nizami Ganjavi (1636), "Divan" by Urfi (17th century), "Divan" by Hafiz Shirazi (1584), "Laila and Majnun" by Maktabi (17th century), "Divan" by Amir Shahi (1573) and "Divan" by Mohammad Fuzuli (17th century).

These colorful miniatures show various scenes of hunting, listening to music, dancing, eating, gardening, fighting and love, as well as natural landscapes, flowers, gardens, nightingales and flowering apricot trees. The most famous miniatures, found in Nizami's "Khamsa", portray the love stories of Laila and Majnun and Khosrov and Shirin.

Scenes include: "Beggar Woman Brings Majnun to Leyli," "The Meeting of Laila and Majnun," "Laila Visits Majnun in the Desert," "Khosrov Sees Shirin Bathing" and "Khosrov and Shirin Listen to the Girl's Tales." The miniature named "Hunting" shows how the shah and his huge band of raiders tracked large herds of game (gazelles, deer and wild horses).

The most influential medical manuscript housed at the Institute is a 12th-century copy of Avicenna's "Canon of Medical Sciences." Avicenna (Abu Ali Ibn Sina) (980-1037) was born in Bukhara, in what today is Uzbekistan. He did much of his medical observation later on in Persia.

The "Canon", written in 1030, is an encyclopedia of medical knowledge considered to be the single most famous book in medical history. The Institute's version of the manuscript was copied in 1143, a little more than 100 years after the text was written. It is one of the oldest Avicenna manuscripts in the world and is considered to be the most reliable.

14
INSTITUTE OF ORIENTAL STUDIES, TASHKENT

Uzbekistan is one of the cradles of human civilization like most of Central Asia,. Archaeological investigations show that the process of inhabiting the territory of Uzbekistan dates back to the Stone Age, and the most ancient information on the nationalities of Central Asia is documented in the Avesta-the code of holy hymns of the Zoroastrians. Many researchers consider Central Asia as the native land of this religion. According to original sources, these lands were inhabited by Soghdians, Bactrians and other nationalities. During the fourth, fifth, and sixth centuries B.C., a greater part of the Central Asian lands was under the power of the Persian dynasty of Akhemenids. The above mentioned nationalities are described in Persian original sources. Greek writers mentioned the existence of Marakanda city (today's Samarkand) and Kiropol in Ferghana. Archaeologists have studied many other cities of that period situated in North Bactria, Khorezm, and Marghilan.

From ancient times, the wealth of the land attracted foreign conquerors. In the third and fourth centuries B.C., Central Asia was conquered by the Macedonians. Conquest by Alexander the Great had a great effect on the economic and cultural development of the peoples of the East, West and Central Asia.

In the middle of the third century B.C., the conquered regions became independent and local dynasties came to power. Bactria, which included the southern parts of Uzbekistan and Tadjikistan, became the hub of the Greek- Bactrian empire and later came under control of the Kushan empire. After the conquest of Central Asia by Alexander the Great, studies of the subsequent period depict development and the heyday of architecture, painting, handcrafts, and music.

During the seventh and eighth centuries, Central Asia was conquered by the Arab Khalifat. The Arabs took over these countries under the mission of spreading the new religion of Islam. As a result, their conquest entirely changed the region's way of life. Building construction, art and science declined under the pressures of war and continued only in the middle of the nineth century. This was connected with the creation of independent empires ruled by the dynasties of the local aristocracy: the Tahirids and Samanids. In the l0th century, the Arabs were forced to withdraw their troops and the Samanids rose to power.

Ismail Samani, the founder of the Samanid dynasty, chose Bukhara for his capital. Architects of the region created their own unique cultural structure - mosques covered by a dome. The nineth, tenth, and eleventh centuries (A.C.) were the heyday of life in the ancient city centers, such as Bukhara, Samarkand, and Termez. A most interesting example of 10th century architecture is the Mausoleum of lsmail Samani in Bukhara. This is believed to be one of the greatest monuments in the Islamic world, built in the nineth century. The K-alon minaret in Bukhara is another masterpiece of the period.

In 1220-1221 Central Asia could not withstand the invasion of Genghiz-Khan's army. Many cities, such as Bukhara, Khorezm, and Samarkand were destroyed. Thousands of people perished (in Samarkand, only 50,000 out of a population of one million survived).

In the middle of the 14th century with the help of the famous warlord Tamerlane the local people were freed from the Mongols. Tamerlane began his succsessful marches to Iraq, India, Turkey, and noth Africa that led to establishing one of the most powerful medival empires, with Samarkand as the capital. Restoration and development of the cities (Samarkand and Shakhrisabz, Tamerlane's native town in particular), revived commerce, handyerafts, sceince and the arts. Monuments belonging to that period and still stand today are the Bibi Khanum mosque, the Shahi Zinda complex of ancient mausoleums, Registan Square, the Gur Emir mausoleum which was built as the burial place for Tamerlane. After Tamerlane's death, the empire existed for another century, then collapsed and fell into a number of small states.

In the 14th century Uzbek nomadic tribes invaded from the north, conquering the small feudal states of Timurids and formed thier own state (later to be called Uzbekistan). The term " Uzbek" means "master" or "lord" of oneself.

Later on, two large khanates - Bukhara and Khiva - were formed. Isolation decreased, and trade and other relations with foreign countries and slowed down the economic development of the region. The economics of Central Asia in the past owed to stable relations with China, India and Europe. In the 2nd century B.C. caravan trade routes connected South-East Europe, Iraq, Caucasus, and Central Asia with Mongolia and China, and is now known as the great Silk Road. The Silk Road passed through the centers of Central Asia - Samarkand, Bukhara, Marghilan, Shakhrisabz, and Andijan.

Through the trade ties of the Central Asian states with foreign countries, world civilization grew enriched with the sceintific and spiritual works of such great thinkers as lbn Sino (Avicenna), Beruni (Albiron), AI- Termezi, Ferghani, Farabi, Ulugbek, Navoi, Babur, AI-Khorezmi and others.

Central Asian architects made a considerable contribution to the global field. A unique style of architecture is spread all over the region and its ancient capitals: Samarkand, Bukhara, and Khiva, that concentrated the very best designing skills and arts of the age. One can feel the atmosphere of medieval Asian cities with squares, caravan-sarays, trade centers, and handicrafts created over many centuries.

In the second half of the 19th century the Bukhara, Khiva

and Kokand khanates were joined to the Russian Empire. During this period agriculture was highly developed in Uzbekistan for one specific reason: it was more economical to grow cotton in Central Asia instead of importing it from the US. Cotton became the most important agricultural item. The construction of railroads made its impact on the development of trade and cultural relations between Asia and Europe. That was when the country began to overcome its earlier period of stagnation.

The Russia Revolution in 1917 changed the political situation in Turkestan and in 1922 Uzbekistan became one of the republics of the USSR. Uzbekistan announced its independence and September l, 1991 was proclaimed as its Independence Day. Upon gaining its statehood, Uzbekistan began to work out its own way of becoming a renewed, developing sovereign democratic republic. The country is a multinational state: more than 129 nationalities and national minorities live there as well as 15 different confessions that have coexisted peacefully for several centuries. People here are also known for their ancient ethic of working hard in order to achieve a better life.

Collection of Manuscripts

The Collection of oriental manuscripts of the UAS Institute of Oriental Studies named after Abu Reyhan Beruni forms one of the richest and outstanding treasury of oriental manuscripts in the world.

The most ancient works keeping in the manuscript fund have more than thousand years history. The latest works dates from the beginning of twentieth century.

The works collected in the manuscript fund was written in Uzbek, Arabic, Persian, Tadjik, Urdu, Pushtu, Azerbaidjan, Turkish,Tatar, Turkmen, Uygur and other languages of the East. These works are devoted to the history, history of literature, philosophy, law, astronomy, physics, chemistry, medicine, language, pharmacology, geography, music, mathematics, mineralogy, agriculture, fine arts and others. They are of great importance on studying history, history of Middle Asia culture, India, Pakistan, Afghanistan, Arabian countries, Iran, Turkey and other countries of the East, as well as on studying the diplomatic and political, economical and cultural connections among them.

Presence of the rich manuscript fund made the necessity of deep studying, in order to make of this cultural heritage a property of wide scientific community. The Institute for Study of Oriental Manuscripts was organized in the framework of the Uzbekistan Academy of Sciences established in 1943. All manuscript copies of the East branch of the State Public Library named after Alisher Navoi were passed to the new created Institute.

At the beginning, there was only one department for studying oriental manuscripts. However, steadily widening activity of the Institute required the organization of new ones, like the department for primary scientific working up and systematization, the department for scientific description and cataloguer, the department for research and publication of literary memorials and documents, and also the department for studying political, economical and cultural life of neighboring foreign countries and their connection with the Middle Asia. The name of the Institute has also changed. Now, it is known as the Institute of Oriental Studies named after Abu Reykhan Bruni of the Uzbekistan Academy of Sciences.

All literary works of outstanding classics on oriental literature collected in the manuscript fund of the Institute: Yusuf Hos Hadjib Balasaguni, Rabguzi, Rudaki, Firdousi, Nizami, Gandjavi, Saadi, Amir Hosrov Dehlevi, Abdurahman Djami, Alisher Navoi, Faridaddin Attar, Djalaliddin Rumi, Hafiz, Omar Hayam, Fizuli, Mirza Abdulkadir Bedil, Abu Ali Ibn Sino, Allamai Zamahshari, Mahmud Kashgari, Ulugbek, Kazizadi Rumi, Ali Kushchi, Kutbaddin Shirazi and many others on different branches of natural sciences.

In the manuscript fund of the Institute there are many manuscripts on the history, of Islam, Islamic sciences, Sufizm, written on Arabic language, Persian, old Uzbek and languages concerning to the IX-XIX centuries.

Due to the efforts of research officers, the Institute issued eleven volumes of the catalogue "Oriental manuscripts collection of the Uzbekistan Academy of Sciences". The short scientific descriptions of 7574 various manuscript works on different Eastern languages are given in it, and this work lasts till now.

Research officers prepared and published the catalogues, devoted to the description of manuscript works (from the collection of the Institute of Oriental Studies) of outstanding representatives of science and culture- Abu Nasr al-Farabi, Abu Ali Ibn Sino, Amir Hosrov Dehlevi, Abdurahman Djami ans Alisher Navoi.

Illustrated catalogue, prepared in collaboration with the Institute of Arts named after Hamza, "Oriental miniatures in the Collection of Institute of Oriental Studies of the Uzbekistan Academy of Sciences" has been published.

In connection with 1000 years anniversary of Ibn Sino, the second edition of "Canon of medical science" has been issued. During the last years of independence the third edition of that book was published. As the Institute intensively works on study and popularization of the scientific heritage of the great scientists, it was awarded to the First International Prize of Ibn Sino.

The number of sources on various questions on history, history of culture and science was edited in the translation and in the original by the research officers. The following works were issued by the scientists of the Institute.

-"itab sirr al-asrar" ("Mystery of mystery book") bu Bakra ar-Razi

-"Baburname" of Zahiriddin Muhammad Bobur

-"Hummayunnama"

-"bdurazzoq Samarkandiyning Hindiston safarnomasi" ("Abdurazzoq Samarkandiy's travel notes about his tour to India")

-"Hiva davlat hujjatlari" ("Hiva State Documents")

-"Tarikh-i salatini Mingitiya" ("History of Mangit Rulers") of Mirza Abdalazim Sami

-"Buxoro tarihi" ("History of Bukhara") of Narshahi

-"bdullaname" of Hafiz Tanisha Bukhari

-""arikh-i Mukimhani" ("Mukimhan history") of Muhammed Yusuf Munshi

-"Ubaydullaname" of Mirmuhammad Amina Bukhari

-""arih-i Masudi" ("History of Masud") of Abu-l Fazl Beyhaki

-"“atla as-Sadayn va madjma al-bahrain" ("The ascent of two happy constellations and confluence of two happy seas") of Abdurazzoq Samarkandiy

-"Mehmanname-i Bukhara" ("The book of Bukhara visitor") of Fazlallah Ruzbehan

-geographical part "Bahr al-asrar" ("The sea of mysteries") of Mahmud ibn Vali

-"“0djma al-arkam" ("Fisc directions") of Mirza Badi divan

-"l-ad-viyat al-qalbiya" ("Heart medicine")

-"Urdjuza" and "Salaman i Ibsal" of Ibn Sina

-"Treatise of astronomy" of Ali Kushchi

-"Iyatimat d-dahr" ("Rare pearl") of Abu-Mansur as-Saalibi and others.

In connection with the growing interest to the study of written heritage, a number of catalogues on various tendencies were issued. The catalogues were created on the basis of the collection of oriental manuscripts of the Institute on historical, natural and exact sciences, medicine, Sufism, catalogues of miniatures and documents. Intensively developing relationships on studying and publishing manuscripts were established with the foreign scientists of Germany, Iran, Japan, USA and other countries.

The ancient manuscripts in the fund will take in more than thousand years period of the culture development of the East back from the I% centuries till the beginning of %% centuries. Nowadays the fund of the UAS Institute of Oriental Studies as the richest treasury of manuscripts in the world is included into the UNESCO list.

15
IRAQI HOUSE OF MANUSCRIPTS, BAGHDAD

Iraq has a long and illustrious history. School children in every corner of the world read about the ancient civilization of Mesopotamia, which shaped and inspired the civilizations of the rest of mankind. This history and civilization is preserved in manuscripts that does justice to and honors to its glorious past.

The work of collecting and putting together the ancient and rare manuscripts in Iraq started with the establishment of the Department of Manuscripts in 1962 as part of the Iraqi National Museum in Baghdad. It originally contained 2,526 manuscripts, but expanded throughout the 1970s and 1980s as the government bought manuscripts from collections around the country. In 1988, when the collection had reached 37,083 manuscripts, the state decided to found an autonomous entity, the Saddam House of Manuscripts. Today there are an estimated 50,000 manuscripts of which 7,000 are on loan from other institutions or private collections and there for repair and conservation (information gathered from talk with former director, Usama al-Naqshabandi).

Iraq has a large collection of manuscripts housed in its libraries and archives. Notable among them are the Iraqi House of Manuscripts, earlier known as Dar Saddam lil Makhtutat, Ministry of Endowments and Religeous Affairs Library, National Library and Archives, House of Wisdom (Bayt al Hikmah), Iraqi Academy of Sciences, Quadriya Mosque etc.

Established in 1920, the Awqaf library is the oldest public MSS collection in Iraq. A modern two storyed facility located near the Ministry of Health, the library building was absolutely destroyed. As with Dar al-Makhtutat, the Awqaf staff had taken steps to protect their collection, moving 5250 out of their total of 7000 MSS to a protected storage space prior to the burning and looting. Unlike Dar al-Makhtutat, the Awqaf staff had Ministry permission to move their MSS prior to the war. According to the staff, these 5250 MSS remain under armed protection in an undisclosed location.

In the course of the 1991 uprising about 20,000 MSS were endangered by events in the provinces although only 346 publicly-owned MSS were confirmed lost and subsequently listed as such in an effort to recover them. In addition, 1000 MSS from the Baraki, Kashani, and other private collections of Najaf and Karbala were reportedly taken to Iran in the course of the 1991 uprising. As a result of this experience, and in accordance with longstanding Ministry of Culture efforts to centralize all MSS collections in one facility, several collections were absorbed into the main collection in the 1990's. In addition, in the course of the 1990's Dar al-Makhtutat staff had microfilmed 8 million folios from 15-20,000 MSS and preserved on CD-Roms 250,000 images from illuminated MSS and other rare MSS. Finally, in accordance with the 1974 Antiquities Law, each governorate did a survey of private and public MSS collections. The results of this survey were kept in box files at the Dar al-Makhtutat, which were moved into the shelter along with the MSS prior to the war.

Iraqi Manuscripts Collection and Libraries in 2003

Collection	Holdings	Comments	Contacts
Collections in Baghdad Libraries			
Dar al-Makhtutat al-'Iraqiyya / Iraqi House of Manuscripts [formerly Dar Saddam lil-Makhtutat / Saddam House of Manuscripts]	47,000 own MSS,3,000 other MSS from the Academy, Mosul, Tikrit, Kirkuk, Basra	Collection transferred to Shelter #12, Hayy Dakhiliyya; preservation facilities looted.	Osama NaqshbandiMs. Dhamya
Maktabat al-Awqaf al-Markaziyya /Ministry of Endowments & Religious Affairs Central Library	7000 MSS.	Ca. 5250 MSS transferred to undisclosed location,Ca. 600-700 MSS burned, Ca. 1000-1100 MSS lootedFacility burned.	Buthayna 'Abd Allah QaysiHasan Freih Salah Karim Baqir Hamid Muhib al-Din Yasin'Abd al-Karim Sa'id,
National Library & Archive/ Dar al-Kutub wa al-Watha'iq	12 million documents, published books.	Facility looted & burned. Rumors of some docs saved.	Ra'ad Bardar
Bayt al-Hikma /House of Wisdom	100 MSS,US, French, Ottoman, UK document copies	Facility looted & burned.Some MSS may re-surface.	Adnan Yasin Mustafa, 'Abd al-Jabbar Naji
Iraqi Academy of Sciences/ Al-Majma' al-'Ilmi al-Iraqi	2000 MSS,58,000 published books.	Facility looted, but not burned. Ca. 80% books looted, Some MSS returned.	Mahmud Hayyawi,Ms. Juwan, "Umm Ibrahim," Muhammad Khudeir 'Abbas, Khalid Khadr Qadir, Jalil Wahhab Salim.

Qadiriyya Mosque Collection	1883 MSS	OK	
Deir al-Aba al-Krimliyin	120 MSS	Christian MSS, OK?	
Maktabat al-Hidaya, Baghdad?	500 MSS	Condition unknown	
Univ. of Baghdad Central Library / Al-Maktaba al-Markaziyya	research collection of published works	OK.	
Mustansiriyya University Medical School Library	medical textbooks, research publications	OK	Walid al-Hashimi
Mustansiriyya University Main Library	research collection of published works	Looted.	
Baghdad Medical College Library	medical textbooks, research publications	Looted.	

Efforts to save the collection from the impending war began 4 months prior to the war and continued right up to the week immediately prior to hostilities. In the course of these efforts, all MSS were taken to the shelter, microfilms to a second (undisclosed) location, and CD/Roms to a third (undisclosed) location. According to Mr. Naqshbandi, his staff undertook such protection measures even though they did not have official Ministry permission to move the collection and were asked to slow their efforts by the Minister of Culture, Hamid Yusuf Hammadi.

Today, the shelter contains nearly 800 steel trunks of MSS, including ca. 500 trunks of Dar al-Makhtutat MSS, ca. 200 trunks from other collections, and 83 trunks of rare published books. These trunks contain ca. 50,000 MSS, including ca. 47,000 from the Dar al-Makhtutat collection and ca. 3,000 MSS from other collections, including:

- Iraqi Academy of Sciences: 667 MSS [including 68 unpublished works of Mustafa Jawad]
- Mosul Central Library, 301 MSS
- University of Mosul Library: 122 MSS
- University of Tikrit: 40 MSS
- Kirkuk Central Library, 40 MSS
- University of Mustansiriyya [Baghdad]: ? MSS
- University of Basra: ? MSS

The Iraqi House of Manuscripts was set up after the 1974 Antiquities Act, which rendered manuscripts part of the national patrimony. The collection was originally housed in the Iraqi National Museum (itself constructed in the 1960's), and then it was provided with its own facilities in the 1980's. It emains administratively part of the Iraqi National Museum bureaucracy, but in a separate facility. In the 1990's, after the chaos and dislocations of 1991, the collection was expanded by a campaign to bring together certain regional and private collections. As a result, by 2003 it housed a collection of over 40,000 Arabic, Ottoman, Persian, Kurdish, Hebrew, Syriac, and other manuscripts.

The Iraqi House of Manuscripts was formerly known as Dar Saddam lil Makhtutat/Saddam House of Manuscripts. It had its modest beginning from the foundation of Department of Manuscripts. The department of manuscripts was established in 1962 as part of the Iraqi National Museum in Baghdad. It originally contained 2,526 manuscripts, but expanded throughout the 1970s and 1980s as the government bought manuscripts from collections around the country. In 1988, when the collection had reached 37,083 manuscripts, the state decided to found an autonomous entity, the Saddam House of Manuscripts.

Today there are an estimated 50,000 manuscripts of which 7,000 are on loan from other institutions or private collections and there for repair and conservation. The bomb shelter reportedly has 4 sets of doors and is under continuous armed guard. On 3 occasions looters tried and failed to force the doors and loot the shelter. On each occasion the "neighborhood" chased the looters away and burned their vehicles (including a Mercedes).

In recent years, several MSS were transferred to Dar al-Makhtutat from other libraries of the country. A sizeable collection of them was transferred from Iraqi Academy of Sciences. A catalogue of the entire Academy MSS collection was published prior to the collection's partial transfer to Dar al-Makhtutat. In addition, there was a hand-written catalogue of Academy MSS, but this catalogue disappeared along with the MSS. Finally, although the entire collection had been preserved in photostat copies (?), these copies were looted along with the originals. The MSS room itself was completely empty during my visit.

The manuscript center has a well trained professional staff that knows how to preserve and conserve manuscripts. The center appeared to be administered and run efficiently. The center seemed to have benefited from financial, technical and professional support for several years before the war. In the past two years state support enabled it to accomplish the task of not only collecting, preserving, repairing but also of microfilming 50,000 manuscripts.

16
JAMIA AL AZHAR, CAIRO, EGYPT

Egypt has been the home of a very rich civilization. Alexander the Great conquered it in 332 BC. He founded Alexandria in 331 BC and it became a major center of civilization and trade in the Hellenistic ancient world with a famous library and intellectual life. The Ptolemy dynasty succeeded Alexander. The Ptolemies apparently founded the custom of marrying their sisters and ruling jointly with them as king and queen. Theyruled Egypt until 31 BC, when Cleopatra's fleet, defending the Roman consul Marcus Antonius, was defeated at Actium by his rival, Octavian, later to become Augustus Caesar. Augustus annexed Egypt as a province of the Roman empire and it was ruled by the Romans until 642 AD. During the Roman period, Christianity came to Egypt. The Egyptian branch of the Christian church, known as Coptic, is one of the oldest in the world. During Roman times Egypt apparently prospered at times, but was burdened by heavy Roman taxation. In particular, Egypt, together with North Africa, supplied a large portion of the grain of the Roman Empire, including the grain given out free to citizens on the dole in Rome.

The unique history of ancient Egypt and visible monuments to that history helped Egyptians to preserve a distinct national consciousness, and to remain a separate entity during the years of Arab, Mameluke and Ottoman conquest. Alexander conquered Egypt in the autumn of 332 BC. He founded Alexandria in 331 BC and it became a major center of civilization and trade in the Hellenistic ancient world with a famous library and intellectual life. The Ptolemy dynasty succeeded Alexander.

The Ottoman Turks conquered Egypt in 1517, and inaugurated a long but mostly undistinguished period in Egyptian history. The Ottomans ruled through a mixture of Janissary and Mameluke soldiers. Copts and Jews found a place in Egypt as merchants and intellectuals, clerks and civil servants. Ottoman rule deteriorated considerably in the 18th century. In 1796, Egypt revolted against the Ottomans and achieved a semi-independent status within the Ottoman empire. However, conditions did not improve. According to some historians, a laborer earned about one-seventh of a piaster per day. The leading Mameluke, Murad Bey, took in fifteen hundred piasters daily for expenses. Coptic villages in Upper Egypt refused to pay their taxes, and in the anarchy of the time, apparently no one tried to collect from them.

Al Azhar University was named after Hazrat Fatima al-Zahraa, daughter of the Holy Prophet of Islam. The Fatimid dynasty governed Egypt from 969 to 1171. The first university courses at Al Azhar were given in 975 and the first college was built 13 years later. Al Azhar University which is known as the highest authority in Sunni Islam is also famous for giving its verdict on Fiqah e Jafria saying that the Jafria School of thought is religiously correct to follow in worship as other Sunni schools of thought.

Al Azhar Library

Al-Azhar library was established in the year 1897,A.D., at the time of Imam Mohammed Abdo, when all books related to Islamic Heritage were distributed to a number of Al-Azhar hostels. An independent building, with an Islamic style, is under construction in an area adjacent to Al-Azhar. At the present time it occupies six areas inside Al-Azhar mosque (Aqabghawiah school, Al-Tabrasia school, Al-Abbasy hostel, Hostels libraries (Magharba,Atrak, shawam).The library comprises of 99,062 books consist of 595,668 volumes of the most precious manuscripts and rare books. The library is considered second to " Dar Al-kotob Al- Masriah" in Egypt, as far as the number of books and the rare literatures is concerned.

The books at the library are indexed according to their

subjects:(Holy books, Readings,Quranic sciences,Tafs.eer, Hadith, fiqh of Abi Hanifa, Al-Shafei', Malek and Ibn Hanbal;inheritances, Scholastic, Logic, language, Grammar, Researches, Eloqnence. ; Literatures and History).

The books were indexed in eight parts consist of 4,650 pages. There are approximately, forty three thousands manuscript back dated to the third century of the Islamic calendar and of later dates. These manuscripts include:

1. A number of hand written Holy Books, in various styles, i.e..(Kufi, Persian, Naskh). Most of the writing are coated with gold, some are overlaid with liquid gold and illustrated with Islamic portrays and drawings.
2. Al-Lae'li Al-F'arida",,written in the year, 706,A.E. "Sharh Al-Shatibia",written by Al-Ga'abary in the year 739,A.H., "Tafseer Gharib Al-Quran", in 514,A.H. "Al Kashaf-' by Zamakhshary" in 654,A.H., "Gharib Al-Hadith- by Ibn Sallam" in 311,A.H., "Omdat Al- Taliben by Ibn Al-Wazeer",in 605,A.H., etc...

Al-Azhar library is known to be the Center of Attraction to the Ulamas and Researchers of Al-Azhar students and all Islamic Universities. It contributes in propagating knowledge by making photo copies of some of the manuscripts available for the benefit of Researchers from Egypt and Arab and Islamic countries.

Collection of Manuscripts

For centuries, Al-Azhar housed one of the world's largest collections of Islamic manuscripts. There are approximately 3 million ancient manuscripts from various Islamic eras in the Muslim world, 1.3 million of which are located in Egypt. Out of the 1.3 million, 42,164 are housed at Al-Azhar University.

It later evolved into a reverend centre for Sunni Islamic learning. In 1897, a central library for Al-Azhar was established, which served as a repository for the vast collection of Islamic works of reference scattered throughout the university's other libraries. Some of the manuscripts date from before 969 AD, when Cairo's founding dynasty, the Fatimids, who ruled Egypt until 1171, entered the country. Because Egypt didn't have printing presses until the early 1800s, many of these old manuscripts are handwritten, in beautiful, surprisingly uniform, Arabic script.

For long centuries, this wonderful treasure house of rare manuscripts was left unindexed and disorganized. They were completely neglected and many were damaged, lost or stolen. Islamic scholars had to travel to Cairo to view these works in person. Even then, gaining access to the yellowing, hand-scripted treasures could be a very tedious and frustrating affair.

Al-Azhar Library is distinguished from other big libraries in the Islamic world by its rare manuscripts and books written by Al-Azhar scholars and Islamic scholars in general. These manuscripts expound on dozens of subjects, including fiqh [Islamic jurisprudence], medicine and other sciences, literature and history. They're written in Arabic and other languages such as Turkish, Persian and Urdu since students came to Al-Azhar from across the Muslim world.

Al-Azhar has decided to rescue its priceless treasures by launching Al-Azhar online (www.alazharonline.org), giving Internet users the chance to access some of the world's oldest and rarest Islamic manuscripts. It will also provide direct access to Islamic culture and heritage as seen through the eyes of the world's oldest university and religious institution. However, the website has been delayed because of the war in Iraq and the time of going to press a launch date has not been announced yet.

The project is being executed in phases. The first featured the construction of the infrastructure at Al-Azhar Library. In the second phase, a training programme will be launched for 100 staff working on the project, in addition to preparing an administrative office within the library itself. The third phase, which has already started, was marked by the opening of the technical laboratory which occupies the entire fifth floor of Al-

Azhar Library. The library is equipped with 90 hi-tech computers for doing the electronic archiving, in addition to other equipment for the developers, web designers and programmers working on the project.

The project management has formed committees of noted scholars from Al-Azhar who will provide the portal with information on various Islamic topics of interest to all Muslims such as fatwas (religious rulings), fiqh and Islamic civilization. Such a prestigious project will allow Al-Azhar scholars throughout the world to interact and be able to receive and answer religious questions. Apart from gaining access to various manuscripts, researchers will also be able to obtain, via the portal, high-resolution copies of the manuscripts for a nominal fee that will go towards funding Al-Azhar projects.

The main objective of the Al Azhar Online project is to preserve the precious manuscripts and books. In addition, the project will provide global access to the invaluable treasure of Islamic culture and heritage from the world's oldest university and religious institution and promote Islamic values and its message of tolerance. The project was launched by General Shaikh Mohammed during his visit to Al Azhar in April 2000 when the Grand Iman of Al Azhar, Dr Mohammed Tantawi, proposed the idea of preserving the priceless manuscripts and books.

Al Azhar has a huge web site which features, in addition to the manuscripts and other publications of Al Azhar, a bank for Fatwa. The site will offer e-learning and virtual reality tours through which the visitor can go round various parts and sections of the old Al Azhar premises, Mr Huwairib said. The project will provide global access to the treasure of Islamic culture and heritage from the oldest university and religious institution worldwide, promoting Islamic values and tolerance. We will launch the web site in Arabic and English languages in the beginning, and later in French, German and two other languages. The portal www.alazharonline.org will create a network for Al

Azhar connecting 10 of its main institutions in Cairo.

Over 42,000 manuscripts of a total of 125,000 books dating back approximately to 1400 years will be featured, 9,000 of which are the only existing copies in the world. These manuscripts and books will be available for viewing on the portal and also for online purchase of genuine copies. AI Azhar will also allow global interactivity with AI Azhar scholars by email and question and answer sessions with them and Fatwas catalogue of Korean materials is planned.

17

JUMA AL MAJID CENTRE FOR CULTURE AND HERITAGE, DUBAI

Juma Al Majid Centre for Culture and Heritage, Dubai is a charitable body for benefit of the public. It was officially established in 1991. In fact, the Centre was started by acquiring sources of knowledge in a variety of forms and their preservation, cataloguing and classification. Since that time, preparations were in progress. Specialists were appointed, and the structure, articles of association and by-laws of the centre were laid.

The Centre was established with full support from its Founder Mr.Juma Al-Majid when he felt that students and researchers, most of them poor, in search of books and references had to spend money travelling and procuring the desired books and copies of manuscripts, often difficult to obtain from Arab and Muslim countries. This was the reason why the library for Islamic, Arabic and humanitarian sciences was established.

The library collection developed gradually into a cultural centre rendering the needed facilities to students and scholars in pursuit of knowledge. It contains a considerable number of copies of manuscripts, university theses and dissertations, printed material, documents, periodicals and other various sources of knowledge. The Centre also publishes books on different subjects as well as a periodical magazine *aafaq at-thaqaafa wat turaath* (Horizon of Culture and Heritage). It also holds seminars on subjects conducing to its goals

The library is the pillar and the foundation of the Centre. On it depends the achievement of its goals: improving the educational level of individuals and the society at large. Hence, the Centre's management is ever ambitious to develop the library and furnish it with everything of educational value from any branch of knowledge existing anywhere in the world, particularly the Islamic world.

The library contains sources of knowledge: multiple kinds and forms of books, audio and visual material, compact discs, etc., in addition to an assortment of old and new periodicals with over three thousand titles, the periodicals ranging from the extinct to the new and the current. It is to be noted that these sources of knowledge are in a variety of languages like Arabic, Persian, English, French, etc.

The library consists of the following sections:

Technical preparation section (includes Supply section, Cataloguing and Classification section, and Periodicals section); Services section ; store-house, depository of principal books, private libraries. The Information Technologies section of the Juma Al-Majid Group of Companies helps the library develop its programmes and computerize its technical operations. This section was pre-eminently effective in building up an automatic system which covered all the material of the library and the technical operations in accordance with internationally recognized specifications.

Library Collections

The printed books which the library has exceeds 320,000 titles in number, the Arabic books numbering about 275,000, that is, 85% of the total number of books; English language books number about 25,000, that is, 7% of the total; Persian language books about 15,000, that is, 5% of the total. The rest are in other languages, French, German and Russian.

The books are on a great variety of subjects covering most of human knowledge. This fact benefits public in a general way and, yet at the same time, enables a specialist researcher to find the subject he is looking for in any field of knowledge, particularly Islamic sciences and its branches, Arabic language, General

Knowledge, Philosophy, Arabic and world literature, Comparative literature, Poetry, Arts, History, Geography, Travels, and Biographies. Books on subjects of General Knowledge including encyclopaedias, language dictionaries, guide-books etc. make up approximately 4% of the total number of the books.

The Library set apart a special section for non-book sources of knowledge including audio and visual material, compact discs (CDs), microfilms, macrofilms, etc. The section has a balanced quantity of these material which have been treated technically, their contents fed into the library database taking into consideration the properties of such materials while preserving them. A special place has been allocated in the library for visitors to view and benefit by these material.

One of the distinguishing marks of the library of the Centre is that it acquired a number of private (personal) libraries which scholars, literary figures and thinkers had set up. These private collections, as they came to the library, enriched it with their rare and choice books together with the comments and marginal notes which the owner of a private library had written in his books while reading them. These comments and marginal notes are mostly expressions of his views, either in the form of criticism, exposition , addition or clarification .

These private collections reached the Centre by different ways: endowments, charity donations, gifts or purchases, and from different countries like Egypt, Syria, Morocco, UAE.

These private libraries numbered over forty and mirrored the tastes of their collectors. In case the owner of such a library was a scholar of language and literature, his collections contained the choicest books of literature; in case he was a religious scholar, he would collect principal books on shariah; or the collector, being a specialist in the field of history and archaeology, had collected important books in that very field.

So each private library has its own peculiar imprint and its own characteristic mark to boast of. For that very reason, the Juma Al-Majid Centre for Culture and Heritage took upon itself the duty of keeping and preserving those libraries in their original shape as they were with their owners, like a necklace intact, none of its beads strewn about. Such preservation is, in fact, an acknowledgement of the merit of that scholar who made efforts and spent his time in learning and instructing and left to us his library as a witness to his merit and initiative.

The Centre committed itself to take care of, maintaining, restoring and cataloguing these libraries to make them available to researchers and students alike.

The library follows a careful policy that insures continuity of that development and those in charge ever try to strike a balance between the flood of knowledge in all fields and the reader's need for information which has no limit.

The Juma Al-Majid Centre for Culture and Heritage applies the most modern automatic/mechanical method of cataloguing and classification, a method that provides researchers with the required information minutely, easily and quickly. This is done by means of a complete database based on Oracle system along with Anglo-American cataloguing rules. The library employs the Dewey Decimal Classification system. It also employs an enlarged thesaurus as a tool for topic-wise analysis of the collection while keeping room to accommodate new terms not found in the enlarged thesaurus, when needed.

Providing information service is one of the main goals of the library of Juma Al-Majid Centre for Culture and Heritage. But, rather, it would be better to say that the library of the Centre has two basic goals: preserving the sources of knowledge available there and presenting these sources to seekers of knowledge quickly and in a way that ensures increasingly higher rates of benefit to researchers from the efforts of other scholars and researchers.

Those who benefit from the library services: the library

follows the same pattern as any public with respect to providing information services. The library offers its services for any one without distinction as to gender, nationality, colour , faith or the academic and intellectual background. The library has also allocated a separate place for females.

Manuscripts

The manuscripts section was established in 1987, the realization of a vision and a deep and moving desire that had overwhelmed Mr Juma Al-Majid's heart and soul since long. His vision materialized and manifested in a collection he made of some precious and rare manuscripts and some important documents. These became the nucleus of this section. Later, he commissioned this job to a special committee consisting initially of the chief of the section, curator of manuscripts, a restoreer, and a cataloguer. This committee, guided by Mr Juma Al-Majid, began to add more and more of the manuscripts and documents. With the passage of time, the committee grew larger and so did the section and the place where the manuscripts were kept. The manuscripts increased in number and kind till the section, by grace of Allah, became the nucleus of one of the great cultural centres of United Arab Emirates.

Purpose and goal

The following are some of the important goals, which this section wants to realize:

1. acquiring and preserving the largest possible number of original manuscripts or their photographs, of historical significance and high international value
2. cataloguing and classifying manuscripts and documents, preparing them for publication and disseminating information about them among researchers
3. Reparing , treating and binding manuscripts damaged or torn or mangled by passage of time
4. strengthening relations with libraries and academic

institutions inside and outside the country, and building up bridges of cultural co-operation between them and the Centre.

5. Improving methodologies of work, adopting everything new and useful for preserving and benefiting the heritage
6. meeting the needs of researchers, going to any length to serve them, giving them scientific advice, providing them with information about the places in the world where manuscripts are to be found, and to show the condition of the print, and helping them to overcome difficulties to get there
7. answering the queries of researchers as to what rules are followed to verify the authenticity of manuscripts.
8. helping researchers attain their goal by corresponding with the libraries of the world on their behalf in order to get copies of manuscripts providing the researcher bears the expenses and ultimately presenting him with a copy of the required manuscript

Important libraries from which the section obtained copies of manuscripts

El scorial library, Spain

Libraries of Princeton and Harvard universities and Library of the Congress, USA

Libraries of majlis al-shoora, Ayatollah Mar'ashi, Shaheed Motahhri school, Aastan Quds Rizvi, Iran

Chester Beatty Library, Ireland

British Museum Library (British Library), Cambridge university and Bodliana, UK

Dar-ul-Kutub National Library, Ahmad Al-Joli (Private) library, Tunisia

Solaimania Library, Ahmad III, Shaheed Ali, Faidhullah libraries, etc, Turkey

Ghazi Khusro Library, Sarajevo

Al-Zahiria, al-Ahmadia and al-Ridhaia libraries, Syria

Arif Hikmat Library, al-Mahmoodia Library, Umm-ul-Qura University, library of al-Imam Mohammad University, library of King Faisal Centre, Saudi Arabia

Library of al-Bayrooni Institute, library of Religious Directorate, Tashkent

Al-Auqaf Public Library, and library of Iraq Museum, Iraq

Library of the Institute for Oriental Studies and National Library, Petersburg

Vatican Library, Ambrosiana Library (Milan), Rome

National Library, France

Yusuf Basha al-Khalidi library, library for Heritage Revival, Al-Ahmadia Library, Izz-ul-Nabuliseen and Aal Tofaha Library, and Aal Al-Rifaa'ee Library, etc..., Palestine

Catholic University library, Lebanon

Al-Azharia library, Dar-ul-Kutub and National Documents library, Municipal library, al-Taimooria library, etc, Egypt

Public Treasury library, al-Nasiria library, al-Jame al-Kabeer library, and other libraries, Morocco

Vienna University library, Austria

Khuda Bakhsh library, al-Mohammdia School library, Indian Education Department library, al-Sa'eedia library, al-Aasifia library, India

Leyden university library, Holland

Al-Ahqaaf library, Tarmeem, and al-Jami al-Kabeer library, San'aa, Yemen

Utilization of manuscripts of the Centre

Any researcher can benefit by the manuscripts of the centre which are dedicated to students, no matter where the researcher is, near or far away from the centre . The former can visit the library centre himself and find out himself through the catalogue of the manuscripts prepared for this purpose in the Reference hall, look at the copy of the manuscript and ask for the copy of the desired manuscript in accordance with the conditions and rules in practice at the Centre.

As for the latter, he should seek help by correspondence or by telephone but he should be very precise and specify the required title, name of the author, his surname and the year of his death.

Conditions for photocopying manuscripts

A special form for this purpose shall be filled in by those inside UAE with a clear and accurate hand, leaving no column blank

An application giving the complete title of the manuscript, the name (three words) of the author, his surname and the year of his death shall be submitted by those living outside the UAE

The application shall be accompanied with a letter from the university or the academic body to which the researcher belongs confirming his need for the manuscript

A photograph of a manuscript, on paper or film, identical to the required manuscript in terms of academic value and unpublished shall be presented in exchange to enrich the Centre dedicated to the service of knowledge

A sum of two dirhams shall be paid for each page in case the required manuscript is illustrated on film and a paper photocopy of it is requested. One dirham and a half shall be paid if photograph is required on another film if there is an alternative manuscript available

The researcher shall undertake to present to the Centre a copy of the book after its publication containing an acknowledgement of the efforts of the Centre and the services being offered by it to the researchers in this field. In the event of failure to abide by this undertaking, the Centre has the right to refuse the subsequent requests of the researcher.

Photocopying of more than three manuscripts shall not be permitted with one application

Requests accompanied with a photo of an alternative manuscript shall take precedence over others

Money remittances shall be made by those living outside the UAE by bank draft to Account no. (0490906523) of the Juma Al-Majid Centre for Culture and Heritage, Mashreq Bank, Hor-al-Anz branch, Dubai, UAE

18

KHUDA BAKHSH ORIENTAL PUBLIC LIBRARY, PATNA

Khuda Bakhsh Oriental Public Library was founded by Khuda Bakhsh Khan, who donated his entire personal collection to the nation by a deed of trust. It was opened for public in October, 1891 with 4,000 manuscripts, of which he inherited 1,400 from his father Maulvi Mohammed Bakhsh Acknowledging its rich and rare collection the Govt. of India declared the Library as an Institution of National Importance by an Act of Parliament in 1969. The Library is now fully funded by the Ministry of Culture.

Mohammad Bakhsh, hailed from Siwan (Chhapra) a district of Bihar. He was a man of letters and law and had a great passion for books. He collected about 1,400 manuscripts including some rare printed books. When he was on his death-bed in 1876 he entrusted the whole lot to his son and wished him to open a library for the public whenever he should find himself in a position to do so. Khuda Bakhsh, thus, inherited from his father love for books and dedication to public service. He made it a mission of life to establish a public library so as to fulfil his father's dream. He made all possible efforts to acquire rare books and manuscripts. He also borrowed services of a book-hunter to collect manuscripts from the learning centres in the Arab world. He devoted himself to this noble cause.

With the acquisition of books he laid foundation of a two-storied building for the library. It was ready in 1888 at the cost of Rs. 80,000 and the books were shifted to this newly constructed beautiful building. To fulfil the long-cherished desire of his father,

Khuda Bakhsh opened it for the people of Patna rare manuscripts in Arabic, Persian and Turkish, apart from the printed books in Arabic, Persian and English.

The library was donated to the public and the Govt. of Bengal, Bihar being a part of Bengal those days was made its trustee. It was modestly named as Oriental Public Library according to the Trust Deed. The people, however, prefixed his name in view of his great service to the public. Since then it is officially known as Khuda Bakhsh Oriental Public Library. But popularly it is called Khuda Bakhsh Library.

Khuda Bakhsh was born in Siwan (Chapra) on 2nd August 1842 and was brought up under the guidance of his father who dedicated his life for the betterment of humanity. Educated at Patna and Calcutta he started his professional career as Peshkar. In 1880 he was appointed the Government Pleader of Patna and in 1881 the title of Khan Bahadur was conferred upon him for his social service. He was elevated to the post of Chief Justice of Nizam's Court Hyderabad for a period of three years in 1895. He was also honoured with another title of CIE in 1903. In spite of having all these titles and honours he was a very simple man with determination and vision. The library was his life-long achievement for which he was committed and devoted. He spent whatever he earned on its growth and as a result he was penniless. He had to borrow money for his medical treatment.

The Government of Bengal made him a generous grant of Rs. 8,000 to liquidate his debts. He died on 3rd August 1908 at the age of 66, and was buried in the premises of the Library. In 1969 it was raised to the status of an Institution of National Importance by an Act of Parliament. Being an autonomous body it has been working since then under the control of the Govt. of India, Department of Culture, Ministry of Tourism and Culture. The raised status played an important role in accelerating the pace of overall development of the library over the years.

A very special feature of Khuda Bakhsh Library is its publications, which have created history in the academic world.

Since 1977 it has been issuing regularly a multi-lingual research quarterly Khuda Bakhsh Library Journal. The main aim of bringing out this Journal is to advance research in Oriental and Islamic studies and also to promote research in Literature. Hence it includes scholarly articles, reprints of articles from old research periodicals and prints original articles on the subjects in which the library specializes.

Simultaneously, the Library also undertook a project of publishing research treatises, its manuscripts after getting them edited by scholars, facsimile edition of manuscripts, indices of Urdu periodicals, catalogues of the manuscripts, books bridging the communal gap and also books on Indian culture, history, literature and Islam.

It has brought out so far about 400 titles in the following languages

* Arabic
* Hindi
* English
* Persian
* Urdu

About thirty collections of manuscripts and books have so far been acquired as donation from the owners in addition to those purchased by the Library. The Printed collection has, on the other hand, its own value covering a wide spectrum of subjects in English, Arabic, Persian, Urdu and Hindi, etc. One significant part of this collection is the Periodical Section which contains around 35,000 bound volumes of old and new periodicals.

International seminars have been organised on manuscript literature on Tibb (Unani Medicine), Tasawwuf (Islamic Mysticism), Quranic sciences, Medieval Indian history followed by the seminars on Urdu Manuscripts, Indic religion and on Indo-Uzbek relations.

The Library encourages scholars and provides them all

research facilities including accommodation. It awards 10 research fellowships - 3 Senior and 7 Junior - for a period of 2 years and helps them do Ph.D./D.Litt. It also assigns different projects to them, for example, editing of manuscripts, compilation of descriptive catalogue of manuscripts, indexes of Urdu periodicals, subject bibliographies, etc. Besides, it also offers lump sum amount to retired professors to work on our manuscripts.

The Library has started a 1 year PG Course in Oriental Librarianship and Manuscriptology to help produce well trained staff to manage any oriental library. Three batches comprising of people selected mostly from in-house staff has been successfully concluded and work is going on to improve the scope of this course even further. The Library facilitates exchange of scholars with other countries and takes steps for sharing its resources with other libraries either in India or outside to enrich its collection.

Collections of the Library

Presently, the Library holds about 2,25,000 books in Urdu, Persian, Arabic and Hindi languages. It subscribes to 527 Journals. There are about 12,000 volumes of serials, which has great value in research. As far as the collection of manuscripts is concerned, the Library holds about 22,000 invaluable manuscripts. Now one of the richest collections of Arabic and Persian manuscripts and Mughal and Central Asian paintings-presently possessing the Khuda Bakhsh Library is fast becoming a centre for preserving and dissemination of knowledge in its special fields of Arabic and Persian learning and Islamic and Medieval Indian Studies.

The Library, with its relentless efforts of acquisition, preservation and dissemination, has emerged as one of the richest collections of Persian and Arabic manuscripts, and of rare printed books and invaluable paintings of Mughals, Rajputs, Turkish and Iranian schools. With over a hundred years of service to the world of scholarship and keeping pace with modern concept of librarianship, the Khuda Bakhsh has also brought into the gamut of its services such activities as may play significant role both on the national and the international planes-using knowledge for the betterment of humanity at large, rising above the traditional concept of the Library, the Khuda Bakhsh has become a centre of academics for acquisition of knowledge and dissemination of ideas and ideals. Scholarly workshops, symposia, talks, lectures and, of course, its yearly international seminars on significant manuscripts have been successfully creating research-based awareness of knowledge both on national and international levels.

The Library has also build up a comprehensive collection of audio and videocassettes of distinguished writers and poets, and eminence of Ganga-Jamni composite culture. Mass Communication Research Centre, Jamia Millia Islamia, New Delhi has extended cooperation in serving this national cause by making video films of such eminent persons and events that have not been covered directly by the Khuda Bakhsh. Maintaining its pace to record the living eminent poets and writers the sub-continent, the Library had added a large number of cassettes both audio and video to its collection,

With a century long span of services to scholarship to the nation and the humanity at larger, the Khuda Bakhsh remains the centre of attraction for seekers of knowledge from round the globe with something worthy to offer to every one from its priceless collection of manuscripts, original paintings and rare printed books in oriental as well as in English, French and German languages.

Acquisition of significant material relevant to the Library's specialized fields is a regular feature of the Library. With efforts spread over two decades of persuasion and pleading the following collections have so far been acquired since its take over by the Union Government:

1. Khujwa Collection (Siwan)

2. Idara Tehqiqat-i-Urdu Collection (Patna)
3. Dr. Shamim Collection (Arrah)
4. Prof Akhtar Orianvi Collection (patna)
5. All India Radio Collection (Patna)
6. Kako Collection (Gaya)
7. Koniber Collection (Navada)
8. Prof. Kalimuddin Collection (Patna)
9. Sir Fakhruddin Collection (Patna)
10. Khanqah Sulaimania Collection (Patna)
11. Dr. A. R. Kidwai Collection (Patna)
12. Mr. Yunus Salim Collection
13. S. A. Salam Collection (Patna)
14. Sajjad Jafri Collection (Bihar Sharif)
15. Sabzposh Collection (Gorakhpur)
16. Madrasa Azizia Collection (Bihar Sharif)
17. Sughra Estate Collection (Bihar Sharif)
18. Khanqah Qadiriya Collection (Islampur)
19. Khalid bin Saeed Collection (Bihar Sharif)
20. Zainul Abidin Collection. Chapra
21. Sasaram Collection
22. Dr. Zaki ul Haque Collection (Patna)
23. Ahmad Husain Collection (Sahasram)
24. Iran Collection (Iranian Students at Patna)
25. Kalimur Rehman Collection (Begu Sarai)
26. Hakim Syed Yusuf Collection (Phulwari Sharif)
27. Qutubuddin Collection (Sahsaram)
28. Muzaffar Gilani Collection (Patna)
29. Zainuddin Collection (Saharsa)

There are some more collections of books and manuscripts through regular purchase. These includes:

Akhtar Ansari Collection (Aligarh)

Saeed Akbarabadi Collection (Aligarh)

Mukhtaruddin Ahmad Collection (Aligarh)

Meher Ilahi Collection (Aligarh)

Kalam Haidri Collection (Gaya)

The Library specializes in Islamic Studies, Tibb (Unani Medicine), Tazkira (Biography), Tasawwuf (Islamic Mysticism), Comparative religions, Medieval Indian History, South East Asian History, West Asian History, Central Asian History, Medieval Science, Literature on Freedom Movement and National Integration as also Urdu, Persian and Arabic Literature.

It contains valuable manuscripts in Arabic, Persian, Urdu, Turkish, Hindi and Sanskrit and Palm-Leaves. It includes splendours of arts of Iranian, Mughal, Central Asian, Kashmiri and Rajasthani schools besides Calligraphic Masterpieces.

Manuscripts

The Library has emerged as an outstanding research library embracing a large number of rare manuscripts, some of them richly illuminated viz. "Tarikh-e-Khandan-e-Timuriya", the only copy in the world, contains 132 beautiful paintings by the famous court artists of Akbar the Great and a writing of Shahjahan. Intellectuals and scholars always speak very high of the Library's precious collection and also acknowledge its prompt services.

Cataloguing of manuscripts is one of the major activities of the Library. The Library prepares subjectiwise descriptive catalogues of its manuscripts. The scheme was started by the scholar-administrator Lord Curzon in 1905 ubder the supervision of scholar Sir Denison Ross. So far, 36 volumes of catalogues have been brought out.

Most of the old volumes of catalogues were out of print since long. During the last two decades all the above volumes of old and out-of-print catalogues have been reproduced. A catalogues of printed books in European Languages in the Library was also released afresh.

The Library is active toward compilation of a union catalogue in order to provide information at one centre, regarding collections of Arabic, Persian and Urdu language manuscripts scattered through out the world. It is making efforts in preparing brief handlist of all such manuscripts which still remain uncatalogued. About more than a dozen of such collections were covered earlier.

Compilation of descriptive catalogue of manuscripts is also a research work. The catalogues published so far contain rich information about the manuscripts and hence they are highly valued in the academic world.

The Library has so far published 36 volumes of Descriptive Catalogue of Manuscripts covering about half of the total collection. Moreover, a hand-list of manuscripts in Arabic (4 vols.), Persian (4 vols.) and Urdu (1 vol.) covering the library collection in its entirety have also been compiled and printed for the benefit of the readers. More volumes of Descriptive Catalogue are likely to be published soon.

Persian Volumes

Poetry (vol. 1)

Poetry (vol.2)

Poetry (volume 3)

Poetry (vol. 6)

Indian History (vol.7)

Biography, Romance, Tales and Anecdotes (col. 8)

Philosophy and Science (vol. 9)

Science and Arts (vol.11)

Commentaries on the Quran, Hadis Law, Theology and Controversial works (vol. 14)

Sufism, Hinduism and the History of Creeds and Sects (vol. 16)

Mixed Contents (vol. 17)

Persian Poetry, History, Biography and Tales (vol. 13)

Encyclopedia of Natural Sciences, Medicine, Logic and Ethics (vol. 13)

Quranic Science Arabic Volumes

Arabic Catalogues

Medical Works (Vol-4)

Tradition (Vol-5)

Theology (Vol-10)

Biography (Vol-12)

Sufism (Vol-13)

History (Vol-15)

Quaranic Science (Vol-18)

Principles of Jurisprudence (Vol-19)

Philology (Vol-20)

Encyclopaedia, Logic, Philosophy and Dialectics (Vol-21)

Science (Vol-22)

Poetry and Elegant Prose (Vol-23)

Ethics and Prayers (Vol-24)

Miscellanies (Vol-25)

Philology (Vol-26)

Miscellanies (Vol-27)

Miscellanies (Vol-28)

Quranic Science (Vol-29)

Tradition (Vol-30)

19
KING FAISAL CENTER FOR RESEARCH AND ISLAMIC STUDIES, RIYADH

Arabs were renowned for scholarship and their love for knowledge. They contributed equally to the field of religion as well as sciences. The contribution of Arab to mathematics is no parallel to any other country. Most of their works containing researches were taken out of the country during the political upheavals. Early, handwritten Arabic texts were delicate by nature and few copies of them existed. It was therefore considered vital to minimize wear and tear on the manuscripts, produce further copies if possible, and store them as suitably as prevailing conditions allowed. For this purpose libraries were established, thereby making available information about a wide range of subjects in central locations and preserving a growing number of manuscripts for future generations of researchers.

The King Faisal Center for Research and Islamic Studies is an operational arm of the King Faisal Foundation. The Center has its own identity and is independently financed. It has its headquarters in Riyadh and was founded in 1983.

Aims and Mission of the Center

In keeping with the goals of the King Faisal Foundation, the Center is dedicated to the service of Islamic civilization, to supporting continuing research, and to encouraging cultural and scientific activities in a number of fields. The mission of the Center may be summarized as follows:

* To raise awareness about the contribution of Islamic

civilization to human heritage and to highlight the main distinguishing features of Islamic civilization.

* To raise public awareness about the late King Faisal b. Abdul Aziz, of his great humanity and remarkable qualities of leadership, and to highlight his central contribution to, and continuous support for Islamic Solidarity. To this end, the Center has established The King Faisal Memorial Gallery, to preserve our memory of him and to document his contribution to Islam in the twentieth century.
* To support research in areas related to Islamic civilization, to develop it along scientific lines, and to encourage researchers and students at all academic levels. The Center provides comprehensive logistical support to students and researchers, offering library and bibliographical services, books, manuscripts, and other materials at the Center, and helps to locate materials elsewhere in the Kingdom or abroad when these are not available locally.
* To help train a new generation of scholars, specialized in the fields of Islamic studies, Arabic language, and the social sciences.
* To help promote and preserve our Islamic Heritage by organizing annual exhibits at the Center.
* To organize lectures, conferences, and symposia, of both a general and specialized nature, on issues vital to Islam and to Muslins and to their roles in the present and in the future, linking today's Muslims to the roots of Islamic culture.
* To continue to build our libraries through the acquisition of manuscript resources – original manuscripts, microfilms, and original sources in other formats – and through the purchase of books, periodicals, and audio-visual material relating to any aspect of Islamic civilization. By enriching our libraries and improving our library services we aim to make the Center one of the principal

resources on Islamic civilization worldwide.

* To develop specialized databases in fields relating to the mission of the Center and its areas of specialization, thus enhancing the library services available to researchers and students at the Center.
* To translate scientific treatises and research into foreign languages, and to translate a variety of works into Arabic, when such translation would be of service in achieving the aims and objectives of the Center.
* To support and encourage research that falls within the Center's interest.

The Library

The Main Library provides accommodation for more than one million books. The collection covers the fields of Islamic Studies and Islamic Civilization. The main reading room houses frequently used reference books in Arabic, English and several other languages. There is a separate reading room for periodicals. At present, these number 3,000 volumes in 16 languages, 35% of which are in Arabic. There is also a collection of rare and out-of-print periodicals.

Adopting an unconventional approach, the main library displays few books in the reading rooms. The majority is kept in computerized racks in a special underground storage room, a system that protects the books from unnecessary handling. Subscribers fill out a request form that includes information about the author, title, and/or subject matter. A computer printout lists all the available data on the subject within the Center. The selected information is then brought directly to the reader's table. A wide range of database topics further supplements research. With its storage capacity of more than one million books and a current inventory of 90,000 titles in 160,000 volumes, as well as 250,000 abstracted articles, this library is a vital resource for scholars.

The children's library, geared toward 5-12 year olds, encourages a love of reading and research from an early age and teaches youngsters how to use libraries to full advantage. The well-equipped library contains more than 18,000 books and magazines and 300 audio-visual cassettes in Arabic, English, and French. A hobby section for drawing, coloring, writing, and games, as well as areas for videos and computers provides further stimulation for the young readers.

A separate audio-visual research library has more than 11,000 audio and videocassettes, slides, and films, which contain lectures and documentary material related to the Center's various activities and interests.

Collection of Manuscripts

As part of the Foundation's contribution to preserving Islamic culture and highlighting the contributions made by Muslim and Arab scholars, The King Faisal Center for Research and Islamic Studies has undertaken the challenging mission of locating, authenticating, acquiring, or copying, and indexing all known Islamic manuscripts worldwide. In addition to nearly 23,000 hand-written texts, some of which are more than 1,200 years old, the manuscript archives have more than 18,000 microfilms and hundreds of photocopies. The majority of the microfilms are acquired through mutual agreements with the Bibliotheque Nationale of Paris, the Library of Congress, and the British Library. Databases save researchers up to 70% of the time they would normally spend searching catalogs for information pertaining to manuscripts located elsewhere in the world.

In environmentally controlled manuscript galleries visitors can enjoy the beauty of ancient, illuminated texts, read sources of wisdom that have been passed down for centuries, or simply admire the labor-intensive efforts of people who loved learning. As past generations knew so well, books preserve and propagate knowledge. Their conservation ensures that future generations will benefit from a growing reserve of accumulated learning.

Thousands of rare Arabic manuscripts have been marred

as a result of burning, burying, water damage, and inexpert cleaning. Even with the support of modern technology, the task of restoring these texts can seem overwhelming. It is not just the poor condition of some of the more seriously deteriorated books but the sheer quantity of the volumes. The continuing discovery of ancient manuscripts and the problem of increasing pollution make the need for preservation greater than ever before. The manuscript library currently contains over 13,000 texts in need of repair. It can take anything from a week to six months to restore each book.

In order to increase the number of qualified technicians, the Center instructs suitable candidates in the discipline of manuscript preservation. When they complete their training, these new experts will be sent wherever there is a need for the preservation of Islamic texts. The Center will provide this service free of charge, only requesting permission to make a copy of the repaired books for its own library. These usable copies will make valuable information more accessible to a larger number of scholars, without further risk of damage to the fragile documents.

The continuing discovery of ancient manuscripts and the problem of increasing pollution make the need for preservation greater than ever before. Technology has risen to meet the challenge, and The King Faisal Center for Research and Islamic Studies is actively applying it. As past generations knew so well, books preserve and propagate knowledge. Their conservation ensures that future generations will benefit from a growing hoard of accumulated learning.

20

LIBRARY OF TIBETAN WORKS AND ARCHIVES, DHARAMSHALA

Library of Tibetan Works and Archives (TWA) is an autonomous body under direct supervision of H.H. the Dalai Lama registered with the Government of India under the Registration of Societies Act of 1860 recognised by Himachal Pradesh University as a Centre for Research in 1991 accorded status of National Library, Achieves and Museum by Tibetan Parliament in Exile in 1996

The Library receives part of its funding from the Department of Culture and Ministry of Human Resources of the Government of India. The Library generates some of its own funding through the sale of books and publications, accommodation rental and class fees, and this is used to meet the 'major part of its budgetary needs. Public and private foundations and other philanthropic organisations such as the Ford Foundation, OXFAM India, the Smithsonian Institution, C.A.R.F., Swedish Development Co-operative, J.D.R. 3rd Fund and Uli Franz Trust, Netherlands Embassy, have provided substantial funding for specific projects in the past.

The Library of Tibetan Works and Archives (LTWA) is one of the most important institutions in the world dedicated to the preservation and dissemination of Tibetan culture. The foundation stone for the Library's Tibetan style building was laid on 11th June 1970, in the hill station of Dharamsala, north India. Located within the compound of the Tibetan Government-in-Exile, the Library serves as a repository for Tibetan artefacts and manuscripts and a centre for language and cultural education.

Its holdings include more than 80,000 manuscripts, books and documents, hundreds of thangkas, statues and other artefacts, 6,000 photographs, and other materials.

As a centre for the study of Tibetan culture, the is firmly dedicated to a threefold vision of preservation, protection and promotion. The Library looks forward into the next century, confident of its role to preserve, and educate others about, a culture threatened with destruction. More than 25 years after its founding, the need for such an institution as the Library of Tibetan Works and Archives has continued to grow.

The primary objective of the Library of Tibetan Works and Archives is to provide a comprehensive cultural resource centre and to promote an environment fostering research and an exchange of knowledge between scholars and students. This is of the utmost importance in a contemporary world shaped by political and spiritual confusion. In trying to fulfil its objectives the Library's priorities include:

* Acquiring and conserving Tibetan books and manuscripts, artefacts and works of art;
* Providing access to books, manuscripts and reference works (in Tibetan and foreign languages) in study areas within the Library;
* Compiling bibliographies and documentation of library holdings and related literature available worldwide;
* Providing copies and prints of library holdings, and acting as a reference centre for such source materials
* Publishing books and manuscripts under the Library imprint;
* Supporting research and study of the Tibetan language, classical and modern, and the traditional arts and crafts.

The Tibetan Library has been in operation since Ist November 1971. It has opened its doors to numerous scholars from many countries. It has launched educational programmes in language, philosophy, culture and the traditional arts. It has encouraged computer projects, and other initiatives aiming to preserve Tibetan thought and culture. The Library sponsors international seminars. It engages in book exchange programmes with other libraries and distributes its own publications, in Tibetan and English, throughout the world. Library holdings increase every year and class enrollments in the Centre for Tibetan Studies continue to climb.

The Library is home to one of only two Tibetan Oral History projects in the world. Its dynamic thangka painting and woodcarving programmes are indica-tive of the fact that cultural preservation includes the arts as well as letters. LTWA works in close collaboration with the Central Institute for Higher Tibetan Studies (deemed a university) in Sarnath and the Department of Religion and Culture of the Central Tibetan Administration. With each year of operation increasing numbers of visitors, researchers and students are drawn to this institution which is able to provide them with an educational and cultural experience available nowhere else in the world.

Departments of the LTWA

The Library is organized in eight distinct departments:

1. The Library itself, which consists of the Tibetan Manuscript Collection and. The Foreign Language Reference Library.
2. The Archives, consisting of the Document and Photographic Archives.
3. The Museum.
4. Education, operating the Centre for Tibetan Studies, which administers courses in Philosophy and Tibetan Language.
5. Research and Translation.
6. Publications.
7. Oral History.
8. Administration.

Manuscripts

The Library holds 70,000 manuscripts and documents in Tibetan and 10,000 books in English and foreign languages dealing with Buddhism and Tibet related affairs.

Between them, the Tibetan Manuscript Collection and the Foreign Language Reference Library contain more than 80,000 items, ranging from handwritten manuscripts and centuries old documents to contemporary books and periodicals. Parts of the collection are open to the public, while access to others is restricted to accredited scholars and researchers. Study areas are provided in the respective wings housing each collection. Research guidance is available from many resident scholars at the Library. General information about the libraries is available at the reception desk on the ground floor.

The Tibetan Manuscript Collection maintains holdings of more than 70,000 manuscripts, xylographs, documents, illuminated manuscripts and microfilm records. This is the most important collection of such materials in the world. Of special value are several handwritten editions of the Kangyur and Tengyur, the Tibetan Buddhist Canon; sixteen handwritten volumes of sundry collected works from Phudrag Monastery and sixteen additional volumes commissioned by Tsagta, Chief of Eastern Kongpo in the 15th century. The major works of Tibet's four Buddhist traditions, the Nyingma, Kagyu, Sakya and Gelug, as well as the indigenous Bön tradition, constitute the main body of the collection.

The Library maintains manuscript exchange projects with many institutions around the world. These include the Gorky Scientific Library in Leningrad; the Ulan Bator State Library in Mongolia; the Sikkim Research Institute in Gangtok; the National Library of the Royal Government of Bhutan; Toyo-Bunko in Japan, and the Beijing National Library. In special cases these institutions provide and exchange photocopies of rare and important works which are otherwise unavailable for general circulation or loan.

The Tibetan Manuscript Collection acquires new materials from among those donated to His Holiness the Dalai Lama as well as from direct acquisitions in Tibet. Several hundred volumes are added each year, ranging from rare and original manuscripts to contemporary reprints in book form. The Tibetan Manuscript Collection is in the process of completing a general catalogue of all materials in the collection. This task is made more difficult by the nature of the holdings and the tendency for works to have elaborate titles containing similar epithets and for authors to be known by a variety of names. The entire collection is also being catalogued in a computer database in the Tibetan language, which will be available to the public. This makes it the only collection of its kind catalogued by computer in Tibetan.

The Foreign Language Reference Library has a collection of more than 10,000 volumes predominantly dealing with language, philosophy, arts and culture, medicine, geography, travel, history and politics of Tibet and the Himalayan region. These materials are primarily in English, but include some in major European and Indian languages, as well as Japanese, Chinese, Russian, and Mongolian. More than 120 journals and periodicals of related interest are currently received and displayed. There is a modest collection of rare and out-of-print books, files of newspaper clippings covering the past 25 years of the Tibetan diaspora, bound collections of periodicals, and files of pamphlets, brochures and other materials concerning the Tibetan community dating back to 1959. Holdings can be accessed through an online cataloguing system. Books are kept in a separate stack room, from where librarians retrieve them on request. The reading room is divided between an area of large open tables and a set of individual study booths.

The continuing expansion of the Foreign Language collection is matched by its growing number of patrons. New acquisitions are received each year from various sources in addition to outright purchases. Publication exchange programmes provide volumes from other publishers and libraries in exchange for new books brought out by the LTWA's Publication Department. Copies of doctoral dissertations are regularly received from University Microfilm International. Books are also donated each year by visiting scholars and by other institutions not formally part of the publication exchange programme. On average, 2,000 people enrol as members of the Library each year for a small fee. They are entitled to use the resources within the reference room. Only accredited research scholars are allowed to borrow materials. Limited photocopying can be done by request on the Library premises.

The Archives

Several thousand legal and social documents in Tibetan, some dating back as far as the 10th century and 6,000 photographs, negatives and slides of Tibet.

The Document and Photographic Archives have seen rapid growth in recent years. Documents include government edicts and court proclamations, marriage and land contracts and others, which reveal otherwise unrecorded aspects of Tibetan life. Many scholars consult these, and the Photographic Archives' collection of negatives and slides, which includes black and white and colour photographs taken by American travellers Tolstoy and Dolan in the 1940s. Many photographs are displayed in the Library itself.

An important new project for the LTWA is the launch of the Central Archives of the Works of His Holiness the 14th Dalai Lama. The purpose of this Archive, as its name implies, is to gather together all materials concerning His Holiness the Dalai Lama's teachings, writings and speeches. Contributions have been received from all over the world.

The Library is also host to a newly initiated Architectural Archive which consists of a catalogued collection of photographs of buildings and architectural features in Tibet and the Himalayan region. Many of the buildings recorded in this Archive no longer exist. Consequently, the collection provides an invaluable glimpse of Tibet's erstwhile magnificent architectural heritage. A Tibetan Architectural Club has been established in this connection to encourage local Tibetan school students with an interest in architecture to develop an appreciation of Tibetan building traditions.

21

MAULANA AZAD LIBRARY, ALIGARH

The Maulana Azad Library is located at the Aligarh Muslim University at Aligarh which is the most respected and important educational centre for Indian Muslims. It was initially founded as Mohammedan Anglo Oriental College in 1875 by Sir Syed Ahmed Khan (1817-1898) and subsequently raised to the status of Aligarh Muslim University (AMU) in 1920. This University, being the representative body of the upwardly mobile middle class Indian Muslims created a significant impact on Muslim politics in India. The University was the outcome of the Aligarh Movement.

It is a known fact of Indian history that Sepoy mutiny of 1857 had made a significant impact on the contemporary social history of this sub-continent. For Muslim elite it caused great mental turmoil as "they were reduced to the position of hewers of woods and drawers of water by the British" (The Aligarh Movement by Dr. Shan Muhammad, 1978, page IX). They took the fall of Mogul Empire as a defeat of the Muslim community.

After dislodging the Muslim rulers from the throne, the new rulers, the British, implemented a new educational policy with drastic changes. The policy banned Arabic, Persian and religious education in schools and made English not only the medium of instruction but also the official language in 1835. This spawned a negative attitude amongst the Muslims towards everything modern and western, and a disinclination to make use of the opportunities available under the new regime. This tendency, had it continued for long, would have proven disastrous for the Muslim community.

Seeing this atmosphere of despair and despondency, Sir Syed launched his attempts to revive the spirit of progress within the Muslim community of India. He was convinced that the Muslims in their attempt to regenerate themselves, had failed to realize the fact that mankind had entered a very important phase of its existence, i.e., an era of science and learning. He knew that the realization of the very fact was the source of progress and prosperity for the British. Therefore, modern education became the pivot of his movement for regeneration of the Indian Muslims. He tried to transform the Muslim outlook from a medieval one to a modern one.

The establishment of Mohammedan Anglo Oriental (MAO) College in 1875 marks one of the most important events in the educational and social history of modern India. Its establishment is considered as the first significant response of the Indian Muslims to the challenges of post -1857 era. It was an important catalyst in a process of social change among Muslims.

In 1920, an Act of Indian Legislative Council elevated the M.A.O. College to the status of a Central University. Since that time AMU has grown into a major Indian university. It presently covers a very wide spectrum of academic disciplines, having 88 departments, 5 institutions, 13 centres

The University currently has about 28000 students on its rolls, most of whom stay in 16 halls of residences with 70 hostels. It employs about 1400 academic staff, and about 6000 non-teaching staff. On an average, about 500 foreign students come to study at AMU every year. The University has a campus spread over 467.6 hectares of land.

The University Library

The Library complex of the University consists of a Central Library and over 80 college/departmental libraries. Libraries of the colleges, institutes and departments, cater to the needs of postgraduates and students of professional courses.

The University has established Book Banks for the benefit

of students of certain professional courses. The Central Library was set up in 1875, when this institution was established as Madarsatul Uloom. In 1877, the Madarsa became Mohammadan Anglo-Oriental College. Lord Lytton, the viceroy of India, laid the foundation stone, and the library was named after him as Lytton Library. Eminent scholars like Gardner Brown, Arnold, Releigh, Horowitz, Storey and Auchtelpone functioned as honorary librarians in addition to their teaching responsibilities.

In 1960, it was named as Maulana Azad Library when the first Prime Minister, Pt. Jawaharlal Nehru, inaugurated its present building. The Seven storied building is surrounded by 4.75 acres of land in the form of beautiful lawns and gardens. It is the most beautiful building of the University and one of the few very attractive libraries in the country. The Library has over 10,00,000 books.

The collection consists of books, periodicals, pamphlets, manuscripts, paintings and photographs. M.A. Library performs the functions of a National Library so far as its collection of Oriental manuscripts are concerned. It is because of these rich collections of immense research value that this Library is reckoned among major libraries of the world. The oldest manuscript owned by the library is some fourteen hundred years old. It is a fragment of the Holy Quran transcribed by Hazrat Ali, the fourth caliph of Islam and is written on parchment in *Kufi* script. Another rare manuscript is tat of *Halnama* of *Beyazid Ansari*, no copy of which is available anywhere else in the world.

The Library has a sizeable collection of early printed books in various languages. The most outstanding among them is the Latin translation of the celebrated Arabic work on optics, *opticam prafatis,* by Ibn-al-Haitham (965-1039) published in 1572.

There are several *farmans* (decrees) of the Mughal kings like Babur, Akbar, Shahjahan, Shah Alam, Shah Alamgir, Aurangzeb etc. Another prized possession of the library is a "Shirt" on which the whole Quran is inscribed in khafi script.

This shirt is believed to have been worn by a warrior of Mughal army.

Among the large collection of Mughal paintings is the painting of Red Blossom, which is magnum opus of Mansoor Naqqash, the celebrated court artist of Emperor Jahangir. Some valuable Sanskrit works translated into Persian have also been preserved in the library. Other possessions worth mentioning are the Ayurved in Telugu and the Bhasa's in Malyalam script written on palm leaves. Abul Faiz Faizi, an eminent scholar of Akbar's court translated several Sanskrit works into Persian, such as Maha Puran, Bhagvat Gita, Mahabharat and Lila Wati, these are also available.

More than 5,000 students, teachers and other members of the university daily visit the library and utilize its services.

Collections of the Library

Sir Syed Ahmad Khan donated his personal collection for the Library at the time of foundation of this university. From 1924 to 1926 Sahibzada Aftab Ahmad Khan was the chancellor of the university. He paid particular attention to the expansion of the library. He also donated his personal collection of rare law books that he had made while studying at Cambridge University. He allocated a budget for the purchase of useful books for the students. The purchase of these books on different subjects added much to the importance of this library as well as the university. In the same manner, the donation of the valuable personal collections of its professors, nobles and distinguished persons strengthened the scientific works.

In the year 1948 Dr. Zakir Hussain was appointed the vice-chancellor of this university. He paid much attention to this library and felt it necessary to expand the area and create a more suitable place for keeping the books and better facilities for the students and scholars. For this purpose he prepared the ground so that the chancellor of the university might exchange views with the central goverment and University Grants Commission authorities. He succeeded in obtaining a grant of one million and thirty thousand rupees from central government for the new buildings of the library. Its foundation stone was laid in 1955 by Pandit Jawahar Lal Nehru, the first prime minister of India after the independence of the country. The plan of the new library building, which is considered one of the best specimens of Indo-Islamic architecture, was prepared and carried out by Architect Fayyaz ud-Din. The new building was inaugurated in 1960. Taking in view the services rendered by Maulana Azad, the great thinker and literacy figure, it was named after him.

Collections of Manuscripts

The manusscripts collection is the most prestigious and invaluable collection of the Library. This collection also originated from the personal library of Sir Syed Ahmed Khan who had a great passion for collecting manusscripts. The copy of the manuscript 'tarikh-e-guzida' which contains notes of the famous scholar, Abul Faiz Faizi, is infact from the founders's own collection. This collection is the largest on the sub continents is known is to scholars throughout the academic world. Some of its highly important and rare manuscripts have attracted the attention of renowned orientalists who have listed them in their monumental bibliographical surveys (1), Geschicte der Arabischen Litterutur' by Carl Brocklemann; (2) Geschicte das Arabischen Schrifttums' by Fuat Sezgin and (3) Persian Literature: a bibliographical survey by C .A. Storey.

The collection contains source material on a variety of subjects. Its coverage is very wide and extends to numerous fields of human knowledge which may briefly be assumed up as under:

1. Islamic theology; the holy Quran and its commentaries; Hadith (traditions); fiqh and usul-i-fiqh (muslim jurisprudence),' aqaid; translations of other holy scriptures.
2. Sufic literature.
3. Philosphy: logic; metaphysics; ethics; dogmatics philosophy (llmul kalam).

4. History: general history of the world; history of different regions;history of india-sultanate period, mughal and mugal period' bibliographics.
5. Literature: prose and belles letters; poetry-epic, didactic, collective works of poets.
6. Linguistics: dictionaries, grammer (sarf and nahv); rhetoric and prosody (banyan badi, and,arud).
7. Geography and travelogues.
8. Exact sciences; mathmatics; astronomy; chemisty and mineralogy; botany; zoology; agriculture, medicine and veterinary science.
9. Pseudo sciences: astrology sciences: astrology; geomancy; divination; interpretation of dreams;
10. Encyclopaedic works.
11. Varia; music; hunting; calligraphy; art of war etc.
12. Translation of Sanskrit works into Persian.

This magnificent and priceless collection has been built up over a period of more than a century. According to the report of the Pro Vice chancellor, the total number of manuscripts in 1924 was just 628. Today it stands at well over 14,500. The language wise breake –up of the collection is as follows:-

(a)	Arabic	5107
(b)	Persian	8255
(c)	Urdu	1075
(d)	Hindi	116
(e)	Sanskrit	3

In its evolutionary growth the collection is heavily indebted to the munificence of great scholars and bibliophiles who donated their entire personal libraries to the university. There are eleven such donations, which are named after the names of their respective donors. The university has also purchased from its own resources afew thousand manuscripts. The respective strength of the different constituents of the manuscripts collection:

1.	Subhanallah Collection	2,399
2.	Habibganj Collection	1,616
3.	Abdus Salam Collection	575
4.	Firangi Mahal Collection	1,552
5.	Sulaiman Collection	1,412
6.	Qutubuddin Collection	235
8.	Munir Alam Collection	117
9.	Aftab Collection	353
10.	Ahsan Collection	353
11.	Shaifta Collection	209
12.	Jawahar Museum (Etawah) collection	1,643
13.	University collection	4,330

Of these collections, the Subhanallah collection is not only the largest but also the richest so far as the subject coverage is concerned. The collection is also known for its illuminated manuscripts and fine art of calligraphy.

The Habib Ganj collection is another treasure of immense academic and research value, which has enormously enriched the manuscripts resources of the Library. The collection formed part of the library of the late Nawab Sardar Yar Jung Bahadur Habibur Rehman Khan Sherwani saheb. Sherwani Saheb had built up an impressive library of manuscripts and printed books. After his death his illustrious son, khan Bahadur Haji Obaidur Rehman Khan Sherwani saheb, whose association with the university spreads over several decades and who also has held the office of the vice chancellor of this University more than once, made a gift of the Habibganj library to the university library. This collection is very rich in literature on Islamics, mysticism, Persian period. It includes substantial paintings of the Mughal period and very beautiful front pieces and embellished borders.

The catalogue of the Persian poetry manuscripts of this collection has been published. In this catalouge Mathnavi Ma'navi, Bostan-e-Sa'adi,,Diwan-e-Asifi Mazhar-al- Asrar, Diwan-e-Rozebhan Sabri, Kulliyat-e-Urfi, Diwan-e Hafiz Qasaed-e-Faizi, Diwan-e-Saeb, Majma ul Bahrain, Diwan-e-Ibne Yamin, Diwan–e-Amir Shahi, Diwan-e-Baidil, Kulliyat-e-Hazin, Diwan-e-Kamal Khujandi, Saulate-e-Usmania, etc., are very important for more than one reason. Some are quite rare and no copy thereof is available anywhere in the world. Some had been on the shelves of royal libraries and bear the seal or contain notes of the kings and nobles whom they once belonged to. Still others have been copied out by famous calligraphists.

From the point of view of the historical significance, the University Collection and the Abdussalam collection are very important. These collections bristle with original source material in the history of Afghan rule in India and the medieval Indian history. The Habibganj, Subhanalla, Shaifta, Sulaiman and Munir Alam collections also contain quite a good number of manuscripts on history. Some of the important manuscripts of this category are Subh-e-Sadiq by Mirza Momohammad Sadiq Sadiqui bin Mohammad Sualeh Asfahani (d.1651), Mirat-e-Aftab Numa by Abdur Rehman (1217 A.H.), Haqiqat-hai Hindustan by Lachmi Narain Shafiq (1204 A.H.), Zikrul Muluk by Shaikh Abdul Haq Muhaddis Dehlavi (1030 A.H.), Tarikh-e-Tabri translated by Abu Muhammad 1029-30 A.H.), Tazkrat-us- Salatin-e- Chaghta by Mohammad Hadi (1132 A.H.), and Tawarikh-e-Azizi by Shah Abdul Aziz Dehlavi.

The oldest manuscript owned by the library is a fragment of the holy Quran consisting of Surah fateha and a portion of Surah baqrah. It is written on parchment in Kufic script and is believed to have been transcribed by Hazrat Ali, the fourth caliph of Islam. There is another copy of Quran which, it is said is the handiwork of emperor Aurangzeb. Yet another copy of the holy book is the original work of Haddad the famous calligraphist in the court of Shahjahan. The particular feature of one more

Quranic manuscript is the it contains only thirty pages and each page contains one chapter parah of the book note with standing the fact that all the chapters vary length. Besides these copies there is large number of magnificently illuminated copies of the Quran, some of which belonged to the imperial collections of the great Mughals. Other manuscriptsof the Quran are fine specimen of calligraphy. There are some other articles besides manuscripts, e.g. a shirt on which the whole Quran is inscribed in Kufic scripts. According to the annual report of the University for the year 1933, the shirt was receipt as a gift by Sir Ross Masood, the then vice chancellor, from his friend, lord Lothian

A number of manuscripts are pretty old and some of them date back as early as 11th and 12th century and quite a few are so rare that no copy thereof is traceable in any other library of the world. Some example are given below:-

1. Autograph copy of 'Uyunul ajwebah fi fanun-al-aswalah' by the renowned mystic Al-Qushairi (A. H.1072).
2. Nahjul-balaghah in two volumes transcribed in 538 A.H. It is surly the earliest Muslim work on the administration of government and contains the dicourses and instructions issued from time to time his governors by Hazrat Ali. Compiled by Sharif al-Razi 1015 A. D. It is considered to be the second oldest copy of the manuscript available in the world.
3. Hal Namah of Bayazid Ansari which contains a short biography of the famous saint Bayazid Ansari of Akbar's period as also a succint account of Roshana'iyah movement down to the reign of Shah Jahan. It was compiled by Ali Mohammed bin Abu Bakr Qandhari. No other copy of this manuscript is available anywhere in the world.
4. Jamharat–o-ashar,il Arab, compiled by Abul Khattab al-Qarshi is a compilation of Arabic poetry which was transcribed in 998 A.H. No other copy older than this is traceable.

5. Nafais-ul-ma'asir by Mirza Alauddaulah Nami Qazwini 1565-1571 A.D. which contains an account of the poets of the 10th century A.H. and the history of Mughals from Babar to Akbar is also known for its rarity. Only a few extracts from this mss. are available in the British Museum.
6. Autograph copy of al-Jami,us Sahih by Ibn-al-Hajar Assaqalani d 1448 A.D.
7. Madanul- Jawahar by Waliullah Frangi Mahli d.1127 A.D. /1853 A.D. is a voluminous commentary on the holy Quran. It is also a unique mss. as no other copy is available elsewhere.
8. Tafsiri-Yaqub Charkhi is another commentary on the Holy Quran very few copies of which are available only in some European libraries.

Some of the manuscripts have the peculiarity of being transcribed by the authors themselves such manuscripts include Diwan-e-Saeb, Fatah-al-Mut'al fi Madah-al-aan by Ahmad bin Mohammad al Maghrabi 1033 A.H.. Khutbatul Qawaid by Fakhruddin bin Mohammad al–Hasan bin Yusuf Ali bin al-Muthar 900 A. H. etc. There is also one more copy of Diwan-e-Sa'eb which was transcribed by his disciple, Arif Tabraizi in 1085 A. H. This copy was gone through by saeb as is evident from the additions made by him of some of his ghazals on the margin of different pages.

Several manuscripts stand out distinctly because of being profusely illustrated and studded with very fine miniature paintings . Khamsa-i-Nizami by Nizami Ganjvi transcribed by Husain Abdullah in 873 A.H., Mathnavi Husaini 1163 A. H. Diwan-e-Hafiz transcribed by Abdur Rehman in 971 A.H. Mathnavi Maulvi M'navi transcribed by Abdullah bin Qambar Samarkandi in 1019 A.D. and Hamla-i-Haideri by Mohammad Rafi Khan Mashhadi deserve special mention.

Among the illuminated manuscripts is Karima transcribed by Badar Ali in 1277 A.H. Mulfuzati saheb qiran by Afzal

Bukhari and transcribed by Hidayatullah in 1220 A.H. Haft band kashi transcribed by Atarud Raqam in 1280 A.H. and Qasidah dar manqabat Hazrat Ali provide a fine feast for the eyes.

The collection also contains a substantial number of manuscripts which are beautifully transcribed in this context Diwan-e-Lisani transcribed by Hasan Quli in 983 A.H., Khamsa–i-Nizami transcribed by Firoz Mohammad bin Sulaiman in Nastaliq script, Mathnavi Maulana Rum 1089 A.H. and Tabaqat-i-Akbari by Khwaja Nizamuddin Bakhshi transcribed by Abdul Haq Qureshi in 1003 A.H. may be cited as just a few examples.

The collection is rich in the works of Persian translations. Most of the Sanskrit epics including Mahabharat renderd into Persian by Naqib Khan who was one of the prominent nobles of Emperor Akbar. Abul Fażal Faizi translated Maha Purana, Bhagvat Gita, Ramayana, Mahabharata, and Lilavati into Persian. Dara Shikoh was also a Persian scholar who translated Jog Vashisth and Upanishad into Persian.. Besides these works, Persian translation of several Sanskrit works like Hitpdesha entitled Mufarrihul Qulub by Taj Mufti-al- Makki etc are also available in the Library.

The Manuscript Division of the Library also possess several farmans (edicts) of the Mughal Kings. The largest among them is the farman issued by Babar under his own seal. It is the only farman of Babar in existence. The Division also contains about a thousand coins mostly belonging to the Medieval Indian period. Besides this, the Division has some rare paintings, and rotographs and autographed letters from eminent personalities.

The catalogues of some collections have been published. They include the following:

1. Habib Ganj Collection: This is the largest collection of donated manuscripts, preserved in the manuscript section of the university. It consists of 2000 volumes on various subjects in Arabic, Persian and Urdu languages. This collection was donated by Ubaidur Rahman Khan Sherwani son of Nawwab

Sadr Yar Jang Habibur Rahman Sherwani (1867-1950 A.D.) to the university in the year 1960. The catalogue in Arabic and Persian has been published in three volumes so far.

2. Ahsan Marehravi Collection: Maulana Ahsan Marehravi was one of the professors of Urdu at Aligarh University. He taught this language from 1922 to 1940. He compiled his poetic works in two volumes, namely Faiz-e Dagh and Mohavarat. His collection consists of fine and rare printed and unpublished books in Arabic, Hindi, Persian and Urdu. It consists of 447 volumes of manuscripts. He presented all his collection to the university and it is preserved in the library under the name of "Ahsan Collection". Its catalogue was prepared by Sayyed Mahmud Hasan Qaisar Amrohvi and published by the university.

3. Shaifta Collection: The collection was donated by Nawwab Mohammad Mustafa Khan, poetic name Shaifta (1802-1869 A. D.). He was one of the great scholars of his age. After acquiring knowledge in Islamic Studies at Delhi, he went to Mecca on pilgrimage. There he studied Saha-i-Sitta under the guidance of Shaikh Abdullah Siraj Hanafi and learnt principles of Hadith from Shaikh Mohammad Abid Sindhi. When he returned to his home after perfoming the pilgrimage at Mecca, he collected rare and fine books in Arabic, Persian and Urdu. In 1857, when the Indians revolted against the Britishers in Delhi, his collection was partly ruined by a fire, in which many fine and rare manuscripts were destroyed. After sometime his grandson Nawwab Mohammad Ismail, the chancellor of the university, donated it to the university. In 1932 measures were taken to prepare a catalogue of Shaifta's published and unpublished books. In 1982 the catalogue of Shaiftah Collection manuscripts was prepared and printed by Sayyed Mahmud Hasan Qaisar Amrohavi. This catalogue includes the description of 224 volumes of the Shaifta Collection.

4. Jawahar Museum Collection: This catalogue has been compiled by Mohammad Abrar Husain Farooqi and published in 1959. It describes 182 Persian manuscripts of Jawahar Museum, Itawa.

5. Aftab Collection: This collection comprises of 66 Arabic, 162 Persian and 3 Urdu manuscripts. Its catalogue was compiled by Mohammad Hasan Rizvi and Syed Mahmud Hasan Qaisar.

6. Subhanullah Collection: The catalogue of this collection was compiled by Syed Kamil Husain and published in 1930.

7. Mirat-ul-Tasawwaf: It consists of manuscripts on Sufism. The catalogue of this collection was compiled by Syed Mahmud Hasan Qaisar in 1980.

22

NATIONAL LIBRARY AND ARCHIVES OF EGYPT, CAIRO

The National Library and Archives of Egypt is a government research and cultural non- profit authority, whose main concern is to render library services throughout Egypt and the Arab World. It was established as an independent legal entity by virtue of the presidential decree in 1993, with an allocated budget including detailed items for each of its activities as specified by the standards of State Master Budget. A 7-storey building over- looking the Nile Corniche in Ramlet Boulac Districtwas allotted from the very beginning to be a large complex for a variety of cultural activities. However, the annex building is now accommodating the National Archives.

The National Library and Archives, as one of several governmental institutions help implementing the Ministry of Culture's responsibilities in the domains of National and Public Libraries, Legacy, Manuscripts, National Archives, Documentation and Information.

The activities undertaken by the National Library and Archives are therefore designed to achieve the following objects:

1. To make available all facilities necessary for getting acquainted with the world intellectual production and to render library services for that purpose.
2. To take an integral part in the revival of the intellectual heritage by collecting originals thereof, and to assist in making these available for scholars and researchers.
3. To collect, maintain and edit all possible manuscripts, microforms, photographs, recordings, and make these

available for research purposes.

4. To collect all documents pertaining to national history and any other relevant subject matter in all ages, and to prepare and to maintain these for general use.

All activities launched by NLA are properly assisted by the NL's press which is not only responsible for printing of legacy books, but also for the books edited by our research centres. Through more active interest and participation in the national guidance, the National Library must also keep up-to-date with relevant social, economic and technological developments so as to be responsive to the demands of the general public and clientele groups, in addition to cooperating with other institutions of the Ministry of Culture.

The National Library, the oldest government library, houses several million authored and translated volumes covering nearly every field of knowledge, and possesses in addition a vast variety of Arab and other oriental manuscripts. Collections of references open to the public. User needs only a "Reader's Pass" in order to use the readings rooms and consult the catalogues on the NL's premises. The public libraries spread throughout Greater Cairo, and our fleet of Mobile Libraries are responsible for rendering services free of charge to the general public, children, and scholarly community. All users have free access to such facilities and can borrow books.

On the academic level, the National Archives, with its immense variety of documents relevant to the history of Egypt, also renders services free of charge to researchers, scholars, university professors, and to those engaged in the work on political and social history of Egypt.

In pursuance of the NL's policy for the dissemination of Arab culture and fulfilling the requirements of research activity, priority is given to edit, reprint and introduce to as many readers and researchers all over the world to legacy books as possible, as well as edit and publish all documents relevant to the history of Egypt.

Historical Development of the Library

Historical development of the Library began in 1870 with the opening of El Kotobkhana EL Khedawaya. It is a Turkish name which means, in Arabic, (El Khedawya National Library), in the lower floor of The Moustafa Fadel Palace (The brother of El Khedwi Ismail in Darb El Gamamez). In 1873 the first material of the Arabic & Oriental collections in The Library, which consists in a unique collection of handwritten books & copies of precious Holy Qura'an, which were collected from The Mosques, the graves, educational centers, bookcases of El Awkaf, government offices.

The basis stone was placed for the expecting Library of Bab El Khalek in 1899.

In 1904 the Library was opened to the public. In 1914 the opening of The National Library in Bab El Khalek to the public. From (1914-1917) When Hussein Kamel became King of Egyptian "Saltana", the library was known as "The National Library of El Soltania". Its name further changed to "The Egyptian Library" in 1917 and this name remains till the revolution of 1952.

In 1970 the location of the Library was changed to the current building in Ramlat Boulak- Corniche El Nile. A year later, the General Egyptian Book Organization was founded, due to the Republican decision num. 2826, in 1971, concerning the union of The National Library with The General Egyptian Book Organization so as to avail writing and publishing through their both printing- presses, aiming to achieve the goals of The General Egyptian Book Organization. The National Library & Archives got back her private individuality and was separated from the General Book Organization in 1993.

Dar El Kotob (The National Library & Archives of Egypt) has been always a pioneer in its field, due to its long history and intellectual ingenuity, whereas it glows with original values and magnificent traditions. Thus, it was but natural that DarElKotob

(The National Library & Archives of Egypt) presumes the leadership role and takes off with its rich traditions to cope with the current international knowledge system, opening up to its streams and participating in its achievements as well as benefiting from its outcomes and technologies in a manner that creatively maintains the balance between DarElKotob's commitment to the preservation of human traditions, and its rational openness towards the most recent systems applied in science and technology.

The Arabic and Easten manuscripts in Egypt are about 110,000. This collection comes in the second stage after the Turkish one. As far as the National Library is concerned, these manuscripts are considered as one of the best and precious collections in the world for they have different topics and handwritings which were written by the authors themselves or by the religious leaders. They have also a big number of holy Qura'an, some of them are written on gazelle skin.

The oldest of them can be traced to 77 A. H. and belonged to Imam El Hasan El Basry (included in Talaat Collections, no. 50, Qura'an). In addition to that, there is a unique collection of Mamuluks' Qura'ans which were endowed by the Mamuluks' Sultans to their schools in Cairo. This collection was transferred to the National Library in the end of the last century. And, also a unique collection of Persian manuscripts decorated by pictures, golden water and beautiful colors.

The manuscripts of the National Library until the first of April 1916 was 19,000 ones, among them 3458 manuscripts represent Mustafa Fadel collection, and it is symbolized by the Symbol (M). It includes 2473 Turkish manuscripts and 335 Persian manuscripts, and 345 manuscripts endowed by Mohamed Mahmoud Bin El Talamiz El Shankitti, and were added to the National Library after his death in 1322 A. H, 1904 A. D, and are symbolized in the index of the National Library by the symbol (SH). In addition to that, There are 189 Qura'ans (among them 27 written by Kufian handwriting on Gazelle Skin). And Ali Pasha

Muharak's manuscripts which were added to the National Library in 1895, two years after his death.

The oldest of these manuscripts is the only copy of the book A Message to Fiqeh Basis written by Imam Mohamed Bin Adrees El Shafaay, handwritten by El Rabea Bin Soliman El Murady, friend of El Shafaay, in the beginning of the third Arabic century. In 265 A. H, it has an approval from El Shafaay to whoever wants to handwrite it. And it is included in the collection of Mustafa Fadel's manuscripts, and is Kept now under the number of 41 Fiqeh basis (M).

Since 1929, it has been added to the National Library some precious libraries, which tripled its size, and those libraries are:

Kula Library was established by Mohamed Ali Pasha in Kula City, where he was born, and was added to the National Library in 1929, and the number of its volumes are 3440. Ahmed Bey Talaat Library added 9549 manuscripts. The Zakiah Library was transferred to the National Library in 1935 and its manuscripts are 1482 volumes.

Those are the most important private libraries, which were added to the National Library.There are less important libraries were added to the National Library and their manuscripts in 1954, were 38583 volumes such as libraries of Wagih El Ameri, Omer Makram, Sheikh Ahmed Abou Khatoah and Ali Galal El Husseiny.

Bernardo Mortiez, the head of the National Library between 1896-1911, had published a book in which he presented the most precious records of the National Library such as Qura'ans, Arabic papyrus, and manuscripts which presented types of Arabic handwriting and its development through 1000 years.

Collections of Manuscripts

The National Library and Archives of Egypt is one of the oldest libraries in the Middle East and its importance lies in having about 55,000 of the most significant collections of manuscripts and microforms in the world which are rendered in Arabic, Turkish and Persian languages.

These rare collections of manuscripts include a wide variety of the Holy Koran (Qur'an), whose early versions are written on paper and parchment, others are in the early undotted Kufi style. Among them are copies written by celebrated calligraphers as Yaquote-al-Mostaasimi. In addition, there is a magnificent collection containing the largest and most richly illuminated versions of the Holy Koran copied in the Mameluke Text-hand, Trilinear and Rayhani writings.

The National Library's collections also include a wide variety of the most valuable manuscripts in various fields of knowledge such as general information, religion, scientific heritage and literature, amongst which is a unique book entitled as (the Message) by Al-Emam-al-Shafi'ai tackling the principles of jurisprudence, and dating back to the third, fourth and fifth centuries, were privately owned by Taymour Pasha, Ahmed Zaki Pasha, Ahmed Tal'at Bey and Mustafa Fadel, then successively acquired and added to the National Library's stock at the end of the nineteenth century.

The collections contain rare Persian manuscripts, some of which are beautifully illustrated by famous Persian painters, like Bostan Sa'adi illustrated in 893 A. H. by Behzad who was entitled as Raphael of the East, also like Shahnama (Book of Kings) by Ferdawsi and Hayder Nama in 416 H.

Ottoman Turkish manuscripts date back to a few centuries ago and represent an important heritage for the Middle East area.

Also, the Arabic papyri collection, discovered at the end of the nineteenth century and amounts to 3.000 papyri, are written in both Arabic and Greek. The majority of such manuscripts are in Arabic and the earliest of which dates back to 22 A. H, and represents invaluable treasure for those who study the development of Arabic calligraphy as they are rich in information about the economic life in Egypt and include deeds of sale and purchase, marriage lines and title-deeds that extend from the Umawi period to Fatimid period.

Similarly, the National Archives has a rare paper historical collection of documents in both Arabic and Turkish languages. The Library's collection include valuable documents' pertaining to the history of Egypt, the earliest of which is the endowment deed of the Fatimid Minister Talae'a bin Ruzeik, dating back to the Ayyubid era (d.567-648 A. H. / 1058 A.D.). In addition, there are legal documents dating back to the Mameluke era (d.648-923 A. H. /1250-1517 A.D.), 74 legal documents dating back to the Ottoman era (d. 1517-1805 A.D.).

Moreover, the National Archives has a wide variety of documents in English, French and Italian languages. These collections, which cover the 19th. and 20th. Centuries are very important for conducting substantive researches and studies on the history of Egypt, Arab World, Africa and their relations with Europe.

The Library collections are of significant nature as they represent an essential part of the human heritage. All of these have helped to build the NL's outstanding local and international reputation. The National Library and Archives comprises a number of research centers, such as: the Center for Editing & Publishing Arabic Manuscripts,the Center of Documents and Contemporary History of Egypt, the Computer Center, the Documentation and Research Center for Children's Literature and the Restoration Conservation & Microfilm Center, which has recently been provided and equipped through a Protocol of Cooperation concluded between Egypt and the Kingdom of Spain whose cooperation and understanding are thankfully appreciated. Infrastructure works at the NL's premises were mostly financed by the Egyptian Cultural Development Fund.

23
NATIONAL LIBRARY OF RUSSIA, MOSCOW

As one of two national libraries in Russia, the NLR is responsible for the preservation of all the printed matter, manuscripts and other documents, for their retention, editing and scientific processing in order to ensure the citizens' right to use the cultural and scientific heritage as well as to have free access to information. The NLR enjoys the right to receive a deposit copy of every item printed in the Russian Federation. In addition, the NLR purchases various materials from foreign countries. The collections are also enlarged through donations and bequests. The NLR is a Russian center for scientific and research activities in the field of librarianship, bibliography and book science.

The NLR was founded according to the will of Empress Catherine II on May 27, 1795 as the first available Russian Library and national repository. The set-up of the Library took nearly 20 years. A.N.Olenin (1763-1843) the first Director of the Library appointed in 1811 played a significant role in the process. He created the basis of the Library activities which is still topical up to this day. The Library was opened for users on January 14, 1814.

In 1828-1834 a new building comprising two large reading rooms designed by C.Rossi and A.F. Shchedrin was added to the old one. The increase in the number of users created the necessity of opening a new reading room. This was opened in a specially erected building in 1862. In connection with the increase of the collection, the architect E.Vorotilov designed a vast building in 1896-1901. The building of the former Ekaterininsky Institute on Fontanka Embankment was put at the disposal of the Library in 1950. The expansion of the collection and number of readers, the scattered storage, all these lead to the necessity to construct a new building. The construction started on October 28, 1986. The New Building was opened for readers in the year 1998. The National Library of Russia offers all the various library services, including information, bibliography and cataloguing services, lending-library services and international. book exchange. All the main Library material, including catalogues and the Central Reference Library, are available for the users free of charge.

Collections

The NLR collects extensively books, serials and other printed matter published in the Russian Federation on the basis of LDC and supplementary acquisitions

* books, serials of research interest in European languages, according to the acquisitions program of the NLR;
* books, serials and other material of historical and cultural importance wherever published, including oriental languages and countries;
* manuscripts in Russian, European and Oriental languages of historical and cultural importance;
* all kinds of foreign publications on Russia - “Rossica”;
* newspapers, engravings, posters, musical editions, worldwide cartographic material - Russian and wherever published of historical and cultural importance;
* sound recordings.

On January 1, 2002 the NLR collection included 33,110,230 items, with 6,058,418 volumes in foreign languages, 9,668,482 monographs and periodicals, 566,791 newspapers in collections, 437,598 manuscripts and manuscript volumes, 308,151 items of music editions, 250,669 prints, engravings, etc.; 125,556 maps and atlases; 35,503 sound records.

Oriental Manuscripts

Imperial Public Library started acquiring manuscripts in oriental languages as soon as it was established in 1795. By the time it was officially inaugurated in 1812 it had accumulated 183 such manuscripts, 103 of them being from P.P. Dubrovsky's collection.

The largest acquisitions made during the early history of the Library became possible due to the successful action of the Russian Army in its campaigns against Persia and Turkey. The Ardebil, Akhaltsikh, Erzerum and Adrianopolis Collections number 420 manuscripts in Persian, Arabic and Turkish. Further growth of this collection became possible due to collecting activities of diplomats (I.O. Simonitch, D.I. Dolgoruky, A. Zhaba) and Russian and foreign scholars (V.D. Smirnov, I.P. Minaev, N.V. Khanykov, K. Tischendorff, J.-J. Marcele), of missionaries (archimandrite Peter (Kamensky), bishop Porphiry (Uspensky), archimandrite Antonin (Kapustin), Z.F. Leontievsky). The largest private collection is that of the Karaim traveler, merchant and archeologist Avraam Firkovich which numbers some 18 000 items as well as the personal papers of its owner.

Thanks to Firkovich and archimendrite Antonin (1180 item) the collection of Jewish (or be precise, Judiac) manuscripts in the National Library of Russia are: "Codex Petropolitanus", of the year 1010 - the oldest unabridged dated manuscript variant of the Bible also called Codex Leningradensis, Leningrad Bible or Cairo Bible with its 16 decorative illuminated sheets; "The Last Prophets" of the year 916 the first among the known manuscripts with the Babylonian system of vowels in different syllables; the incomplete Bible of the year of 929 decorated with the pictures of two menorah (with seven branches. Christian East is represented by 40 Syrian manuscripts, 13 among which date back to the first millennium (the earliest one being the "Ecclesiastic History" by Eusebius of the year 462); by 64 Coptic manuscripts of the 10th – 18th centuries; by 34 Ethiopian manuscripts of the 16th - 19th centuries; by 236 Georgian handwritten books of 8th-19th centuries (of which the most celebrated is the "Tbetic Gospel" of the year 995); and by 106 Armenian manuscripts. .Many of the Georgian and Armenian manuscripts are decorated with miniatures and illuminations. Of great interest are the 100 Arabian Christian manuscripts, the earliest of which is the Gospel of the year 892 with miniatures. Hand-written Islamic books are also well represented

Over 2000 Arabian codices and fragments include a whole collection of Korans in Kufic alphabet of the 8th - 11th centuries, gorgeous books decorated in "Memeluke Style" of the 14th - 15th centuries, a "Geography" by al-Idrisi with 37 maps, an astronomical work by as-Soufi with pictures of the constellations. Books in Arabic were written and copied not only in Arabic countries but also in Iran, Central Asia, Turkey, Dagestan and other Islamic areas.

Among more than 1000 Persian manuscripts, 140 are decorated with miniatures starting with "Shah-Name" of the year 1333. Especially well represented is the Tabriz school (see, for example, the poem "Gui va chaugan" by Arifi copied by shah Takhnasp in 1525). Some of the miniatures are attributed to Bekhzad and Mukhammedi. There are also works signed by Rizai Abbasi. Among the calligraphists one should note Sultan-Ali Mashhadi, Shah Mahmud Nishapuri, Mir Imad.

The Persian manuscripts produce great impression not only by their miniatures and calligraphy but also by their overall design: by their ornamental illuminations and margins as well as by their stamped and patent leather bindings. Some of the Turkish manuscripts were also designed in Persian tradition. First of all this applies to the works of the Uzbek poet Alisher Navoi (for example, to his "Early Divan" copied in 1465 when the poet was 25 years of age). Over 400 Turkish manuscripts were copied in Turkey, Central Asia, the Crimea and the area of the River Volga.

There are also 56 Kurdish manuscripts of the 19th century. Among the items preserved in the Library there are some 800 documents written in Islamic countries. These are charters written by Persian shahs and Turkish sultans, deeds of purchase, letters, and registers which recorded legal acts. Among the manuscripts and xylographs from Far East, South- East Asia and other Buddhist areas one should note 300 Chinese manuscripts, 70 Manchurian manuscripts, 60 Japanese manuscripts, 400 manuscripts written in the 15th - 19th century in various Indian languages, 160 Tibetan manuscripts, 39 Mongolian manuscripts and 14 Kalmuck manuscripts.

The Oriental collections include archives containing documents and translations into oriental languages made in the 20th century (by Peisakh, Bernstein, Margolin). The collection of Russian archives contains the archives of such orientalists as Samoilovich, Troitskaya, Martinovich, and Shprintsyn.

The Oriental collections are continuously replenished. Over 100 manuscripts including the Arabic manuscript of the 14th century - the "takhmis" "Kasydat al-Burda" which is an excellent sample of a book designed in the "Mameluke Style" - have been acquired in the past five years.

At the moment the National Library of Russia preserves some 27000 oriental manuscripts: codices, fragments, scrolls, documents (charters, letters, etc.), xylographs, and drawings fully illustrating the history of the evolution of writing and of the art of making books in the East. The chronological span of the collections is from the 10th century before Christ (papyri from Ancient Egypt) to the present day: its geographic span is from Japan and Indonesia to Spain, from St. Petersburg to Etheopia.

24

RAMPUR RAZA LIBRARY, RAMPUR

Rampur was a small state but it was very rich in many respects. It contributed a lot to the intellectual and literary world. Such contributions could not be received from larger states as far as the field of knowledge specially music, poetry and education is concerned. The Raza Library of Rampur is the manifestation of such contributions by the rulers of the state.

The Rampur Raza Library is a very rich in the resources on Indo-Islamic studies and arts. The erstwhile 'Rampur State' later merged with the Indian Union, was founded by Nawab Faizullah Khan in 1774. He ruled over the state up to 1794 and formed the nucleus of the library through his personal collection of valuable manuscripts, historical documents, books and paintings kept in the State's Toshakhana. The Nawabs of Rampur State had been great patrons of renowned scholars, poets, painters, calligraphers and musicians. During the rule of Nawab Ahamd Ali Khan (1794-1840) notable additions to the collections were made. Nawab Muhammad Saeed Khan (1840-55) created a separate Department of the library. He was an enlightened ruler and shifted the collection to new rooms. He appointed Agha Yousuf Ali 'Mahvi' , an Afghan scholar, to organize the collection into a Kutubkhana. The Nawab also invited well–known calligraphers, illuminators and binders from Kashmir and other parts of India.

Nawab Raza Ali Khan (1930-66) became the Nawab on 30th June,1930. As he was educated here and abroad, he took unprecedented interest to build the schools and colleges in the State. He was a lover of Indian music for which he purchased several rare manuscripts and books on Indian music. He kept his personal interest in the library affairs after the merger of the State into the Indian Union in December, 1949. He was also responsible for the acquisition of the valuable Loharu Collection of the library. After the independence and the merger of the State in the Union of India, the Library was brought under the management of a Trust on 6th August, 1951. This Trust management continued till June, 1975. Nawab Murtaza Ali Khan was the President of that Trust. Professor Syed Nurul Hasan, the then Minister of State for Education and Scientific Research, Government of India, visited the library repeatedly and took a serious view of the neglected condition of this priceless heritage. At his instance and Nawab Murtaza Ali Khan, the Government of India took over the library on 1st July, 1975 under the Act enacted by the Parliament and assumed the full central responsibility for the management of the library. Mrs. Indira Gandhi, the Prime Minister, proclaimed the library as an Institution of National importance in a packed meeting ground of the people in her public announcement during her visit to Rampur in 1974.

The Central Government took over the library with effect from 1st July, 1975 under Rampur Raza Library Act (Act No.22 of 1975). The affairs of the library are managed by the Rampur Raza Library Board which has been set up under Section 4 (2) of the Act. It is the governing body with His Excellency, the Hon'ble Governor of Uttar Pradesh as the Chairman. There is a provision of twelve other members including one descendant of the erstwhile ruling Nawab family of Rampur, distinguished historians, scholars in Arabic, Persian and Urdu literature besides officials concerned with the affairs of the library in the Central and State Governments.

The Rampur Raza Library management is committed to enrich its collection of books, manuscripts, art objects, historical documents, coins through purchases, gifts or exchanges. The devoted Officer On Special Duty leaves no stone unturned in increasing the items of historical importance to the repository of the organization every year.

A large number of scholars, noted litterateurs and dignitaries visit the library regularly. Reputed personalities in the field of literature happened to visit and observed its collections during the 20th century. They have penned down their observations in the visitor's book of the library and rated it as the unique collection richer than those of such other libraries of the world.

Well-known historian and Islamic scholar Allama Shibli Naumani expressed his views and saw the library on 6th April 1914.

"I have consulted this library several times. There is no better collection in India than this. I have also seen the libraries of Egypt, Syria, Turkey and Europe and I can say that this library is richer than any one of them."

Percy Brown, the author of the famous book 'Indian Paintings under the Mughal' has written about the library on 22nd September 1917. "I have spent a pleasant and most instructive morning in this library with Hafiz Ahmad Ali Khan, the Superintendent as my guide. The pictures have been to me a source of great delight. Some of these are unique.

Manuscripts

The Raza Library has preserved some rare collections like the seventh century AD Quran written on parchment in early Kufic script attributed to Hazrat Ali. Besides, The library houses a large collection of manuscripts, printed books and miniature paintings. The institution is particularly known for its treasure of Indo-Islamic studies and arts.

In 1975, the Government of India declared the library as an institution of national importance by an act of parliament. Presently, the Raza Library is an autonomous organisation, financed by the Ministry of culture, Government of India.

Housed in two magnificent buildings in the fort of Rampur,

the library has a remarkable collection of 15,000 manuscripts, including 150 illustrated ones with 4,413 graphics in them. Besides, there are 205 manuscripts on palm leaves, 1,000 miniature paintings and 1,000 specimens of Islamic calligraphy. The library has more than 50,000 volumes of printed books. It also possesses vast collection of art objects and ancient astronomical instruments. Another feature of the library collection is manuscripts belonging to the libraries of Halb, Makkah, Madinah, Egypt, Iran, Afghanistan and royal libraries of emperors and noblemen.

As per the Annual Report of the Library, more than 1,534 scholars from India and abroad visited the library and over 6,048 books and 474 manuscripts were read by them during the year 2000-2001. The library provided 6,866 photographs and 51,211 photocopies of the material to its readers. Besides this, 27,192 visitors came to the library to view and appreciate its collections.

The conservation laboratory has been equipped with modern equipment. The library fumigated 2,624 old printed books, 54 rare Mughal miniature paintings, 525 old manuscripts, 14 old historical documents, 5 big size paintings, 106 old printed books and 26 specimens of calligraphy were conserved and restored.

Raza Library is more famous for its invaluable collection of manuscripts, mostly in Arabic, Persian, Urdu and other Indian languages. The collection of manuscripts as broken up language wise is mentioned below:

Arabic	5,053
Persian	4,060
Urdu	1700
Hidi and Sanskrit	1,000
Tamil	150
Turky and Pushto	50

Arabic

The collection of Arabic manuscripts here is considered as the oldest with rare specimens of Islamic calligraphy and book binding. Among them is the seventh century AD Quran written on parchment in early Kufic script attributed to Hazrat Ali. Another specimen of the holy Quran written in the eighth century AD is attributed to Imam Jafar Sadiq. Another copy of ninth century Quran written on parchment is attributed to Imam Abul Hasan Musa. The celebrated scholar and calligrapher Ibn Muqla, who served three caliphs of Baghdad as prime minister and died on July 20, 941 AD, copied the Quran in the early Naskh style. That masterpiece has found an important place in the collection. The noted calligrapher has reshaped the Arabic letters into Naskh, which is still in vogue in one or the other form. It is a unique specimen of Ibn Muqla's calligraphy.

The library has a copy of the Quran penned by the master calligrapher of the 13th century AD of Baghdad, Yaqut-al Musta' Simi. It has ornamentation in gold. Another masterpiece of Arabic manuscript by the same calligrapher is Diwan- al- Hadira dated 1221 AD. It was once the part of the royal library of Ibrahim Adil Shah of Bijapur. An interesting work in Arabic of pseudepigraphy and wonderful creations profusely illustrated with strange figures of human beings, animals and birds entitled Ajaibul Makhluqat, was written by Zakaria bin Mahmood al Qazvini (1283 AD) and scripted in elegant Naskh by Ibn Kamaluddin Husain in 1571 AD.

Persian

The Persian collection comprises of books mainly on Sufism, Medicine, History and literature. The first volume of Tafsir-eTibri is available in the only which is unique in antiquity The other book is Tafseer-e-Zahidi which is considered as a specimen of Persian prose. Three copies of this work are available here. Many copies of Kulliat-e Sa'di, Kulliat-eKhusro and Shahnama of Firdausi are available in Library. A book belonging to the period of Firoz Shah is available on Mathmatics entitled Dasturul al Bab fi Ilm-ul Hisaab which is rare.

Zakhirai Khawarizm Shahi is one of the earliest treatises on medicine among the Persian manuscripts of the library. It was scripted by Zainuddin Ibrahim Gurgani (d. 531 AH). Another one is Tafsir-e-Tabri translated from Arabic by Abdul Baqi and scripted by Mirza Muhammad bin Mujtahid in the 12th century AD. It bears the autographs of Shah Abbas of Iran and Qasim Beg Khan in 1621-22 AD. The earliest illustrated Persian work on history of Mongol tribes entitled Jamiul-Tawarikh by Rashidud-Din Fazlullah, includes rare miniatures depicting various aspects of political, social, and religious life of the Mongols. The paintings indicate inspiration of the Chinese and Central Asian early paintings which had influenced the Herat school of painting.

The library has the Khamsa of Nizami Ganjavi (1203 AD) illustrated in 1542-43 AD. It represents the Iranian style and is beautifully painted against a floral background. The manuscript of the Diwan-i-Jami bears a beautiful seal of Hamida Bano Begum, daughter of Ali Akbar, mother of emperor Akbar and that of Nazar Ara, daughter of Shah Jahan, on the colophon. Diwan-i-Hafiz, a rare illustrated manuscript, is among the collections of the library. It was written in Akbar's eventful reign around 1570-80 AD, and was illustrated by celebrated court painters.

Among the other rare Persian manuscripts of the library there is a copy of Risalah Khawaja Abdullah Ansari and Sad Pand-i-Luqman bound together and scribed in elegant Nastaliq by the master calligrapher Mir Ali of Herat, who died in 1544 AD. It bears signatures and seals of several kings and scholars and was graded as being of first category by emperor Shah Jahan and was purchased by him for Rs 1,000. He presented another copy of the same Risalah to Jahan Ara Begum who lavishly praised its importance in her own handwriting in 1588 AD and bears the seals of Shah Jahan and Aurangzeb.

A unique illustrated Ramayan of Valmiki translated into Persian by Sumer Chand and illustrated during the reign of Farrukh Siyar in 1715-16 AD bears 258 miniatures throwing light on the art, architecture, costumes and ornaments of the period, besides highlighting the composite culture of India in the late medieval period.

Palm Leaves

The collection of palm leaf manuscripts is among the valuable assets of Raza Library. Most of them are in Telugu, Sanskrit, Kannada, Sinhala or Tamil. They are generally religious in character. A Tamil script mentions the rules of preparing images and icons and the mode of worship; another leaf manuscript tells the medicinal properties of herbs. One such manuscript in Sanskrit written in Grantha script; is of the Ramayan. It eulogises the Ramayan as Brhahmavachakam. A Kannada manuscript is a treatise on music and yet another manuscript is Periyatine Vaimoli, the sacred hymn of the Vaishnavas. Besides manuscripts and books, the library is also a treasure-trove of antique art objects and rare astronomical instruments. The oldest instrument of the collection is an astrolabe made by Siraj Damashqi in 1218 AD. The instrument was used for measuring the latitude of the sun and stars for navigational purposes and astronomy. Two other astrolabes by the same instrument maker are dated back to 1225 AD and 1230 AD and are found in the collections of Salar Jung Museum, Hyderabad, and National Museum, New Delhi. Apart from these, the Raza library has a vast collection of books in Sanskirt, Turkish, Pushto, Hindi, Urdu and other languages.

25

ROYAL ASIATIC SOCIETY, LONDON

The Royal Asiatic Society has a long and distinguished history. It was founded in 1823 by a group of people led by the Sanskrit scholar Henry Colebrooke, who had worked in South Asia and wished to pursue the objectives set out in the Society's Royal Charter of 1824 relating to investigation connected with, and for the encouragement of, science, literature and the arts in relation to Asia".

During the Nineteenth Century the Royal Asiatic Society was the main centre in Britain for scholarly work on Asia and had many distinguished Fellows including the Duke of Wellington, Rabindranath Tagore, Sir Henry Rawlinson and Sir Richard Burton. Over the years a number of societies with similar purposes and programmes have been established in South Asia, Hong Kong, Japan, Korea, Malaysia and Thailand, and have been recognised as associates of the Royal Asiatic Society. Members of these societies are entitled to attend lectures and use the Library while in London temporarily, and to join as subscribing Fellows without other sponsorship.

The Society has some 700 members, half of whom are based outside Britain. It operates from its own building, a large house in Bayswater, which contains the library and collection, and a lecture room where meetings take place. Now, the Society is run by a Council of around twenty elected Fellows. It currently has a staff of seven, some of whom work part time. The Society's total income in 2000 was £162,000. It is a registered charity (No. 209629) and welcomes support from donors.

The Royal Asiatic Society exists to encourage and facilitate

Asian Studies and is Britain's senior learned society in the field. The Society's main activities are:

* publishing the Journal of the Royal Asiatic Society
* providing access to the Society's extensive collection of books, historic documents, paintings and artefacts, and promoting research into its holdings
* arranging a programme of lectures and seminars
* publishing books and monographs on Asian subjects, in collaboration with the Curzon Press
* organising conferences and exhibitions
* making awards to recognise achievements in the field

Library

The Library is primarily for the use of the members of the Society, both Fellows and Library Associates. Other readers may be admitted, by prior appointment, for a limited period of time. The geographical scope of the library includes all of Asia from Turkey in the West to Japan in the East, from Siberia in the North to Sri Lanka and Indonesia in the South. There is also a certain amount of material on Islamic North Africa.

The time coverage of the collections is very roughly that of the last two thousand years with a few important exceptions. Firstly the Society does not concern itself with Current Events, that is to say roughly the last fifty years. Secondly where there are major continuous civilizations such as in India or China material relating to the origins and ancient history of those civilizations is included, whereas ancient Middle Eastern history is largely excluded.

The subject coverage of the library is, broadly speaking, that of the Humanities i.e. History and Politics, Religion and Philosophy, Languages, Linguistics and Literature (classical rather than modern), Art, and Geography. The natural sciences such as mathematics and astronomy are covered in general works on the histories of various civilizations.

Law is generally excluded, other than that relating to Islam and Hinduism. The library also is not strong on modern ethographic or anthropological material although some relevant information may be found in the accounts of visitors to remote areas. Although the contents of the library are housed in rooms on all floors of the building, access to the Collections is restricted to staff.

Anyone wishing to see an item should first identify it in one of the catalogues and then request a member of the library staff to bring the item to a seat at a table in the Reading Room which is located on the ground floor at the front of the building.

Library - Contents

90,000 Monographs

Approx. 2,250 Bound vols of Periodicals

Over 1,150 Boxes of Periodical Parts

7 bound vols of Early Newspapers

300 bound vols of Pamphlets

200 Boxes of loose pamphlet type material

A small collection of maps.

Over 1,500 Oriental Manuscripts

10 Collections of European language Manuscript Material

Over 2,000 Prints, Paintings, Drawings, Busts etc.

Many albums and boxes of Photographic Prints

800 Glass plates

750 35mm Transparencies and a small number of Ektachromes Glass plates

Archival material relating to the R.A.S. comprising

75 Bound volumes of Minutes etc.

10 Boxes of loose archival material.

Miscellaneous "museum" items including Copper plate inscriptions, 4 "Bronze" figures from S.E.Asia, a Qajar ceramic bowl, a cast of a column with a Chola inscription, a cast of a Lion with a Hittite inscription etc, etc.

Books available in the Library may be lent at the discretion of the Librarian to Members of the Society and Library Associates, in good standing. Bound periodicals and loose periodical parts, Manuscripts, Maps, Prints and Drawings etc. are not normally available for loan. Up to 6 books may be borrowed at a time for up to 6 months (unless requested by another member) before being returned, or returned and taken out again. If a book on loan is requested by another member, the period of the loan is reduced to 1 month. Books older than 100 years are not normally lent and the physical condition or rarity of the book, whatever its age, may preclude outside loan.

Library – Catalogues

Printed Book Catalogues

Manuscript Catalogues

Arabic Script Catalogues

Malay & Javanese Script Catalogues

Sanskrit & Other Indian Language Catalogues

Pali, Burmese, Sinhalese &Amp; Thai Catalogues

Chinese, Tibetan & Mongolian Catalogues

European Manuscripts

Prints & Drawing Catalogues

Periodicals Handlist

Photographs

Other Items

RAS Material now on deposit elsewhere

Index (Language, topic, names)

Main Catalogue. In four parts

Catalogue of Printed Books, published before 1932, in the Library of the Royal Asiatic Society. London: The Society, 1940.

vii, 541p Lists books acquired by the Society between 1823 and c.1932. Entry by Author, with additional entries under translator, editor, or title for anonymous works. Note: includes collections of the Library of the Society of Biblical Archaeology, merged with RAS, 1919. c.21,000 entries

Catalogue of the Library of the Royal Asiatic Society. London, The Society, 1893. Largely superseded by the 1940 catalogue except for c.325 entries for The Bible and c.900 pamphlets bound in 110 volumes.

Card catalogue. Books and periodicals acquired between 1932 and c.1991. Has separate sequence for Storey collection. Mixture of typed and handwritten cards. c. 20,000 entries.

Automated catalogue. Lists books acquired since 1991. In addition older material has been re-catalogued onto the database. Possible to search by Author, keywords in Titles, or Subjects. Re-cataloguing done: Most of South East Asian and Japanese material added and some of South Asian collections c. 5,700 entries

Specialised catalogues

Lovell, Mary S. and Rivett, Bernadette Catalogue of the Burton books in the R.A.S., collected by Oscar Eckenstein. 1999- c.200 entries

Tcheraz, M. The Schrumpf Collection of Armenian books [in the Library of The Royal Asiatic Society] Journal of the Royal .Asiatic Society, 1893 pp.699-716 Note: Some later Armenian books appear in the 1940 printed general catalogue c. 341 items

List of the Malay books bequeathed to the Society by the late Sir W. E. Maxwell, K.C.M.G.; compiled from notes made by C. Otto Blagden. *Journal of the Royal Asiatic Society,* 1899 pp.121-129

Wenzel, H. List of Tibetan manuscripts and printed books in the Library of the Royal Asiatic society. *Journal of the Royal Asiatic Society,* July, 1892 pp.570-579

Blois, F. de. Catalogue of the Storey collection. 1999- Computer based list being converted to "universal system". Large proportion Persian language, some Russian and Arabic. Older card catalogue in existence A I 3 c. 4,800 entries

MANUSCRIPTS

Arabic script catalogues

Codrington, O. Catalogue of the Arabic, Persian, Hindustani and Turkish manuscripts. *Journal of the Royal Asiatic Society,* July, 1892 pp.501-569. Some items now identified as Malay and relocated. Established numbering scheme still in use.

Reade, J. Provisional draft handlist of Royal Asiatic society manuscripts in Arabic script. Typescript. 1996. 102 Arabic, 484 Persian, 16 "Hindustani", 68 Ottoman Turkish. Adds manuscripts given since Codrington.1892. viz.:

R.S. Greenshields 1931 13 Persian, 1 Arabic

G. Ellis, 1940s 48 Persian in 40 vols. 16 Arabic in 14 vols.

C. A. Storey 1967 3 Persian

J. Hansman c.1990 14 Arabic in 13 vols.

Robinson, B.W. *Persian paintings in the collection of the Royal Asiatic Society.* London: RAS, 1998. Detailed catalogue of 15 illustrated Persian manuscripts in collection and one oil painting

Morley, W. H. *A descriptive catalogue of the historical manuscripts in Arabic and Persian languages, preserved in the Library of the Royal Asiatic Society....* London, 1854. Provides a fuller description of the contents of those manuscripts dealing with historical subjects.

Sanskrit and other Indian language catalogues

Barnett, L.D. Catalogue of the Tod Collection of Indian manuscripts. *Journal of the Royal Asiatic Society,* II, 1940 pp.129-178 Sanskrit, Prakrit, Hindi and Gujarati. Lists 171 mss in Hindi, Gujarati and Rajasthani. Does not include some items associated with the Tod Collection at a later date.

Cowell, E. B. & Eggeling, J.B. Catalogue of the Buddhist Sanskrit manuscripts in the possession of the Royal Asiatic Society. *Journal of the Royal Asiatic Society,* 1876 pp.1-52 [Hodgson collection. 79 mss brought back from Nepal by B.H.Hodgson.]

Winternitz, M. A catalogue of South Indian Sanskrit manuscripts, especially those of the Whish collection, belonging to the Royal Asiatic Society of Great Britain and Ireland. London, 1902 (Royal Asiatic Society monographs; 2) Lists 215 mss but further 15 items added in manuscript to Library office copy of catalogue.

Pali, Burmese, Sinhalese & Thai catalogues

Filliozat, J. Survey of the Pali manuscript collection in the Royal Asiatic Society. *Journal of the Royal Asiatic Society,* ser.3. v.9 (i) 1999 pp.35-76. Lists 125 items Pali language but various scripts. Also available as offprint.

Handlist of Burmese manuscripts. Typescript c.1956. 85 mss., c.59 described in more detail in Filliozat survey (d1) We also have one decorative leaf of a Kammavaca mss. treated as museum item by Society in past.

Handlist of Sinhalese manuscripts. Typescript c.1956. 33mss, c.8 described in more detail in Filliozat survey (d1)

Handlist of Thai manuscripts. Typescript c.1956. 27mss, none in Filliozat, 1 of the 2 illustrated mss, has been described in Ginsburg, H. *Thai art and culture: historic manuscripts from Western collections.* London: British Library, 2000

Purchase of the Morris manuscripts [a list of Pali, Sanskrit and Burmese mss from this collection] *Journal of the Royal Asiatic Society,* 1896 pp.212-214. 29 manuscripts and 9 transcriptions, described in more detail in Filliozat survey (d1)

26
ROYAL ASIATIC SOCIETY, MUMBAI

Society's genesis is traced to 1804 when the literary Society of Bombay was established by a great savant, Sir James Mackintosh, The Recorder of Bombay, with the objective of "promoting useful knowledge particularly such as is more immediately connected with India" .Amongst those who attended the first meeting were Jonathan Duncan , then Governer of Bombay, the noted historian William Erskine, Sir Charles Forbes, and the two friends, the artist Henry alt and Viscount Valentina whose journals of travels in the East, published in 1809, with sixty engravings after painting by Salt, have become collector's tem today. In 1829 the Literary Society, thereafter known as the Bombay Branch of Royal Asiatic Society was normally to become an integral part of the Royal Asiatic Society of Great Britain. In 1830, the BBRAS moved into the north wing of the newly constructed Town Hall, on payment of the princely sum of Rs. 10,000. In 1873 , the Bombay Geographical Society and in 1896 the Anthropological Society , donated their libraries and museums, and merged heir activities with those of the BBRAS.

The acquisition of the Library of the Medical and Literary Society of Bombay, which had been founded in 1789, formed the nucleus of the library of the Society. Since then, many rare additions have been made to the collection of the athenaeum through the generosity of inumerable educationists and philathropists ncluding Jagannath Shankartshet , Sir Cowasji Jehangir, Bhau Daji Lad , Pandit Bhagwanlal Indraji, remchand Roychand, Dr. Jivanji Modi, Nassurwanji Dadysett, Sir Dinshaw Petit, Sir Dorab Tata and the heirs of G. K. Nariman and V. Bhandarkar.

Portraits and statues of many of the benefactors line the alls of the famous Durbar Hall of the Society. The museum attached to the library was opened in 16 for the ollection and preservation of antiquities such as eological specimens and archaeological relics.Today his unique collection of inscriptions, copper lates, carvings and specimen of the natural history art and mythology of the East, is housed in the Prince of les Museum, Mumbai. Following the tradition of most clubs, hotels and institutions of the Raj, the ociety initially restricted its membership xclusively to Europeans who were elected by a system of black balling. This quaint practice whereby a ommittee Member voted against a proposed member's candidature by dropping a black ball in to the lection box, was discontinued only a few years ago. n 1840, Sir Maneckji Cursetji was privileged to become the first non - European member.

Membership was then thrown open to Indians and amongst the arliest members elected were Shri Jagannath hankarshet and Sir Jamsetji Jeejeebhoy. Since its nception the Society has sponsored readings and discussions of papers on oriental subjects and has also published a journal since 1841 embodying these papers. The Society is recognised by Mumbai iversity for Ph.d studies. Several noted scholars pursue research in these subjects under the aegis of the Society's Mahamahopadhyaya Dr. P. V. Kane nstitute. Dr. Kane worked in the society's rooms on his seminal publication on the Dharmashastra for which he was honoured with the Government of ndia's highest award the Bharat Ratna.

The Society organises seminars, workshops, and public lectures by outstanding scholars. Every three years, the Society confers Honorary Fellowship for eminent scholars and awards medals to renowned scholars.

Library of the Society

The Library of the Asiatic Society is one of the well known Libraries in the country. It has a collection of nearly 2.5 lacs books, receives nearly 150 current periodicals and has 80,000 bound volumes of periodicals, and maps. Most of the collection is very rare and therefore valuable. At present, the library is used by 2,900 members on all the week days, except on Sundays and Bank Holidays, from 10.30 a.m. to 7.30 p.m. The catalogue has been computerized so also the Library operations. The members are provided borrowing facilities. In addition, they are provided an access to internet. Some of the rare collection is microfilmed and can be accessed through the microfilm reader and reader printer. The Library has a bindery of its own. To provide more space to the books, the Library has introduced the Mobile Racks System. It has a special room where the rare books are preserved.

To enhance the collection of the library, the Society has established 'Gift and Exchange Scheme' and executed it successfully. This scheme has been introduced for receiving gift of books from scholars and bibliophiles. However, the library is interested in receiving only those books which come within the purview of its activities viz. books of a scholarly nature on subjects like Indology, the Social Sciences, Asian Studies, the Arts, Literature and Culture. Others are donated to those libraries in the city which are likely to be interested in them

A special room has been created to house books which need special care, such as, those which are very old, which are oversize or undersize, which contain rare photographs, coloured pictures, which have the autographs of renowned persons, and so on. The Society has set up two laboratories, viz., conservation and microfilming. Both these laboratories are dedicated to prolong the life of valuable material in the library. Each crumbling book is fumigated, opened up, pieces of a page joined when necessary, treated chemically page by page, covered with tissue papers, rebound and returned to the shelf for the reader's use

The Library having been established for nearly 200 years has majority of collection which is rare. In addition it has good number of over size books having beautiful colour plates on various topics . Books like are prestigious books in the rare collection. Some of them are:....

1) Achilles Tatius: Erotica, Leyden,1640;
2) Galilio Galilei Linceo: Diologo, Florence 1632
3) Sir Walter Raleigh: History of the World, London, 1736;
4) W. C. Macnaghten (Ed): Alif Laila or Book of Thousand Nights and one Night, Calcutta, 1839
5) William Shakespeare: Works ed. Charles Knight, with 340 illustrations by John Gilbert, London 1875;
6) Charles Blount (trans): The two first books of Philostratus concerning the life of Appllonius Tyaneus, London, 1680
7) John Gould: The Birds of Asia, London, 1850-83;
8) Henry Lord: Discoveries of the sect of the Banias and the religion of the Parsees London, 1630;
9) M. Eugene Bournouf: Le Bhagavata Puran, Paris, 1840;
10) Captain James Cook: Voyages to the South Pole and Round the World, London, 1777;
11) Francois Bernier: The History of the Late Revolution of the Empire of the Great Mogol and Voyage to Kashmir in 1664, London, 1671;
12) Kathana: Rajatarangini, a History of Kashmir, Calcutta 1892.
13) Sandhya (Upanayana Sanskar of Hindus);
14) The Birds of Asia, in 6 volumes by John Gould;
15) A picturesque illustration of the scenary, animals and native inhabitants of the island of Ceylon in 12 parts by Samuel Daniels, and
16) Painting in the Buddhist Cave of Temple of Ajanta by John Griffiths

Manuscripts

The Society has a rich collection of manuscripts in Sanskrit, Pali, Tibetan, Prakrit, Arabic, Persian and in numerious other languages. The Sanskrit manuscripts are written in various Indian scripts. Some of the manuscripts are illustrated and several of them once belonged to the Mughal imperial library. The Chinese manuscripts consist of translation of the Indian Buddhist ones. Some of them are;

1) Dante Alighieri: Divine Comedy, 1350;
2) Firdausi: Shahanama, 1495
3) Suryasiddhanta with Bhashya of Candelvara, 12th century (Astronomy);
4) Suryasiddhanta with Bhashya of King Madanpala, 12th century (Materia Medica);
5) Atharvaveda samhita 16th century (very rare);
6) Bhagavat Puran with Bhashya of Yogesvara,13th century;
7) Aranyaka Parvan, richly illustrated , 1516;
8) Shadavashyakasutra with commentary by Merusun—dara, 13th century;
9) Kalpasutra of the Jains, 12th century;
10) Gautamprichha (in Prakrit) with Sanskrit Vritti of Srititaka,1350;
11) Vasupujyacharitra, life of the Jain Tirthankara Vasupujya, 1242;
12) Vikramcharita, life of king Vikramaditya in Sanskrit, 12th century.

Library has collection of nearly 1400 maps some of which date back to 18th century such as Map of West Coast part of Ceylon published by A. Dalrymple. There are maps published by Marine Survey Department of the Government of India. It also hold a valuable collection of 11,829 coins. The nucleus was formed around a donation of coins from government and a numismatic collection, formerly belonging to Sir Bartle Frere presented by Sir Cowasji Jehngir. To these, many more valuable gold, silver and copper coins were added. These include a 5th century gold coin of Kumargupta, a very rare gold mohur of

Emperor Akbar and coins issued by Shivaji. It also possesses a precious group of Buddhist bronzes representing the seven Buddhas and Maitraya, the futute Buddha. These eight bronzes were found in 1882 by Pandit Bhagvanlal Indraji in the relic stone coffer from the stupa of Sopara.

27

SALAR JUNG MUSEUM AND LIBRARY, HYDERABAD

The Salar Jung Museum of Hyderabad is the repository of the artistic achievements of diverse European, Asian and Far Eastern countries of the world. The major portion of this collection was acquired by Mir Yousuf Ali Khan popularly known as Salar Jung III, but quite a few items were inherited by him from his father Nawab Mir Laiq Ali Khan Salar Jung II and his grand father Nawab Mir Turab Ali Khan, Sir Salar Jung I .

This eclectic treasure of world art of over 40,000 objects has grown out of the rich and variegated collection acquired by them but more specifically by Mir Yusuf Ali Khan, popularly known as Salar Jung III (1889-1949). He served briefly as Prime Minister (from 1912-14) to Mir Osman Ali Khan, the seventh Nizam of Hyderabad. He spent a considerable portion of his wealth in collecting objects of art and other curios in staggering profusion. He was indeed a consummate dilettante and a shrewd connoisseur of everything pertaining to art & antiquities, as the collection in the museum testifies.

After his death, in the absence of any direct descendents, the Indian Government appointed a committee to administer the Salar Jung Estate. To perpetuate the name of Salar Jung, a private museum of that name came into being in December 1951, in the Diwan Deodi, the ancestral palace of Salar Jung III. It was declared open by the first Prime Minister of India, Pundit Jawaharlal Nehru. The control and supervision of the Salar Jung Estate was fully passed to the Indian Government in 1960 and for a year the Museum was administered directly by the Ministry of Scientific Research & Cultural Affairs. By an Act of Parliament , known as the Salar Jung Museum Act, 1961, the Museum with the Library were declared to be an "Institution of National Importance."

The Museum then shifted to it's present premises in 1968, and was declared open by Dr. Zakir Hussain. Under the Salar Jung Museum Act of 1961, the Indian government transferred the administration of the Museum on July 1, 1961 to a Board of Trustees with the Governor of Andhra Pradesh as ex-officio Chairperson.

The Salar Jung Museum Act has empowered the Board of Trustees, which is an autonomous body, not only to manage the Museum efficiently, but also to plan, promote, organize and implement programs for the proper development of the Museum. Moreover the Board has been fully authorized to take such measures, as it thinks fit for providing instruction and research in activities bearing on museums & libraries, and for the advancement of learning.

Salar Jung museum is the fantasy of an art visionary come to life which waited for its consummation for another great lover of art Jawaharlal Nehru to visit the historic city of the Quli Qutab Shahs and inaugurate it on 16 December, 1951 when the collections were hurriedly assorted and housed in Diwan Devdi, residence of the Salar Jungs. Every year a million visitors pay homage to this great repository of art and history. The priceless collections were moved in 1968 to a new site from the 100-year-old palace Dewan Devdi of the prime ministers. Legend has that the museum houses art collections of three generations of the Salar Jung family, beginning with Salar Jung, who was prime minister under...

The incomparable treasures of the museum, consisting only of a part of the original collection, are an amazing amalgam of antiquity and modernity, the three Salar Jungs scouring continents for objets d'art and returning home with shiploads of artefacts. It is believed that during the colonial period a lot of the art wealth of the country was shipped to the metropolitan countries and the Salar Jungs are credited with bringing back some of it to enrich the collection. The museum represents, in popular belief, the largest one-man collections of the world. They reflect the stunning range of time and place of these treasures, some of them belonging to different civilisations and dating back to the first century and retrieved from nearly every nook and corner of the world. However, the chief architect of this great and magnificent congeries of art is believed to be Salar Jung III, i.e. Nawab Mir Yusuf Ali khan.

The marvellous expose unveils the art heritage of India, Asia, Middle East and Europe and includes Persian carpets, Chinese porcelain, Japanese lacquer ware, sculpture, invaluable collections of jade, bronzes, enamelware, paintings, wood and inlay work from Tibet, Nepal and Thailand etc. There are Aurangzeb's sword, daggers belonging to empress Noor Jehan, emperors Jehangir and Shah Jehan, the turbans and chair of Tippu Sultan, furniture from Egypt, paintings etc. Among the sculptures stands out the world famous statue of Veiled Rebecca, her beautiful face hazily visible through; hold your breath, a marble but gossamer veil. The visitor may mistake it for a gorgeous woman draped in a wet garment. Equally captivating is a double-figure wood sculpture done by G.H. Benzoni, an Italian sculptor, in 1876. It stands before a mirror and shows the facade of a nonchalant Mephistopheles and the image of a demure Margaretta in the mirror.

Every form of art in its ancient glory finds its representation in the museum. Statuary includes a standing Buddha image of limestone from Nelakondapalli (2nd or 3rd century A.D.); Mukhalinga from Kausambi (4th or 5th century A.D.); Ananthasayi Vishnu with his ten avatars carved on top (12th century A.D., Kakatiyaa, Warangal); Jain, Buddhist and Hindu bronzes dating back to later Pallava and Chola periods and the two most famous exhibits of the museum – the Veiled Rebecca and a sycamore wood carwing portraying a double statue of

Mephistopheles and Margaretta. The mammoth collection includes paintings such as "Soap Bubbles" by Fransesco Hayez of Italy; "Piazzo of San Marco" by Antonio Canaletto (1697-1768) and "Venice" by Marc Aldine of Italy. Pottery items range from Dresden (Germany), Sevres (France), Capodimonte (Italy) to Wedgewood and English porcelain.

In short, the museum is a standing monument to the artistic genious of mankind throughout the space-time spectrum.

The Library

The museum is home to 43,000 art exhibits and 50,000 books collected from all over the world. Old timers believe that the present collection constitutes only half of the original art wealth amassed by Salar Jung III. His employees siphoned off part of it, since Salar Jung was a bachelor and depended upon his staff to keep a vigil. Some more art pieces were lost or stolen during the shifting of the museum from Dewan Devdi to the present site. The museum, declared an institution of national importance by an Act of Parliament in 1961, overlooks another landmark, the languid Musi, of the four hundred-year-old city founded by Mohammed Quli Qutub Shah. This great treasure trove is a tribute to man's eternal quest for beauty and elegance, particularly India's remarkable cultural diversity and heritage.

The library collection is very rich in histories, biographies ornate prose and official letters and documents which through light on the political and cultural life of the Deccan from the 17th to the 19th centuries. Some of the works are very rare indeed.

Other attractions are a gallery exclusively devoted to the celebrated family of the Salar Jungs, a children's section, a reference library and a section devoted to rare and ancient Arabic Urdu and Persian manuscripts, including a handwritten miniature Qoran. On display are unique mementos like the panegyric in Urdu presented to Sir Salar Jung and Nizam VI in memory of their visit to Delhi to witness the Imperial Proclamation of Queen Victoria in 1877. The first room houses the personal items of the

Salar Jung household such as various mementoes received by the Salar Jungs, embroidered sherwanis and a commodious and arresting masnad (ceremonial throne-like chair used by Salar Jung III). In the room, one can also see a large portrait of Mir Yousuf Khan, the clothes of the nobility, their books and furniture and bric-a-brac.

In the field of poetry also the Library is very rich. It contains about 1200 manuscripts which are catalogued n three volumes: IV to VI A good few Diwaans and anthologies are extremely rare and valuable. A wealth of information is available for research scholars.

Manuscripts

The Library contains 7,742 manuscripts out of which 4,146 are in Persian. This collection is one of the ppremier private treasures in India which ranks next to the great oriental manuscripts libraries and serves as an auxiliary to the Khuda Bakhsh Library, Patna, The National Library, The Asiatic Society Library, Calcutta and other important oriental collections in India and elsewhere.

The following is the number of manuscripts available in the Library

Persian	4,146
Arabic	2,459
Urdu	1,045
Hindi	2,000

The following works deserve special mention and the Library is proud of to own them:

1. Tarikh-e-Qutub shahi by Khurshah b. Qubad al-Husaini is the general history of the World compiled by Ibrahim Qutub Shah of Golconda. It is a Royal copy. An other known copy of this work is in the British Museum.
2. Tajul Maasir, A history of the Early Sultans of Delhi 1191-1217. It is the oldest known copy having been transcribed in 1325.

3. Shah Jahanama: It is the history of the first ten years of rein of shah Jahan. An imperial copy written in excellent nastaliq on gold sprinkled paper. The authors name in not known. It appears to be the only known copy.
4. Shahinsha nama-e- Shah Jahan. A collection of prose and poetry pertaining to the life of the Mughal emperopr. It is the only knpown copy.
5. Mirat-e-Sadiq by Mohammad Shafia Wearid c1736. It is the history of Mughal India written as an appendix to Farishta's gulshan-e-Ibrahimi. It is the only known copy in existence.
6. Tabsira-e Ulin-nuha, by Mir Mohammad Ahsan entitled Ma'ni Yab Khan. A history of Farrukhsiyar's reign that throughs light on the condition of the country on those troublesome days. The other known copy is in the British Mnuseum.
7. Tadhkira-e Asifiya: It is the history of first three Nizams by Vir Rai, the Chronicler who gives detailed account of those days as he found them. It is the only copy available.
8. Tarikh-e-Mahabat Jung. An anonymous compilation of the history of Bengal under Aliwardy Khan Mahabat Jung. It is a rare work.
9. Mah Nama c 1814: A history of the Nizams of Hyderabad written for Mahlaqa Bai the favourate courtisan of Asif Jah II. The copy was transcribed five years after it was compiled.
10. Beklarnama: A history of Sindh compiled for Capt. Stock of East India company.

A catalogue for Arabic and Persian manuscripts was planned to be brought in 20 volumes representing the following subjects in each language;

Catalogue of Arabic Manuscripts

I. Philosophy, Logic. Theology etc

II. Holy Quran. Fragments, Commentaries etc

III. Principles of Tradition, Jurisprudence, Fiqh, Fatawa of all Sunni Scholls etc.

IV. Principles of Tradition, Jurisprudence, Fiqh, Fatawa of all Shia Schools etc.

V. Sufism, Homiletics, Preaching etc.

VI. Philosophy, Literature, Poetry and Prose and Biography of Poets

VII. Mathematics, Astronomy, Chemistry, Useful Arts, Secret Arts, Fine Arts, Medicine etc.

VIII. Geography, History, Biography, Compendiums.

Catalogue of Persian Mnauscripts

I. Philosophy, Logic. Theology etc.

II. Quranic Science , Recitation, Translations, Commentaries, Traditions, Law of all Schools.

III. Sufism, Ethics, Homiletics, Prayers and Preachings and Biographies of Sufies.

IV. Mathematics, Astronomy, Chemistry, Secret Arts, Useful Arts, Fine Arts etc.

V. Medicine Vetenary Science etc.

VI. Lexicon, Grammar, Rhetoric, Prosody, etc

VII. Poetry

VIII. Poetry

IX. Biographies of Poets, Prose Works, etc.

X. Geography, History, Biographies Works of Mixed Contents and Miscellany.

XI. Geography, History, Biographies, Works of Mixed Contents and Miscellany.

The manuscripts have immense value for the lovers of arts and learnings and scholars devoted to the study of Eastern civilization, history, philosophy, religion, literatyre and culture of the Asian people embedded in Arabic Persian and Indian languages.

The collectin abounds in several antiquities, relics of Asian countries, masterpieces of Asian arts and learning, works of great thinkers, artists and unique specimenof book-arts collected from various Islamic countries of the Middle East. The rarities present various apochs, styles, schools and centres patronage and show the development of the art of calligraphy, miniature painting, decoration and illumination, gliding, binding, papermaking and preparation of ink of all colours.

The special feature of the collection is that it is rich in de-luxe Codexes of the Holy Quran representing Muslim Calligraphy at its highest from the 8th to 18th century A.D. It also containd genuine manuscripts and autograph copies of royal and historical personags and famous calligraphers like Yaqut-i-Must'asimi. The rarities of the collection may be grouped as under:

1. Manuscripts of unique, original and highly intrinsic literary and historical value hitherto unknown.
2. Rare works as well as material for research produced by distinguished authors and compilers.
3. Works of contemporaneous value, containing accurate and reliable texts.
4. Works containing special external features, e.g: records of ownership, endorsement, autographs, seals of special owners, collections and libraries, and colophons bearing the date, place and name of the scribe etc.
5. Works of artistic value bearing calligraphic and other decorative features mentioned below.
6. Other manuscripts of outstanding value from the intrinsic and extraneous point of view.

The cata logue of the manuscripts provide brief description of each manuscript in order to reveal the author, title external features, and bibliographical information at a glance for the researchers. Entries are arranged alphabetically under each subjects as mentioned above. The main object is to acquiant scholars working on several Islamic subjects in different countries with the real nature and content of the Collection.

28
SARASVATI BHAVAN LIBRARY, BENARAS

The Library has been named after the Goddess of learning i.e. Sarasvati. It is located at the Sampurnanada Sanskrit University campus in Benaras. The genesis of the Sarasvati-Bhavana Library and its manuscripts collection can be traced back to 1791 and after its long journey, it has grown from the 5852 manuscripts to 1,11,132 from purchase, gifts and donations, etc. The first landmark took place in the year 1791 when the Banaras Government Sanskrit College was established. At the same time, the establishment of Sarasvati-Bhavana Library was sought keeping in view the use and proper preservation and conservation of the manuscript collections of the Institute although there was no independent building of Sarasvati Bhavana Library or the Institute at that time.

At first "The Banaras Government Sanskrit College" was started in a big building at Karnaghanta in Varanasi with its Sarasvati-Bhavana Library in the same building and there was no provision to appoint a separate Library Officer. Consequently, the teachers and students were given the responsibilities for procuring and preserving the manuscript collections of the Sarasvati-Bhavan Library and it was maintained separately for a long time from the year 1791 up to the year 1813 in the present existing Sampurnanand Sanskrit University premises.

With the passage of time the manuscript collections grew up to the great extent which created the need to appoint a pertinent expert towards the proper organization and conservation of the manuscripts. In the year 1811, a meeting was organized by a committee where it was finally decided to establish a separate building of Sarasvati_Bhavana Library and its librarian post was created. As per the Committee Report of 1813, one post of Librarian and two posts of Library Assistants were sanctioned. Pandit Mathuranath Shukla was appointed as the first Librarian of Sarasvati-Bhavana Library, although there was no separate building of this library during this period. After the retirement of Pandit Mathuranath Shukla, the Principal, Pandit Ramanandji took the charge of the Librarian and who subsequently managed the Sarasvati-Bhavana Library and its manuscript collection.

Maharani Srimati Ram Kuar of Aashanganj donated a piece of land to the Institute for the construction of the Sarasvati Bhavana Library, and then on the 6th November 1907 the foundation stone of this library was laid down by Sir John Hibbet. With 7 years of continuous efforts of the Officers and the staff a beautiful classical building of the Sarasvati Bhavana Library was erected in the year 1914 under the present campus of the University. The respected contemporary Principal Dr. Arthur Vennis efforts in beautifying the Library building are always appreciable.

The Sarasvati Bhavana Library building was inaugurated on the 6th February 1914 by Lt. Governor General Sir James Scorgi Meston of United Provinces where he gave its name as "Princess of Wales Memorial Sarasvati Bhavana Library".

Maha Mahopadhyay, Padmavibhusan, Sahitya-Vachaspati, Pandit Gopinath Kaviraj was appointed the first president of this library on the 24th April 1914, when it was established in separate building. The collection and circulation of the manuscripts and the printed books was started under the supervision of Pandit Gopinath Kaviraj with its total 3204 printed books and 5852 manuscripts.

M. M. Pandit Gopinath Kaviraj M. M. Pandit Gopinath Kaviraj devoted himself deeply to develop the library and he started to carry out the two famous granthamalas (i.e. book series) namely :-

A. SARASVATI BHAVANA TEXTS SERIES

B. SARASVATI BHAVANA STUDIES SERIES.

Dr. Mangaldev Shastri and Pandit Vishvambhar Jharkhandi were appointed as the Librarian of the Sarasvati Bhavana Library respectively after the retirement of Pandit Gopinath Kaviraj.

The responsibility of circulation and control of manuscripts were handed over to other suitable experts during the period of Sri Vishvambhar Jharkhandi and this responsibility was aptly handled by Pandit Vindheshvari Prasad Dwivedi and Pandit Sri Narayan Shastri Khistey.

Collection of Manuscripts

The manuscript collections in Sarasvati Bhavana Library grew from 5852 to 50000 in the year 1948, and in the same year one post of the Chief Librarian and the other two posts of the Deputy Librarians were sanctioned. The year 1963 may be taken as the most crucial year because in this year basic reorganization schemes were undertaken keeping in view the proper utilization of the Library materials acquired in Sarasvati Bhavana Library by the scholars and the users. As a result, a second annexe building was built in the name of Sarasvati Bhavana Library under the UGC aid in which all the printed books of the main building of Sarasvati Bhavana were shifted. Apart from this, the administration, microfilming and binding sections were established in this new building.

In the year 1948, Pandit Sri Subhadra Jha was appointed as the Chief Librarian of Sarasvati Bhavana Library and after few years the existing Kashi Government Sanskrit College was renamed as "Varanaseya Sanskrit Vishvavidyalaya" on the 12th March 1958, which is now popularly known as Sampurnanand Sanskrit University, Varanasi. Pandit Sri Vibhuti Bhushan Bhattacharya was appointed as the Chief Librarian of this Library just after the retirement of Dr. Subhadra Jha in the year 1967.

The Contemporary Registrar of Sampurnanand Sanskrit University Sri Lakshmi Narayan Tiwari was appointed as the

Chief Librarian of Sarasvati Bhavana Library in the year 1970. After few years he was appointed on the post of Dean, Faculty of Shramana Vidya followed by Dr. Vijay Narayan Mishra who worked till his retirement. After Dr. V. N. Mishra the charge of the librarian post of Sarasvati Bhavana Library was given to the heads of different teaching departments of the University to look after the duties and the responsibility of the librarian time to time.

The material acquired in the Sarasvati Bhavana Library may be grouped among three major categories such as, manuscripts and thesis, printed books and important journals and many local and national daily newspapers etc. In other words, this library acquires all major sources of information whether it is of primary or secondary or tertiary in nature.

During the year 2000 there were

a) 1,11,132 Manuscripts,
b) 2,03,934 printed books,
c) A large number of famous journals,
d) Newspapers,
e) Dissertations and
f) Thesis

Descriptive Catalogues of Sanskrit Manuscript

More than one lakh Sanskrit manuscripts are presently available in the Sarasvati Bhavana Library. The detailed information concerning these manuscripts has been systematically published in the form of the Descriptive Catalogues in 13 volumes and each volume of this catalogue comprises different parts. The total volumes of the descriptive catalogues may be treated as the manuscripts database of the Sarasvati Bhavana Library. The compilation work of the Descriptive Catalogues of these manuscripts was started from the year 1953.

This valuable manuscript collection is stored in fully

airconditioned environment in the Sarasvati Bhavana Library, where the microfilming and lamination activities are carried out by suitable professional experts.

The total number of manuscripts stored in the library catalogued in 13 volumes, comprise 34 parts. These 34 descriptive catalogues of the manuscripts have now so far been published consisting of more than 15 subjects of Indology and Orientation Learning.

The following are the major subjects of these valuable manuscripts such as:-

1. Veda and Upanishad described in 4 parts;
2. Karmakanda described in 4 parts;
3. Dharmasastra described in 2 parts;
4. Puranetihasa and Gita described in 2 parts;
5. Stotra Sahitya described in 4 parts;
6. Tantra-Sastra described in 3 parts;
7. Samkhyayoga, Purvamimansa and Vedanta-Darsana described in 2 parts;
8. Nyaya-Vaisesika-Darsaan described in 2 parts;
9. Astrology described in 2 parts;
10. Vyakaranasastra described in 1 part;
11. Sahityasastra described in 2 parts;
12. Jain-Darsan, Bhakti-Sampradaya, Ayurveda, Kamasastra, etc. described in 3 parts;
13. Appendix and supplement volumes described in 3 parts.

The above mentioned descriptive catalogues cover more than 80 thousand manuscripts of the Sarasvati Bhavana Library and the rest of the volumes in the press which will be published soon. All the manuscripts in the Descriptive catalogues are enlisted on the basis of the following 12 major elements/ steps such as :-

1. Serial Number

2. Title of the manuscript
3. Name of the author
4. Details of the letter Number
5. Size of the manuscript
6. Line Number
7. Letter Number
8. Nature of the script
9. Base
10. Year of Script
11. Remarks of script
12. Special remarks

For ease of the scholars and educators information need is being created. A suitable environment which can enhance the use of these manuscripts to a greater extent in the present society, is being created.

Detailed List of Catalogues:

The following are the detailed lists of published descriptive catalogues analyzed one after another taking into consideration the nature of the subjects, authors and so on.

1. Descriptive Catalogue (Volume I, Part I): It comprises manuscripts on Veda and Upanisad. In this volume the catalogued manuscripts have been classified under their general heads. Research scholars and information seekers may be able to find several remarkable manuscripts catalogued in this volume, such as :-
   a. Kapisthala Katha Samhita
   b. Kapisthala Katha Grhya Sutra
   c. Jatapatala, a work of Vyadi most probably the pre-panini grammarian of ancient India Srutivikasa, a commentary on Rgveda by Sri Govinda Batta
   d. Commentaries on some of the major Upanisads by Prakatarthakara.

2. Descriptive Catalogue (Volume I, Part II) is the continuous part of this volume which contains the same nature of manuscripts on the subject "Veda" and "Upanisads" but, has no place in its first part. It includes a list of books in an alphabetical order in the end. Many famous Sanskrit and other regional languages manuscripts were catalogued in this volume. Some of the authors such as Sri Sankaracharya' ; Sankarananda; Sri Brahmananda Sarasvati, Narayana and Sri Narendra Sarasvati whose famous work enlisted in this part. Besides, there are some other equally remarkable manuscripts catalogued in this volume.

   1. Descriptive Catalogue (Volume I, Part III) helps us to know is the last part of about the manuscripts on "Veda-Sastra" of Sarasvati-Bhavana Library .More than 3000 manuscripts concerning "Veda-Sastra " has been catalogued in this part and the scripts of these manuscripts are in Devanagari with few of them in Bengali and other regional languages.

4. Descriptive Catalogue (Volume I, Part IV) is the 1st volume which also includes all the remaining manuscripts on "Veda Sastra" other than listed in its preceding parts, with an alphabetical list of the manuscripts occuring in Part III and IV in the end.

5. Descriptive Catalogue (Volume II, Part I) deals with the manuscripts on the subject "Karmakanda" and its related subject fields. The total number of manuscripts i.e. 3365 have been catalogued in this volume. Some of the manuscripts in this volume were written by the famous authors such as:-

   Sri Gangadharendra Sarsvati;

   Sri Dattatreya; and Sri Apayaya Diksit

6. Descriptive Catalogue (Volume II, Part II) relates to the manuscripts on "Karmakanda" having an alphabetical list

of the manuscripts of Sarasvati-Bhavana Library in the end occurring in part I and II. This part comprises 1700 manuscripts approximately and its alphabetical index given in the end can help the scholars as the major source of information concerning these manuscripts.

7. Descriptive Catalogue (Volume II, Part III) also represents the manuscripts on "Karmakanda" of Sarasvati-Bhavana Library. More than 4000 manuscripts have been catalogued in this section.
8. Descriptive Catalogue (Volume II, Part IV) contains the list of manuscripts on "Karmakanda" with a list of the manuscripts appeared in part III and IV is given in the end in alphabetical sequence.
9. Descriptive Catalogue (Volume III, Part I) deals with the manuscripts on the subject "Dharmasastra," having an alphabetical list of manuscripts of the Sarasvati-Bhavana Library in the end. More than 2000 manuscripts concerning Dharmasastra have been catalogued in this part. Some of the popular manuscripts such as Mittaksara by Vijnaneshvar, "Danamayukah by Nilakantha and Vivadacintamani by Vacaspati" are enlisted in this part.
10. Descriptive Catalogue (Volume III, Part II) represents all the remaining manuscripts of Dharmasastra in this part, with an alphbetical list of manuscripts of Sarasvati-Bhavana Library in the end.
11. Descriptive Catalogue (Volume IV, Part I) deals with the manuscripts on the subject "Puranetihasa~' and "Gita~', with an alphabetical list of the manuscripts in the end of Sarasvati-Bhavana Library .Many famous writers such as Sri Agniveshmuni, Sri Ballabh Dikshit, Sri Damodar Shastri and Vimalbodha and their manuscripts such as Ramayanarahasyam, Bhagavatatatvadipa, Bhagavata Niranaya, and Adipuranam are catalogued in this volume.
12. Descriptive Catalogue (Volume IV , Part II) Comprises

all the remaining manuscripts on "Puranetihasa" and "Gita" other than listed in its first part. An alphabetical list of the manuscripts of Sarasvati-Bhavana Library is given in the end.

13. Descriptive Catalogue (Volume V, Part I) helps the researchers to know about the manuscripts on '.Stotra'. The term "Stotra' is equivalent to holy poems. The total number of 3552 manuscripts concerning stotras have been catalogued in this part, while the remaining manuscripts on "Stotras" is available in the further parts of the same volume.
14. Descriptive Catalogue (Volume V, Part II) represents with the manuscripts on "Stotra" stored in the Sarasvati-Bhavana Library , with an alphabetical list in the end of the manuscripts catalogued in its part I and II.
15. Descriptive Catalogue (Volume V, Part III) also deals with the manuscripts on "Stotras" of Sarasvati-Bhavana Library other than listed in its preceding part I and II nd. Hence, it includes 4940 manuscripts of stotras in this part. Sri Sankaracarya, Valmiki, Balwanta, Anantananda Nath, Nanapattavardhana, Nandanath, Bhaskar Pattavardhana, Upmanyu, Sri Vyas and Brihastpati are the famous stotras manuscripts writers whose work are catalogued in this part.
16. Descriptive Catalogue (Volume V, Part IV and V) is the last part of the volume V which comprises the last portion of stotras manuscripts of Sarasvati-Bhavana Library, along with an alphabetical list of manuscripts in the end occuring in its part III and IV.
17. Descriptive Catalogue (Volume VI, part I) may be taken as the major information source of the manuscripts on "Tantra-Sastra" which is stored in Sarasvati-Bhavana Library of Sampurnananda Sanskrit Vishvavidyalaya, Varanasi. In addition, it has an alphabetical list of

manuscripts in the end of the Sarasvati-Bhavana Library .This first part of volume VI comprises 2362 manuscripts on "Tantra- Sastra". Some of the famous manuscripts of "Tantra-Sastra" such as, Batukbhairavapuja Prayoga, Sarasvati-mantra, Bagalamukhikrama written by Bhaskarrai, Mantramahodadhi, Ajapajapa and Shivasaktitarapithadinyasha written by Mahidhar , along with other remarkable manuscripts of tantra-sastra.

18. Descriptive Catalogue (Volume VI, Part II) deals with the manuscripts on "Tantra-sastra" other than listed in its first part. All the manuscripts on "Tantra-sastra" catalogued in this section are fully completed. Sri Kashi nath Bhatta, Sri Nityanath, Sri Rambhadra, Sri Shiv, etc. are the famous writers of Tantra-sastra whose work are recorded in this part, along with many other prominent manuscripts writers work.

19. Descriptive Catalogue (Volume VI, Part III) also represents with the manuscripts on "Tantra-sastra", other than listed in its part I and II. Apart from this, it has an appendix of the list of manuscripts on 'Tantra-sastra" occuring in its Part I and II, which are stored in the Sarasvati-Bhavan Library .

20. Descriptive Catalogue (Volume VII, Part I) deals with the manuscripts on the subjects "Samkhya- yoga" "Purva-mimamsa" and "Vedanta Philosophy" with an alphabetical list of the manuscripts in the end stored in the Sarasvati-Bhavana Library. The manuscripts are catalogued in this volume according to the subjects such as :-

    Sankhyayogagranthatantrasuci ;

    Vedantagranthasuci;

    Mimamasagranthasuci;

    Vedantagranthanamaksaranukramani

    Mimamsagranthanamaksaranukraman

    Sri Anandgnan, Sri Sankaracharya, Vamanasram, Sri

Dharmaraj Dikshit, Sri Ramanand Sarasvati are some of the famous manuscripts writers related with the vedanta. Sri Narayan, Rameshwar , Sri Apodeva, Sri Kumarila Bhatt, Sri Khanddeo, Madhava Bhatt, Sri Partha sarthi, Sri Shabar Swami are some of the famous writers who has worked on Mimamasa.

Sri Vachaspati Misra, Sri Ganesh, Sri Vijnan Abiksu, Sri Nagoji Bhatt, Sri Mahadev, Sri Atmaram Yogindra and Patanjali, Sri Raghvananda are some of the famous writers who worked on Samkhyayoga.

All the manuscripts of the authors as mentioned above enlisted in this part of this volume.

21. Descriptive Catalogue (Volume VII, Part II) is also related with the manuscripts on "Mimamsa" and "Vedanta", philosophies with an alphabetical list of manuscripts in the end of Sarasvati- Bhavana Library.
22. Descriptive Catalogue (Volume VIII, Part I) deals with the manuscripts on "Nyaya- Vaisesika. which were acquired upto 1950 This part of volume VIII describes not only the manuscripts included in the catalogue of Pandit Gopinath Kabiraj, but also all other Nyaya- volume are Sridhar, Neelkantha, Varahmihir Trivikrama, Balabhadra, and Sripati Bhatta
23. Descriptive Catalogue (Volume IX, Part II) also describes with the manuscripts on the subject "Jyautisa.sastra" other than listed in its preceding part. The following are the some of the famous astrological writers such as Sri Jagannath, Sri Bhaskaracharya, Sri Durga Prasad, Sri Ramakrishana, Sri Haridev, Sri Dinkar whose manuscripts have been enlisted in this part. An alphabetical list of the manuscripts of Sarasvati.Bhavana Library has been added for facilitating the further reference to the users and the scholars.
24. Descriptive Catalogue (Volume X, Part I and II) relates to the manuscripts on "Vyakarana.sastra" of

Sarasvati.Bhavana Library. With the help of this catalogue it becomes easy to locate many famous linguists and their important work, contemporary of Panini. All the manuscripts of works on Vyakarana described here have their titles arranged in an alphabetical order to facilitate reference to the users/ scholors.

25. Descriptive Catalogue (Volume XI, Part I) deals with half of the total manuscripts on "Sahitya.sastra" of Sarasvati-Bhavana Library in this part which is followed by an alphabetical list of manuscripts is mentioned at the end concerning the works on Kavya, Alankara, Kosa and Chandah. The first 287 pages are devoted to Sahitya manuscripts, that are followed by the descriptions of Kosa manuscripts and at the end Chaandah manuscripts.

The following are the list of manuscripts based on the subjects in this volume such as :-

a. Sahityagranthasuci;
b. Kosagranthasuci;
c. Chandogranthasuci, etc.

26. Descriptive Catalogue (Volume XI, Part II) deals with the remaining half manuscripts on "Sahitya-sastra" with alphabetical list of manuscripts of Sarasvati- Bhavana Library .

27. Descriptive Catalogue (Volume XII, Part I) is an important volume which includes the manuscripts on different topics such as "Jainism", "Bhakti-Sampradaya", " Ayurveda", "Kama-sastra", "Silpa", "Sangita", "Niti", "Dhanurveda", "Panji", Prasasti", and "Citra". Besides, it also relates some of the manuscripts in regional languages with the alphabetical list of manuscripts in the end of Sarasvati-Bhavana Library .

28. Descriptive Catalogue (Volume XII, Part II) is a continuous part of this volume and it comprises the same nature of manuscripts on different topics such as 'Jainism', 'Bhakti-

sampradaya', , A yurveda' 'Kama-sastra', 'Silpa', 'Sangeeta Niti', 'Dhanurveda', 'Panji', 'Prasasti', 'Citra' and manuscripts in regional languages with a descriptive narration, followed by an alphabetical list of manuscripts of the Library .2650 manuscripts of 13 different subjects have been catalogued in this volume although the number of manuscripts of these subjects was not quite sufficient. But for the scholars of the modern Indian languages it may become a major source of information.

29. Descriptive Catalogues (Volume XIII, Part 1/11) comprises I to II parts of volume XIII concerning Appendix and Supplements of these descriptive catalogues and now these are in the press which will be published soon. Certainly this lightened stream of knowledge, backed with rich heritage will assume the goal as aimed in our motto "Srutam me Gopaya" accompanied with the eternal message 'Tamaso ma Jyotirgamaya".

The following are the list of some famous printed manuscripts which are procured in the Library-

1. Siddhanatas'iromani-with Vasana Bhasya and Vartika
2. Satvatasamhita-with Bhasya
3. Sisyadhivrddhidam-with Vivarana
4. Tattvacintaman- (Mula)
5. Rasamanjari-with commentary
6. Manisaramanjusa-with Abhiddhammattha Vhbhavani commentary
7. Kaccayana Vyakarana- with Kaccyana Vannana
8. Atta Salini-with Atthayojana
9. Abhidhamma-Mula Tika
10. Jnanasiddhanta Candrika
11. Buddha Stotra-Samgrahah
12. Karunapundarika Sutra

13. Baithaparibhasa
14. Kautaliya Arthasastra (in four parts)
15. Nyaya Kandali (with Tippanika)
16. Nyaya Ratnamala (with vrtti)
17. Nyaya Rahasya
18. Mahabhasya Tika Suktiratnakara
19. Paribhasendusiromani
20. Siddhantasarvabhauma
21. Tarkamrtacasaka
22. Advaitadipika (Savivaranam)
23. Khandanabhusamani
24. Tattvakamalakara
25. Mimamsakautuhala
26. Parijatacampu
27. Suryasiddhantasauravasara
28. Rasamimamsa (with Tika)
29. Nrsimhaprasadadevapratisthasara
30. Rgvedakalpadrumah
31. Danakelicintamani
32. Krsnakutuhala, etc.
33. Uttarsatkarna
34. Jnnanadipavimarsini
35. Samvitprakasah
36. Parasaropapurana Samiksatmakam Sampadanam
37. Sahitvamimamsa
38. Vrttivarttikam
39. Krsnakutuhalam
40. Janakiparinayah
41. Parijataharanacampuh

42. Pratilinaparisistam
43. Vaiyakaranasiddhantamanjusa
44. Paribhasendusekharah
45. Kaccayana- Vyakaranam
46. Vyomavati
47. Kiranavalirahasyam
48. Pragalbhi
49. Paksatavadah
50. Navyamatiyaparamarsakaranatavadah
51. Dharmasamuccayah
52. Jatakatakatha
53. Saradatilakam
54. Tripurarnavatantram
55. Gautamiyamahatantram
56. Sundarimahodayah

The above mentioned descriptive catalogues are presently stored in the Sarasvati-Bhavana Library of the Sampurnanand Sanskrit University, Varanasi under the control of the Chief-Librarian. There is a provision for accessing all these materials via INTERNET or online networks from any place in the world on request.

29

SARASWATI MAHAL LIBRARY, TANJORE

Tanjore or Thanjavur as it was earlier called, was the capital of the chola empire from the 10th century to the 14th century A.D. later is become part of the Vijaynagar kingdom, then passed into the hands of the Marathas and later still went to the British. For ages it has been the chief political, literary and religious centre of the South. The celebrated temple Brihadeshra built by the Chola King during the 11th century is its major attraction. The Saraswati Mahal Library, dating back from the time of the Marathas, contains a rare collectins of books and manuscripts on paper and plam leaves.

The Library has been named after Maharaja Serfoji's. It is located at the palace of the Maharaja. The Library contains paper manuscripts on different subjects such as science, medicine, engineering, astronomy, painting, dancing, etc. in various languages such as Sanskrit, Tamil, Telugu, Marathi and some European languages. Around 8,000 of these are on palm leaves. This is the result of the efforts of the Nayak and Maratha rulers for over 300 years. This palace library was originally developed by the Nayak rulers. The Maratha rulers especially Raja Serfoji made a major contribution, organising a massive collection of good books.

In the old days palm-leaf manuscripts were preserved in almost every house in India. They contained the texts of the epics, the Puranas, Sthala Puranas, and so on. When the palm-leaves were in danger of being damaged, their contents would be copied with a stylus on new leaves. The damaged leaves would be consigned to the Kaveri or some other sacred river, or to some pond on the occasion of Patinettam Per.

The Library has been described by Dr. Burnell " to be perhaps the largest and the most important in the World" and which Dr. Buhler says " contains a great many useful and a number of many rare or nearly unique books many of which are quite unknown or procurable only with great trouble and expense". It was a private property earlier under the possession of Rajas of Tanjore.

Beginning of the Library

The earliest beginning of the Library must have been about the end of the 16th century when Tanjore was under the rule of Telugu nayakas who collected Sanskrit manuscripts written in Telugu characters. In the eighteenth century the Marathas conquered the country and since then the Library has been increasing. By far the greater portion of the collection was made by Serfoji during a visit to Benaras during 1820 to 1830. Sivaji, his successor added a few. There has practically been no addition of any value till recent times. A good number of Sanskrit manuscripts including rare and valuable manuscripts representing the collection of generations of a family of scholars known as "Jumbunatha Bhatt, Landagai collection" was added to the Library in 1921.

The attention of the Government of India and through it the Government of Madras was directed in 1868 to the importance of the examination, purchase or transcription of manuscripts in Sanskrit language available in Indian libraries and the framing of printed lists or catalogue of the same. In December of the same year, the Government of Madras asked Mr. Pickford, Professor of Sanskrit to carry out the instructions of the government of India. He commenced to catalogue the manuscripts at Tanjore; but he felt seriously ill and had to return to Europe in March 1870 and never came back to India. It is not known how much he had done as his unfinished catalogues could not be found.

Thereupon Dr. Burnell, District and Session Judge, was appointed to catalogue Sanskrit manuscripts at Tanjore. This learned scholar devoted a great deal of research and labour to the task and his catalogue which he styled " a classified index to the Sanskrit manuscripts in the Palace at Tanjore" was published in three parts between 1878 and 1880 in London. This is now chief key to the Sanskrit collection in this Library. But unfortunately great many manuscripts, above 4000, seem to have been omitted and his catalogue cannot be said to be complete.

It is became a public library in the full sense of that term, because the Government of Madras through the treasurer of the Charitable endowments being responsible for its administration. The collection belonged to the reigning princes of Tanjore-the Maratha Maharajas. When the least of them died leaving no direct male heir and after the death of the last surviving Rani, this collection together with the other properties formed the subject of litigation in civil courts. The collection attracted the attention of some wealthy patron of learning from other countries. And it would appear that arrangements were very nearly ready to sell the whole collection outright at an assessed value, when public attention was focused on certain remarks of Dr. Burnell to the effect that "it would not be possible to form a collection like that at Tanjore at a less cost than L 50,000. The parties concerned had perforce to wake up and the deal was not immediately concluded. The public of Tanjore also began to take interest in the affairs adequately. Then the Government of Madras took possession of the collection under the Charitable Endowments Act in 1918.

In respect of the magnitude and the range of subjects dealt with, not to speak the diversity of languages employed, the Tanjore Library is perhaps second to none among oriental libraries of the country.

As regard the origin of collection, Dr. Hultzsch has the following interesting information in "No. 3 report on Sanskrit manuscripts in Southern India " edited by him in 1905 at Madras:

"The manuscripts described in the report belong to Jumbunathan Bhatta, a Maratha brahmana at Tanjore, who is the elder son of a certain Mannabhatta. He is a no mean Sanskrit scholar and knows the whole Rig Veda by heart. As he is continually teaching the text of this sacred book to students, even his blind daughter has learnt recite portion of it. The existence of this Library was brought to my notice by Mr. T. S. Kuppuswami Sastri, of the Educational Department, who is favorable known to Sanskritists by his paper on Rama Bhadra Dikshita. During my absence furlough in Europe, my first assistant, Mr. V. Venkayya, M A was deputed to Tanjore in order to catalogue Jambunathas collection. He spent three months at this work, in which he received the valuable help of Mr. Kuppuswamy Sastri. Both the lists and the extracts testify to the thoroughness at care with which he has accomplished his task."

In 1922 the Library received other valuable collection of rare interest, known as the "Kagalkar" and the 'Patanga Avadhuta" collections. The former is about 159 and the later, about hundred years old. The collection made by the Kagalkar family of learned Sanskrit scholars specially works in Sanskrit grammar contains the auto graph copies made some of them of the works composed by themselves and others. Its prominent feature is the collection of works on Sanskrit grammar. The collection made by Patangavadhuta whose descendents settled at Tiruvadamarudur in Tanjore district contains a large number of works on Vedanta and bhakti. Both these collections comprise several manuscripts whose do not exist in this Library. There has been a marked improvement in the working of the Library ever since it became a public trust. Many influential persons came forward and took interest in its development. The manuscripts are either on palm leave or on paper. They are of very different value and have come from many sources. A large collection of them are recent Nagari copies of manuscripts in South Indian characters and are at least are a century old.

These manuscripts are in more than eleven distinct

alphabets being from all parts of India. On the whole, one may easily say that the total number of manuscripts in this library is likely to accede.

A large number of original records belonging to the last reigning house of Tanjore which will be of very great importance for reconstructing the political and social history of Maratha rule in Southern India has recently been transferred to the care of this Library from the civil court by the order of the judge.

Nature of Collection

India has a long tradition of creating and preservation of knowledge for the posterity. The earlier generations of the Indians went on inscribing on palm - leaves with their stylus until their hands ached. They copied old texts to be preserved for posterity. This tradition lasted until perhaps the time of our fathers. People of our generation have thrown these precious manuscripts into the river without making copies of them. So much so it is doubtful whether the texts of many Puranas will ever be available to us. Not only Puranas, but also a number of sastras. However, some scholars have taken great pains to go from place to place to collect manuscripts and preserve them in libraries. The Sarasvati Mahal Library in Tanjavur, the Oriental Manuscripts Library and the Adyar Library, Madras, have good collections of manuscripts. The Theosophical Society Library, Adyar, has done commendable work in this respect. Sarabhoji and other rulers of Tanjavur took great trouble to collect manuscripts for the Sarasvati Mahal.

A large number of the manuscripts in the Library are on palm leaves. The palm-leaf is called edu in Tamil. It has two sides with a rib in between - either of the two sides after the removal of the rib is called an edu. The plantain leaf also has a rib. When it is split across the rib, each part is an edu. For long the palm-leaf was our paper, nature's paper which was not easily damaged. The letters had to be inscribed on it with a stylus.

The palm-leaves containing the text of Jnanasambandhar's

Tevaram compositions went upstream against the current of the river Vaigai and were laid ashore. The spot where the manuscript lodged itself is called "Tiruvedakam" ("Tiru +edu + akam"). Here the deity lord Siva is called "Patrika Paramesvara". Nowadays the word "paper" is understood as a newspaper, magazine, periodical, etc. "Patrika" means a magazine today. The lord associated with the spot where the palm-leaves, nature's paper, were laid ashore is "Patrika Paramesvara", which could be taken to mean "the Lord the journalist". "Patra" and "Patrika" mean the same, a leaf. In the past letters were written on palm-leaves. That is why a letter also came to be called "patra".

The Englishmen, Frenchmen and others had a thirst for knowledge and research and were anxious to learn even from foreign sources. The Germans came to our country and searched for palm-leaf manuscripts to take home with whom. We must be grateful to some of these foreigners through whose efforts a number of our sastras were rediscovered. There was, for example, Mackenzie who was surveyor-general of India. He went from place to place to collect palm-leaf manuscripts. There was at that time no special department to deal with them but Mackenzie had them read by experts and took steps to have them preserved. Mackenzie's men even came to our Matha at Kumbakonam to gather information.

It is believed that Westerners took with them some of our science manuscripts from the Sarasvati Mahal especially those pertaining to the art of warfare. It is further claimed that Hitler made some type of weapons and aircraft on the basis of knowledge contained in these texts.

There are palm-leaf manuscripts still with us like Bhojaraja's Samarangana Sutra. From these we learn that we had long ago not only "astras" to be employed with mantras but also "sastras" that were product of science. Digests like Varahamihira's Brhatsamhita bring together the various disciplines of our land.

Some of our ancient palm-leaf manuscripts contain texts not only of our religious systems but also of various arts and sciences. But we have lost many of our Sthala Puranas. We must do our best to preserve what remains and, at the same time, continue the search for more manuscripts.

The Puranas give us instruction, in the form of engrossing stories, on the truth of the Paramatman proclaimed by the Vedas, the dharmas, and the moral and ethical codes of conduct that they lay down. The teaching they impart touches our very hearts. The lessons of the Puranas, the stories of noble men and women contained in them, have shaped our lives. The Puranas have indeed served as a source of our inspiration for our people from time immemorial. We must no longer be apathetic to them and must make a determined effort to preserve them as a treasure. Let us make a comparative study of puranic literature and take an integrated view. This will be to our own benefit as well as to that of all mankind.

Preparation of Catalogues

The Library holds a large number of books and manuscripts in almost all Indian and European languages and almost on all branches of human knowledge. Special mention here may made to the books and manuscripts in Telugu, Tamil, Marathi and English on account of their number and importance.

Dr, Burnell issued what he modestly styled " A classified index to the Sanskrit manuscripts in the Palace at Tanjore", between 1878 and 1880. Between 1880 and 1918 for very nearly 40 years, the Library has been the victim of many an outrage. Those who were in possession gave out of loan many rare manuscripts which did not return to the Library.

A Committee appointed by the Government of Madras took charge of the Library early in 1919. Since then they have been busy pushing forward the work of revising and publishing fresh catalogue of all the works available in the Library. According to the latest scientific methods. Each work is described in detail in a card index form which contains all the necessary particulars.

In 1920 a catalogue of printed book in French, Latin, Italian and Greek was published. In 1926 three volumes of a catalogue of Tamil manuscripts in the Library were published. From the year 1924 a catalogue of Marathi manuscripts and books of the Library was prepared: the first volume was published at that time. the catalogues are available on sale.

Administrative Committee of the Library approached the Government of Madras, year after year with the request for a special grant to prepare and publish the descriptive catalogue of Sanskrit manuscripts in the Library. In 1927, the government allotted the necessary funds for a three year programme for carrying out the work of preparing and printing of the catalogue.

Present Collection

The Library has been enriched with several very fine collections of manuscripts every one of them rare, valuable and very interesting manuscripts. The Kagalkal collection, Jambunatha Bhatt Landagaya collection and the Patanga Avadhuta collection on these three alone numbers 2181 manuscripts. Besides these, the Tyagaraj Swamy collection which alone contain more than thousand manuscripts than the minor collections the Subramanya Sastri collection, Subramaniya Rao collection, Ramchandra Ganapat collection, Neelakantha Sasri collectionTawker Collection, Mehta Ccollection all are of great and paramount importance.

Now, the Thanjavur Maharaja Serfoji Saraswati Mahal Library, Thanjavur has a rich collection of manuscripts numbering 40,000 in Sanskrit, Marathi, Telugu, Tamil and other languages. Besides manuscripts, it has a collection of over 23,000 books in the Indian and European languages covering various disciplines. There is a large number of illustrated manuscripts in Saraswati Mahal Library, Tanjavur, Tamil Nadu. Long before the illustrated story telling began in the modern era, multi-colour paintings, drawings and sketches have embellished manuscripts.

While such illustrated manuscripts, several centuries old, are available throughout India, the Archives of IGNCA has a collection of about 800 slides from select illustrated manuscripts in the Saraswati Mahal Library. The slides are from four manuscripts selected from the list. They are:

1. Nayaka nayaki bhava
2. Citra Ramyana
3. Prabodha Chandrodaya
4. Bhavartha Ramayana

These illustrations are not a mere visual treat. They tell their own story about the date of the manuscripts, the social customs, costumes, jewellery, adornments, the hairstyles, the colour techniques and painting styles.

It is with a view to make there accessible to researchers that IGNCA had undertaken a project of slide documentation of the illustrations of the manuscripts, though the entire manuscript collection has been microfilmed. These slides have been arranged in the order of series. For instance, the horse series, bird series, nayaka nayaki bhava, Hindu mythology, palanquins, Rg Veda manuscripts etc. This way the illustrations can be approached in two ways. Reader who knows the title of the manuscript can reach them, or researcher, for a comparative study can pursue a series, a theme, in various manuscripts.

The maximum number of slides are in the Hindu mythology series followed by horses. Some precious manuscripts of Maratha origin are in this library. There are 26 slides of illustrations from these.

The slides collection does not cover the entire illustrated manuscripts collection. Only some select manuscripts were allowed to be photographed for the purpose. While anyone can see the slides for interest and reference in IGNCA, the permission to publish them rests with the Saraswati Mahal Library.

30

SULEYMANIA LIBRARY, ISTANBUL

Turkey has a very ancient and rich civilization. Earliest records of the Turkish people show that their ancestors in Central Asia date back to some time before 2000 B.C. Roaming widely throughout Asia and Europe, the Turks established vast empires throughout these continents. By the 10th century, most Turks adopted the religion of Islam. Following this substantial change, the Karahanid Empire of central Asia (10th and 11th centuries) and the Ghaznavid Empire (10th and 12th centuries) developed in areas known today as Iran, Afghanistan, and Northern India.

As the time passed, some Turks travelled south-west to Anatolia (Asia Minor) considered to be the cradle of civilization because it has embraced more than 20 cultures and civilizations. These civilizations included: the Hitites, Assyrians, Lydians,Greeks, Persians, Macedonians, lonians, Romans, Byzantines and Turks. In A.D. 1071, the Turks fought a crucial war with the Byzantine Empire. Settling in Anatolia (which today covers most of Turkey), the Turks established many small feudal states and some empires.

The Seljuck Empire was the first Turkish empire in Anatolia. After the Seljuck's influence declined, Anatolia fragmented into a number of small states. The Ottoman Turks unified these separate units, which eventually became the largest empire in recent history, the Ottoman Empire.

The Ottomans ruled for more than six centuries (1281 - 1922), in part because their system of government allowed flexibility in the practice of diverse religions, languages and cultures.

The magnificent reign of Sultan Suleyman I (1520 -1566) is known as the golden age of the Ottoman Empire. Born during a turbulent age of continual political and military conflict, Suleyman became a dynamic leader at a very early age. To prepare for his reign that would begin after the death of his father (in 1520), Suleyman became governor of a province in Northwest Anatolia at the age of 15.

The Ottoman Empire more than doubled the boundaries of its realm under Suleyman the Magnificent's direction and was transformed into a full-fledged Muslim world empire. By his death in 1566, the empire included most of Eastern Europe, Western Asia and North Africa.

But land and power were only part of what made the empire years golden. As a principal patron of the arts, and as a poet himself, Suleyman supported societies of painters, architects, metal workers, weavers and ceramists who produced works of extraordinary quality. Suleyman was a catalyst in the cultural legacy that has lasted for centuries.

The 18th century marked the beginning of the decline in Ottoman power. Weakening continued until World War I (1914-1918), when Ottoman armies fought and lost on several fronts throughout the empire. Eventually, Anatolia was divided and occupied by allied forces. Although the Ottoman Empire was dissolved, the fight had just begun for the Turkish people.

Mustafa Kemal Ataturk, a highly respected army general from World War I, led the Turkish people in their War of independence (1919-1922) against the allied occupiers. It was the first successful war of national liberation in this century.

The Suleymania Library

The Süleymania Complex was built by the chief architect at the royal court, Mimar Sinan (Koca Sinan) for Sultan Süleyman the Magnificent, and was completed in 1557. Today, the Süleymania Library occupies the First and Second Madrasas (colleges or seminaries, especially ones connected with a mosque) of the original complex. Each room in the Medrese has a rectangular window that looks out on the Mosque. In the back yard there are a number of rooms surrounding a garden, each having a door opening to the underside of the portico and with a fireplace inside. On both sides there are six rooms facing one another. On the west side, there is a classroom in the middle above the portico. Both Madrasas have the same architectural characteristics. Each of them has a classroom, a corridor stretching beneath three domes, a large room with its entry from the corridor, and twenty more rooms. The classroom of the Second Medrese is the reading room of the present Library. The rooms are used today as stacks, with illumination and humidity regulators, for storing the Library's collections, and from where material is served to the reader on request.

In 1918, books in the library were moved to the Second Medrese of the Süleymania complex. Several foundation libraries like Asir Efendi, Besir Aga, Çelebi Abdullah Efendi, Hafiz Ahmet Pasa, Kiliç Ali Pasa, Laleli, Merih Pasa, Molla Çelebi were added to the main library which was then named Süleymania Umumi Kütüphanesi (the Süleymania General Library). It has continued to grow with the addition of many other foundation libraries, including a very important one, the Ayasofya Library. This rich library, founded in Ayasofya (St Sophia) by Sultan Mahmud I in 1739-1740, was joined to the Süleymaniye Library in 1967.

The Süleymaniye has now five affiliate libraries: Atif Efendi Library, Haci Selim Aga Library, Köprülü Library, Nuruosmania Library, and Ragup Pacha Library. Apart from the manuscripts, the library includes printed books, books in foreign languages, and Turkish books in Latin script under the title of "contemporary works".

The reading room, with a capacity of thirty readers, has reference books such as encyclopaedias, histories, anthologies, dictionaries, local and foreign catalogues, and copies of master files belonging to other libraries in Anatolia that have no catalogues.

Binding and pathology service, where worm-eaten or worn-out books are repaired, was founded in 1962. The service occasionally offers courses in classical binding, headband weaving, book restoration and marbling.

Microfilm service and archive was founded in 1950. Microfilms and photocopies, if requested, of manuscripts in the archive are prepared for readers. The microfilm archive, therefore, has been formed in two basic ways: 1. through exchange or 2. from manuscripts in the Süleymania or from other libraries through the intermediation of the Süleymania. It is also possible to have digital copies of manuscripts from Süleymania Library.

Computer service provides bibliographical descriptions of manuscripts and printed books held in public and manuscript libraries in Turkey. The search programme of the computer is based on a vast range of criteria. In addition to title or author, the system also enables the reader to search, for example, by century, gilding, miniature, copyist or type of calligraphy.

Collection of Manuscripts

Housed within the library are over 67,000 manuscripts. As they often contain more than one work and, thus, the number of actual works in the library could be estimated at over 100,000. These documents date from the 8th century to the early 20th century and include rare items relating to Islam, laws in the Ottoman time, Ottoman foreign policy, the sciences and medicine, literature and culture, among others. The majority of the manuscripts are in Arabic, respectively in Turkish and Persian. Many of these manuscripts have unique and beautiful bindings, gold gilded and miniature illuminations. Numerous manuscripts are on rare papers. The manuscripts display a number of calligraphy styles. Some of the manuscripts were translated from other languages, recording the ideas of other areas of the world at the time.

Besides a lot of autograph copies and unique manuscripts, muraqqas of famous calligraphers like Seykh Hamdullah, Izzet

Efendi, there are works in every kind of subjects such as astronomy, mathematics, geography, literary and historical subjects, chronicles, anthologies of songs and theory books for music, etc.

Each collection at the library has its own master file and also card indices. Each collection has its own numbering system for identification. For this reason, cart indices contain collection names as well. Both donated or bought manuscripts are registered under the name, Manuscript Donations (Yazma Bagislar) or Printed Book Donations (Basma Bagislar). All items are registered in the Turkish national library computer system, which provides a description of the manuscripts and printed books. In addition to title and author, the search program of the computer allows the reader to search by century, gilding, miniature, copyist or type of calligraphy. There are microfilms, negatives, positives, facsimiles, photographs, photocopies, videotapes and digital representations.

Approximately 5,000 of the manuscripts have been microfilmed by the Directorate of the Süleymania Library. It also includes a collection of photographs on old Istanbul.

The centre of the project, Union Catalogue of Manuscripts in Turkey (TÜYATOK), set up in 1978, is in Ankara. The Istanbul branch of this centre was formed in 1978 in Süleymaniye Library, and started work in 1979. The aim of this project is to prepare and publish catalogues of bibliographical descriptions of the manuscripts collections (in Turkish, Arabic, Persian and in other languages) held in libraries at present. Twenty two fascicles have been published so far.

Bibliography:

The following work is the publication describing the Süleymania Library:

- Halit Dener. "Süleymaniye Umumi Kütüphanesi". Istanbul: Maarif Basimevi, 1957. (The Süleymaniye Public Library).

The followings are some publications on the collections or using the manuscripts of the Süleymania Library: These volumes are printed under the title Union Catalogue of Manuscripts in Turkey:

- Giresun Yazmalari, Ankara, 1980. (Giresun's Manuscripts. These manuscripts are preserved at the Süleymaniye Library);
- Ali Nihat Tarlan Dermesi, Ankara 1981. (The Collection of Ali Nihat Tarlan. These manuscripts are preserved at the Süleymaniye Library);
- Antalya Tekelioglu Dermesi, Istanbul 1983 and 1984. (The Collection of Antalya Tekelioglu. These manuscripts are preserved at the Süleymaniye Library);
- Amcazade Hüseyin Pasa and Hekimpasa Musa Nazif Efendi Dermesi, Ankara, 1987. (The Collection of Amcazade Hüseyin Pasa and Hekimpasa Musa Nazif Efendi).

Fuat Sezgin has published the facsimile of 54 works (in 53 volumes) in Germany. The original copies of some of these facsimiles are in the Süleymania Library.

To prevent loss, the manuscripts are protected in the library stacks by security guards. The reading room of the library is open from 8:30 a.m. to 4:30 p.m. everyday except Sundays and there are three librarians in the reading room. 5,000 of the manuscripts have been copied onto microfilm. Researchers can use manuscripts in the reading room with the exception of damaged or unique manuscripts (they can reach these through microfilm services). The manuscripts and microfilms are stored in fireproof steel boxes. Humidity is controlled at 50-60% and the temperature at 15-18° centigrade to protect the manuscripts. Dehumidifiers reduce the humidity when it gets high. The Turkish Ministry of Culture has also built an annexation to the Süleymania Library specifically for the preservation, restoration and conservation of the materials. Preservation costs are included in the annual budget appropriated to the Library by the Ministry of Culture.

The 67,000 manuscripts of the Süleymania Library consist of 118 different collections, gathered from the libraries of wakfs of the Ottoman Empire. There are manuscripts of the Ottoman period and collection of poems (divan) produced by and various works for the Ottoman Sultans, statesmen and others. These wakf collections include manuscripts related to Islam, including rare and unusual copies of the Koran, Koranic interpretation and the traditions of the Prophet Mohammed (hadis), religious ordinances (fetva), manuscripts on Islamic laws (fikih), catechism (akaid), theological works (kelam), philosophical works (hikmet), logic (mantik), astronomy, astrology, mathematics, ethics, politics, history, rules of Islamic conduct, medicine, dictionaries, grammar and literature. There are also various miscellanies. These manuscripts are rare in terms of their age, subject matter and visuality (binding, calligraphy, gilding and miniature illuminations). For works with miniatures see Nezihe Seyhan. "Süleymaniye Kütüphanesi'ndeki Minyatürlü Yazma Eserler Katalogu, A Catalogue of Miniatured Manuscripts at the Süleymaniye Library". Unpublished MA Thesis. Bogazici Üniversitesi, 1991.

Some important items are: a copy of the Koran attributed to Ali, the cousin and son-in-law of the prophet Mohammed; rare manuscripts from the 9th century, such as the book Al-asl fi'l furuq (Ayasofya 1026) by Imam Mohammed al-Shibani (b. 189/804 or 805) and an important and rare book of the Turkish language entitled Atabetu'l-Hakayik (Ayasofya 4012, 4757). Most manuscripts were presented to the Ottoman Sultans or written in their names.

In terms of content and number, the Süleymania Library perhaps houses the largest and most important manuscript collections of the world. The collections are essential to studies on religion, history, culture, languages and hard sciences. The

Süleymania Mosque Complex, with its library, was a major educational and cultural institution of the period.

Experts can find materials on each subject of scientific or cultural importance. Following are some works that rely extensively on the sources at the Süleymania Library:

- Ahmet Ates. Istanbul Kütüphanelerinde Farsça Manzum Eserler I. Istanbul, 1968.

  (Persian works in verse at the Istanbul Libraries.)
- Fuat Sezgin. Geschichte des arabischen Schrifttums, I-IX. Leiden, 1967-1984.
- Carl Brockelmann. Geschichte des arabischen Literatur, I-II. Leiden, 1943-1949.
- H. Ritter. "Ayasofya Kütüphanesinde Tefsir Ilmine Ait Arapça Yazmalar".

  Türkiyat Mecmuasi 7-8. Part II. pp. 1-93. Istanbul, 1945.

Each wakf collection in the Library has a unity in itself. Beginning with heavenly works, they were taken numbers in a peculiar order including anthologies. But the collections of Manuscript donations and Printed book donations were taken numbers according to their dates of donation or purchase. The unity of subjects was not taken into consideration.

The Süleymania Library serves Turkish and foreign scholars, by providing microfilm, photocopies and slides of the materials. Access is permitted under certain rules and regulations and, for foreign scholars, with the permission of the Ministry of Culture. A digital imaging programme of the manuscripts was begun at the start of 2000. The library has a microfilm archive of works from other libraries in Turkey and around the world.

The Library houses manuscripts by famous Ottoman calligraphers, manuscripts dating to the early centuries of the first millennium AD, miniatures and autographes, all of which occupies a significant value for historians, art historians, literary historians and the historians of hard science as well as those who are interested in the study of orient.

31
UNIVERSITY OF CAMBRIDGE LIBRARY, CAMBRIDGE

The University of Cambridge is one of the oldest universities in the world and one of the largest in the United Kingdom. Its reputation for outstanding academic achievement is known worldwide and reflects the intellectual achievement of its students, as well as the world-class original research carried out by the faculty members of the University and the Colleges. Its famous Colleges and University buildings attract visitors from all over the world. The University's museums and library collections hold many treasures which give an exciting insight into some of the scholarly activities, both past and present.

The University Library

The University Library was originally founded in the 14th century but there were no oriental books in the Library's earliest collections apart from Bibles. From the 1630's and for the next two centuries many books from individual oriental scholars (from both Britain and Europe) were added to the Library's collections. Other early bequests to the Library from Britain and Europe also contained some oriental items. The Library also acquired the libraries of many Cambridge oriental scholars, some of whom collected extensively abroad. The end of the 19th the oriental collections began to be developed more extensively and during the 20th century purchasing from abroad increased with the aim of forming a more consistent coverage of the areas and subjects involved.

The Library houses extensive oriental collections which relate to and derive from all areas of the Middle East, South and

Southeast Asia and East Asia. Not all areas are covered in equal depth and some particular areas and subjects are covered more thoroughly than others. The scope of the holdings embraces all periods from pre-history to the present day. The collection aims at extensive coverage of works which are important contributions to scholarship in the areas of the humanities and social sciences. It also collects representative collections of literature written in Asian languages. The collection is primarily a book collection but serials also form an important part of the provision. There are also significant holdings of manuscripts, archives and rare books, many of immense value and significance.

The oriental collections are administered in four separate language groups i.e. Chinese, Japanese (and Korean), Near and Middle Eastern, Indian and Southeast Asian. The Library also houses the Taylor-Schechter Genizah Collection, a priceless accumulation of centuries-old Hebrew manuscript material and Judaica, recovered from the Cairo Genizah in 1896-97. There are also many other special named collections within all the area groups which are listed and described in more detail under separate headings. The present stock of the oriental collections is estimated to number over 350,000 volumes. In addition, there are considerable holdings relating to all areas of Asia in the Library's western language book collections, in the Library's manuscript and rare books collections and in the Official Publications Department.

The collection aims to satisfy the present and future research and teaching needs of the staff and students of the University but its resources are also available to visitors from outside the University who would benefit from their use.

Collections held in the University Library

* Ancient Near Eastern Languages
* Arabic, Persian and Turkish printed books
* Chinese Collection
* Hebrew and Jewish manuscripts

* Hebrew Printed Books
* Japanese Collection
* Korean Collection
* Map Department
* Oriental Manuscripts. Near Eastern Collection: Islamic languages
* Oriental Manuscripts. Near Eastern: General
* Printed books in Iranian languages
* South Asian Collection
* Southeast Asian Collection
* Taylor-Schechter Genizah Research Unit
* Tibetan Collection

Arabic, Persian and Turkish printed books

* Collection Details
* Description of Collection
* Subjects of the Collection
* Collection Material and Size of Collection
* Collection Management Information
* Collection Catalogue Information

Collection Details

This large collection (in excess of 16000 titles) includes primary sources and studies in Arabic, Persian and Turkish on all aspects of Islam and Muslim theology, history, literature and language. It includes material on all traditional branches of Islamic learning.

Works in the principal Islamic languages came first came into the library around the year 1620. Since then, the collection has been expanded systematically, through purchase and donation. Because of its long history in collecting Oriental material, the library has large numbers of early imprints, with many Bulaq editions, Ottoman Turkish texts and early European publications of Islamic texts. The collection is particularly strong in the Islamic sciences (tafsir, hadith, fiqh etc..), early history and classical literature ('adab' in the widest sense).

Approximately 80% of the material in this collection is accessible through the main library OPAC. This includes books published after 1979, all of which have records in the online catalogue. Material published prior to 1979 has not been entered fully into the OPAC, and readers must refer to the old guardbook catalogue next to the main reading room. This applies especially to Ottoman Turkish books.

Regions covered under this collection include; Central Asia and the Caucasus, East Asia, Near & Middle East and North Africa, South Asia, South East Asia. The countries included are: Bngladesh, Bhutan, Brunei, Cambodia, China, East Timor, Egypt, India, Indonesia, Israel, Japan, Laos, Malaysia, Maldives, Myanmar (Burma), Nepal, North Korea, Pakistan, Singapore, South Korea, Sri Lanka (Ceylon), Thailand, The Philippines, Vietnam, Yemen.

Archival materials (includes non-published & mixed material), Audio materials (includes cassettes & CDs), Books, Computer files (includes CD-ROMs & other electronic material), Manuscripts, Maps (includes all types of cartographic material), Music (only includes printed & manuscript music), Newspapers (includes microfilm editions), Official publications, Public records, Serials, Theses, Visual materials (includes photographs, prints, drawings, videos & films).

Access to the main catalogue is via a web or telnet link which provides a number of search menus and access points. There are separate catalogues of the Chinese collections and of the Japanese Union Catalogue which can be accessed from the main catalogue menu. For other material, and most books printed before 1979, readers must refer to the guardbook catalogue in the library

Oriental Manuscripts

The Near Eastern manuscripts include important collections, representing a full range of literature in Arabic (over 1500 codices), Hebrew (over 1000), Persian (over 1200), Syriac (c. 300) and Turkish (c. 450), and E.G. Browne's collection of c. 480 codices (Arabic, Persian and Turkish). There are also major collections of documents, most notably the Taylor-Schechter Cairo Genizah, over 140,000 fragments of documents and texts, principally in Hebrew and Judaeo-Arabic from the Taylor-Schechter Genizah Collection and the Michaelides collection of some 2,000 Arabic and Coptic fragments. The papers of E.G. Browne contain an important archive of original and unique Persian material on the first constitutional period in Iran. Papers of other Orientalists and those interested in the Middle East should be searched for among the Western manuscripts. Armenian, Georgian, Ethiopic, Malay and other Near and Middle Eastern languages are also represented - see guide at the end of this leaflet.

Most of the Islamic and Syriac codices, and many of the Genizah fragments, are described in the published catalogues. The Hebrew manuscripts catalogue will be published in 1996; a catalogue of the Persian, Arabic and Turkish content of the Browne papers is being prepared for publication, also a union catalogue of the Turkish manuscripts in Cambridge, and a handlist of the Michaelides collection.

The Library also holds on deposit a collection of Islamic manuscripts belonging to Corpus Christi College and the two halves of the Pote collection which are the property of King's College and Eton College respectively. Papers of E.G. Browne which are the property of Pembroke College are housed alongside the Library's collection and included in the catalogue.

The Indian, Tibetan and Southeast Asian Collections

These manuscripts include important collections, representing a full range of literature in Sanskrit & Prakrit (over 1,000), Sinhalese (111), Tibetan (109), Malay (93), Pali (64),

Malayalam (52), Burmese (50), with smaller collections in Bengali, Cambodian, Javanese, Lolo, Lao, Gujarati, Hindi, Marathi, Moso, Newari, Punjabi, Shan, Sindhi, Tamil, Telugu, and the like. A major focus of the collections is on Buddhist manuscripts.

The private papers of Lord Crewe, Sir Samuel Hoare, Lord Mayo and Lord Hardinge are among the Western manuscripts relevant to South Asia. The Jardine Matheson archive is also with Western manuscripts. Thomas Erpenius' manuscripts include early Southeast Asian manuscripts. Sir George Scott's collection is very significant for Southeast Asian material.

The Library also holds on deposit the Sanskrit manuscripts of Corpus Christi College.

Bibliographical Guide to Oriental Manuscripts

Arabic, Persian, Turkish

E. G. BROWNE: A hand-list of the Muhammadan manuscripts, including all those written in the Arabic character, preserved in the Library of the University of Cambridge. Cambridge, 1900.

E. G. BROWNE: A supplementary hand-list of the Muhammadan manuscripts, including all those written in the Arabic character, preserved in the libraries of the University and Colleges of Cambridge. Cambridge, 1922.

R. A. NICHOLSON: A descriptive catalogue of the Oriental MSS belonging to the late E.G. Browne. Cambridge, 1932.

D. S. MARGOLIOUTH: Catalogue of Oriental manuscripts in the Library of Eton College. Oxford, 1904. [On deposit.]

Arabic, Persian

J. ARBERRY: A second supplementary hand-list of the Muhammadan manuscripts in the University and Colleges of Cambridge. Cambridge, 1952.

Arabic in the Taylor-Schechter Genizah Collection. See under *Hebrew.*

Persian

E. G. BROWNE: A catalogue of the Persian manuscripts in the Library of the University of Cambridge. Cambridge, 1896.

S. HOPKINS: A miscellany of literary pieces from the Cambridge Genizah collections. Cambridge, 1978.

S. MORAG: Vocalised Talmudic manuscripts in the Cambridge Genizah collections. Cambridge, 1988.

S. C. REIF *et al.*: Published material from the Cambridge Genizah collections. Cambridge, 1988.

G. KHAN: Karaite Bible manuscripts from the Cairo Genizah. Cambridge, 1990.

M. L. KLEIN: Targumic manuscripts in the Cambridge Genizah collections. Cambridge, 1992.

G. KHAN: Arabic legal and administrative documents in the Cambridge Genizah collections. Cambridge, 1993.

Hindi

G. NIEMANN: Uncatalogued Indian manuscripts of Corpus Christi College, Cambridge: the Honner collection. (*IAVRI Bulletin*, 9 (1980), pp. 3-15.) [On deposit.]

Pali

T. W. RHYS DAVIDS: List of Pali manuscripts in the Cambridge University Library. (*Journal of the Pali Text Society*, 1883, pp. 145-6.)

Pashto

J. F. BLUMHARDT & D.N.MACKENZIE: Catalogue of Pashto manuscripts in the libraries of the British Isles. London, 1965.

Sanskrit

BENDALL: Catalogue of the Buddhist Sanskrit

manuscripts in the University Library, Cambridge. Cambridge, 1883.

D. WRIGHT: List of my collection of Sanskrit manuscripts; pp. 316-324 in History of Nepal..., ed. D.Wright. Cambridge, 1877.

C. BENDALL: List of MSS, with notes; pp. 39-53 in his A journal of literary and archaeological research in Nepal and northern India. Cambridge, 1886.

C. BENDALL: Notes on a collection of MSS obtained by Dr Gimlette...at Kathmandu. (*Journal of the Royal Asiatic Society*, N.S. 20 (1888), pp. 549-551.)

Syriac

W. WRIGHT: A catalogue of the Syriac manuscripts preserved in the Library of the University of Cambridge. 2 vols. Cambridge, 1901.

A. E. GOODMAN: The Jenks collection of Syriac manuscripts in the University Library, Cambridge. (*Journal of the Royal Asiatic Society*, 1939, pp. 581-600.)

32
UNIVERSITY OF PUNJAB LIBRARY, LAHORE

The land where the Islamic Republic of Pakistan is situated today had been a seat of world's leading Civilizations from the time immemorial. There is plenty of evidence from the pre-historic and historic period to support this argument, e.g., fossil jaws of apes, circa 14 millions years old found from Pothohar. They belong to a species named "Sivapithecus Pakininsis", said to be the ancestor of Man. A 2 million years old earliest stone hand axe. Now on display in Islamabad Museum, Islamabad.

The present Pakistan is the seat of some of the most important institutions including the Liaquat Memorial Library, the Central Secretariat Library, and the University of Karachi Library. Also of note are the National Archives of Pakistan, in Islamabad, and the Punjab Public Library, in Lahore. The National Museum of Pakistan, in Karachi, contains important materials from the Indus Valley civilizations, as well as Buddhist and Islamic artifacts. Cultural materials also are displayed in the Lahore Museum and the Peshawar Museum. The Industrial and Commercial Museum, in Lahore, contains exhibits on the manufactures of Pakistan.

The legacy of the predecessors at the time of independence, on August 14, 1947, came as a treasure which may be called as Pakistan's National Heritage. So rich and diversified is this heritage that Pakistani nation can be proud of its glorious past, be Islamic or pre Islamic as far back as pre-historic times.

However, what has been excavated in Pakistan already makes an important and a huge collection. Now it is incumbent upon us to save this national heritage for the future generations and let them be proud of their glorious past as well as let the national heritage for the future generations a source of inspiration for their brighter future. It is for this reason that the government of Pakistan has established a fund called "National Fund for Cultural Heritage"(NFCH). The National Fund for Cultural Heritage was established in April 1994 for the conservation and preservation of the Pakistan's national heritage and its proper maintenance and matters connected therewith.

There is a department of Archaeology whose sole purpose is to look after the national heritage. However, the department is a governmental institution and at times people raise objections to the progress of the department of Archaeology. As in some people's opinion there can be much more achievement in a better way. Hence the government in response to this objection & to supplement the task of the Department of Archaeology and for the worthy cause of conservation and preservation of Pakistan's national heritage has at long last established a fund under the name of "National Fund for Cultural Heritage".

The establishment of NFCH is much appreciated and a great interest is shown by the general public hence since its establishment in 1994 hundreds of proposals were received from different agencies and individuals for the conservation, preservation and publication of the Pakistan's national heritage.

University of Punjab

The University of the Punjab was formally established with the convening of the first meeting of its Senate on October 14, 1882 at Simla. It was the fourth University to be established by the British colonial authorities on the Indian Subcontinent. The first three universities were established by the British rulers at their initial strongholds of Bombay, Madras and Calcutta. The University of the Punjab came into existence as a result of a long drawn struggle of the people of Punjab after the war of independence in 1857. Contrary to the three previously established universities, which were only examining institutions, the University of the Punjab was both teaching as well as examining body right from the beginning.

The contribution of Dr. G. W. Leitner, an enlightened Hungarian and a naturalized British, was instrumental in the establishment of this University. He became its first Registrar. Prof. A. C. Woolner, who remained Vice-Chancellor of this University during 1928-1936, played a key role in its development during the initial decades of this century. His statue still stands in front of the Allama Iqbal Campus of the University.

Until independence in 1947 the University of the Punjab fulfilled the educational needs of a vast region of the Subcontinent. Partition of the Subcontinent somewhat reduced the geographical limits of the jurisdiction of the University. However, for many years after independence it still ranged over vast areas including Punjab, NWFP, Baluchistan and Azad Jammu & Kashmir. New universities were set up later in the country to share responsibility for imparting higher education with the University of the Punjab.

The strength of the University Faculty was greatly reduced because of the migration of non-Muslim teachers and scholars at the time of independence. The University functioning was restored, mainly due to the efforts of the eminent educationist like Dr. Umar Hayat Malik, who became the first Vice Chancellor after the independence. Academic programs were initiated soon after the independence under many new departments.

Some of the biggest libraries are those of Oriental College, Law College, Hailey College of Commerce and department of Islamic Studies, Department of English and Institute of Chemistry where 57,335; 48, 725; 36,845; 20,149; 15,738 and 13,130 books, respectively are available. In addition, these libraries also receive many periodicals and research journals. The total number of books in all the University libraries is over 720,000.

University Library

Punjab University Library is the largest resource center of knowledge and information in Pakistan, which came into existence in 1882. The library remained in its old building upto 1988 and in the same year it was shifted to its present two-storied building. The total area of library is 1,02,000 sq. feet with a basement of 10,000 sq. feet.

The strength of the Library collection increased by donations from the various corners of the country specially undivided Punjab of the pre-independence India. Private collections played a major role in its development and the collection also expanded by the purchased collections containing manuscripts and published books. The notable collections purchased for the Library are many but some of them are worth mentioning here. To start with, the Percy Collection comprising of about 650 books was purchased in 1911.

The collection of Maulana Mohammad Husain was also donated to the Library of Oriental College which later transformed into this University by his son after the demise. It contained 389 manuscripts and 3150 books published books. Pirzada Mohammad Arif of Rohtak also gave his collection comprising 205 manuscripts and 777 books. The famous Urdu literary figure Braj Mohan Duttatriya Kaifi also donated his personal collection of 130 manuscripts and 877 books.

In 1936, an important contribution to the collection of the Library was made by Alfred Woolner and his wife by contributing 8000 manuscripts and 1575 books. The collection of a famous Urdu scholar Hafiz Mahmood Shirani was purchased by the Library and the catalogue of this collection has been published separately. In 1948, the collection of Haji Mehboob Alam was also donated by his son. It contained 363 manuscripts and 6825 books. In 1952, the collection of Prof. Sirajuddin Azar comprising of 1500 manuscripts was purchased for the Library. Hakim Abdul Hameed Atiqui also donated books to the Library from time to time. Likewise, a former principal of the college. Prof.

Mohammad Iqbal donated 1713 books in 1952. Sir Sirajuddin, Sir Moham Lal, Sir Ganga Ram and Prof. Singh also donated 4000; 2154; 5000 and 2000 books respectively.

The position of Library collection as a whole in 1982 was as under:

English Books	189405
Urdu Books	23749
Arabic and Persian Books	25308
Sanskrit Books	28000
Misc. Pamphlets etc.	7225
Microfilms Manuscripts	11260
Sanskrit Manuscripts	8671

The catalogue of 1122 Arabic manuscripts was compiled by Abdul Nabi Kaukab and Syed Jameel Ahmad Rizvi and published in the year 1982.

In 2002, the Library contained a collection of 402634, which includes 22,574 manuscripts and 65200 bound volumes of national and international research journals covering various disciplines taught in the University. This prestigious library has more than 50,000 volumes of old documents published during the later half of 19th and first two decades of 21st century. The library has 1750 microfilms of rare material. It is a depositary library for the UNO publications.

33
AL-ZAHIRIYA LIBRARY, DAMASCUS

Al-Zahiriya Library is located in Damascus, the capital city of Syria. The country is located on the east coast of the Mediterranean Sea and is bordered by Turkey to the North, Jordan and Israel to the south, Lebanon to the southwest, and Iraq to the east and southeast. It covers an area of 185,180 sq. km., with an estimated population of over 12 million. Syria has seen a rapid growth in population since its independence in 1946.

Syria has a rich cultural heritage. Its strategic location makes it a bridge between the Mesopotamian and Nile Valley civilizations. It is also a link between Asia, Africa, and Europe. Throughout history, conquering armies introducing different cultures have passed through Syria, leaving their cultural marks. The cultural diversity of Syria today reflects its rich history. Islamic armies came to Syria in the seventh century and gradually the country adopted the new religion. Most of the people in Syria today are Sunni Muslims (75%), followed by the Shi'ite Muslims (15%). The Kurds, Turkmen, and Circassians are Sunni. The 'Alawis, the Druze, and the Isma'ilis are Shi'ites. The rest of the population is divided among several Christian denominations: Greek Orthodox, Armenian Orthodox, Greek Catholic, Syrian Catholic, Syrian Orthodox, Armenian Catholic, Maronite, and Protestant. Syria also has a few thousand Jews living mostly in Damascus.

Arabic is the official language of Syria. Some 85% of the people speak Arabic as their native language. Kurdish is spoken in the northeast and northwest of the country. Turkish is spoken in villages around the border with Turkey. Armenian is spoken mostly in Aleppo and other major cities. Circassian and Syriac are spoken by other minorities in various places in the country. English, French, German and Russian are taught to children after their elementary education.

The Umayyad Mosque has been a hub for Muslim scholars since the first Islamic century. Under the Ayyubids and Mamluks, a flurry of *madrasa*-building brought professional scholars to Damascus from all corners of the Muslim world. During the late 19th and early 20th centuries in Damascus, many scattered manuscript collections were consolidated into the National Library, housed in the Mamluk-era Madrasa al-Zahiriyya, the pride of Syrian scholars in the age of Arab nationalism. With French rule in 1920 came an army of researchers and catalogers who established one of the region's best library collections at the Institut Français des Études Arabes à Damas.

There are four main research institutions for historians in Damascus: the Asad Library, Institut Français des Etudes Arabes à Damas, Markaz al-Watha'iq al-Ta'rikhiyya (Center for Historical Documents) and the Dar al-Kutub al-Zahiriyya (Zahiriyya Library).

Al-Zahiriyah Library was established in 1880. It has issued over twelve indexes of Syrian manuscripts. These indexes can be used as selection guides for manuscripts. The history of the building, which dates from the late 13th century, is probably more interesting than the holdings of the library itself. One of the largest and best preserved of the Damascene *madrasas*, al-Zahiriyya was named for Sultan al-Zahir Baybars, the first of the Mamluks sultans. In 1876 it was turned into a general library. Along with al-'Adiliyya Madrasa, across the street, it was also headquarters of al-Majma' al-'Ilmi al-'Arabi, the premier institution of the Syrian literary renaissance of the late 19th and early 20th centuries.

The Zahiriyya collection was decimated, however, by the creation of the Asad Library when the manuscript collection, rare books and periodicals relating to Syria were transferred to the Asad Library. The Zahiriyya now contains about 70,000 volumes mostly related to Islam, the Arabic language, history and biography. The library is now used mostly by high school and college students. There are no conditions for using library except that some form of identification must be deposited at the circulation desk in order to use books.

Legal deposit was established in Syria in 1949. The intention of the law was that two copies of every work published in Syria be deposited in al-Zahiriyah National Library. The law was not enforced until July 1983, when a presidential decree required the deposit of 5 copies of each work published by a Syrian author in the Asad Library.

The manuscript collection at the Asad Library is the largest in Syria, comprising almost 20,000 volumes. Most of the manuscripts were gathered from the *madrasas* of Damascus and housed in the Zahiriyya *madrasa* until the founding of Asad Library. The manuscripts in Asad Library from the Zahiriyya collection are indexed in a series of indices to the Zahiriyya collection under the general title *Fihris makhtutât Dar al-Kutub al-Zahiriyya*. A list of the indices follows:

Yusuf al-'Ishsh, *al-Tâ'rîkh wa-mulhaqâtuhu* (Damascus, 1947)

Khalid al-Rayan, *al-Tâ'rîkh wa-mulhaqâtuhu* (Damascus, 1973)

'Izzat Hasan, *'Ulûm al-Qur'ân* (Damascus, 1962)

'Abd al-Ghani al-Daqir, *al-Fiqh al-Shâfi'î* (Damascus, 1963)

'Izzat Hasan, *al-Shi'r* (Damascus, 1964)

Sami Khalaf Hamarnah & Salah Muhammad al-Khiyami, *al-Tibb wa-l-saydala*, 2 vols. (Damascus, 1969)

Ibrahim Khuri, *'Ilm al-hayâh wa-mulhaqâtu*

Muhammad Nasir al-Din al-Albani, *al-Muntakhab min makhtutât al-hadîth* (Damascus, 1970)

'Abd al-Hamid al-Hasan, *al-Falsafa wa-l-mantiq wa-adab al-bahth* (Damascus, 1970)

Ibrahim Khuri, *al-Jughrâfiyâ wa-mulhaqâtuhu* (Damascus, 1970)

Asma' al-Himsi, *'Ulum al-lugha al-'arabiyya*, 2 vols. (Damascus, 1970)

Muhammad Salah Ayidi, *al-Riyadiyât* (Damascus, 1973)

Muhammad Riyad al-Malih, *al-Tasawwuf*, 2 vols. (Damascus, 1978, 1980)

Mustafa Said al-Sabbagh, *'Ulum wa-al-funûn al-mukhtalifa 'inda al-'Arab*

Muhammad Muti' al-Hafiz, *al-Fiqh al-Hanafi*, 2 vols. (1978, 1980)

Salah Muhammad al-Khiyami, *'Ulûm al-Qur'ân al-Karîm*, 3 vols.

Riyad 'Abd al-Hamid Murad & Yasin Muhammad al-Sawwas, *Qism al-adab*.

There is also an index to manuscripts in the Zahiriyya collection that came from the 'Umariyya *madrasa*, one of the largest libraries in Damascus until the creation of the Zahiriyya collection: Yasin al-Sawwas, *Fihris makhtutât al-madrasa al-'Umariyya al-mahfûza fi-l-Zâhiriyya* (Kuwait, 1987). Most of these indices are available at research libraries in the US and Britain. The Asad Library is preparing a collection of indices of its own because, in addition to the Zahiriyya collection, the Asad Library has acquired manuscripts from the general library in Aleppo, from cultural centers around the country and through purchase and gifts since the establishment of the library.

Two catalogues to the Aleppo collection are Salman Qutliyya, *Makhtutât al-tibb wa-l-saydala fi-l-maktaba al-'âma bi-Halab* (Aleppo, 1976) and *al-Muntakhab min al-makhtutât al-'arabiyya fi-Halab* prepared by Markaz al-Khidmat wa-l-Abhath al-Thaqafiyya (Beirut, 1986). IFEAD is also compiling indices to manuscripts related to history-writing contained in the Asad Library. The library says it has 35,000 manuscripts copied on film from other collections through the *Ma'had al-Turath al-'Ilmi al-'Arabi* (Institute for Arab Heritage and Science) in Aleppo.

Conditions for use of the manuscript collection are different. One needs a letter from a university or research institution stating that the researcher requires use of the manuscript collection. Users are not allowed to see originals unless special permission is granted by the director of the library. Instead, they must avail themselves of copies of manuscripts on microfilm and microfiche. If a manuscript has not yet been microfilmed, the researcher must still make a formal request to see the original. Requests for copying must be made in writing to the director of the library.

The Asad National Library

In 1984, the Asad Library was established in Damascus to serve as a national library and to house manuscript collections from all over the country. The mid-1990s was an auspicious time for American researchers in Syria because of the establishment of the American Research Institute in Syria (ARIS), a consortium of American universities that has been working for the past several years to establish an institute for research with residential facilities for them in Damascus at par with the European facilities there.

The Asad Library replaced al-Zahiriyah Library. The Asad Library has published annual issues of the *Syrian National Bibliography* (*al-Bibliyuqhrafiya al-Wataniyah al-Suriyah*) since 1985. The bibliography is a comprehensive list of Syrian publications. It includes short annotations for some entries and author, title, and subject indexes. A list of all Syrian publishers and a list of newspapers and periodicals are also included. The Asad Library is attempting the publication of a Syrian retrospective bibliography. The first issue was published in 1987.

The Asad Library also publishes a quarterly index to Syrian periodicals (*al-Kashshaf al-Tahlili lil-Suhuf wa-al-Majallat al-Suriyahi*).

The Asad Library is playing a major role in promoting the distribution of Syrian publications outside the country. The library has established exchange programs with many institutions around the world, and willingly continues to do so. The Library of Congress Middle East Cooperative Acquisition Program (MECAP) has established a good relationship with the Asad Library. For the first time in many years MECAP has access to Syrian publications through their representative in Damascus. MECAP provides a blanket order plan that includes Syrian publications. The program's diplomatic connection makes it easy to obtain Syrian publications.

The library also holds all manuscripts and rare books and periodicals previously held at Dar al-Kutub al-Zahiriyya. The Asad Library has special departments devoted to music, fine arts, film and old periodicals and has reading rooms with reference materials in history, literature and the sciences. Complete collections of newspapers, including the contemporary dailies, *al-Ba'th*, *al-Thawra* and *Tishrin,* are available. There are facilities for photocopying and microfilming but copying manuscripts and entire books requires special permission.

34
BUDDHIST MANUSCRIPTS IN NEPAL

Buddhist literature was created in Sanskrit beginning right from the period starting from Buddha's Mahaparinirvana and continuing till the 11th century AD. Out of this vast literature only a small portion of it was translated into Tibetan between 7th and 11th century. Unfortunately, with the passage of time, the great treasure of Buddhist Sanskrit literature was lost or destroyed due to various historical conditions.

An exhaustive history of the Sanskrit Buddhist literature has long been needed. The reasons behind the scarcity of research in Sanskrit Buddhist literature are many. One of the major reasons is the disappearance of Buddhism from major parts of India and the unavailability of the original Sanskrit Buddhist works.

In 1824, Mr. Brian Hodgson, a British diplomat in Nepal, discovered a great number of Sanskrit Buddhist manuscripts in Nepal. The existence of these before his time was unknown, and his discovery entirely revolutionized the history of Buddhism, as it was known to Europeans in the early part of this century. Copies of these works, totaling 381 folio manuscripts have been distributed so as to render them accessible to European scholars.

Of these eighty-six manuscripts comprising 179 separate works, many were presented to Asiatic Society of Bengal: 85 to the Royal Asiatic Society of London; 30 to the Indian Office Library; 7 to the Bodleian Library, Oxford; 174 to the Société Asiatique, and to French scholar Eugene Bern ouf. The last two collections have since been deposited in the Bibliothèque Nationale of France.

Prof. Jaya Deva Singh writes in his Introduction to Madhyamika Philosophy:

Books on Mahayana Buddhism were completely lost in India. Their translation existed in Chinese, Japanese and Tibetan. Mahayana literature was written mostly in Sanskrit and mixed Sanskrit. Scholars who have made a study of Buddhism hardly suspected that there were also books on Buddhism in Sanskrit.

In a similar manner Suniti Kumar Chatterji writes:

One great service the people of Nepal, particularly the highly civilized Newars of the Nepal Valley, was to preserve the manuscript of Mahayana Buddhist literature in Sanskrit. It was the contribution of Sri Lanka to have preserved for human kind the entire mass of the Pali literature of Theravada Buddhism. This went also to Burma, Cambodia, and Siam. It was similarly the great achievement of the people of Nepal to have preserved the equally valuable original Sanskrit texts of Mahayana Buddhism.

It is in Nepal that most of the Sanskrit Buddhist documents have been found. Concerning Nepalese Buddhist literature, as many as 20 reports have been published.

Most of the manuscripts originally preserved in Nepal have been carried out of the country by the pioneers of the modern Indology. An earliest illustrated Manuscript of Astasahasrika Prajñaparamita dated 1015 AD is now in the collection of the Cambridge University Library. This Manuscript offered new material to students of South Asian and Central Asian art history. It is difficult to know exactly when the tradition of illustrated manuscripts began. But from available documents it seems that copying and writing manuscripts began as early as the tenth century in Nepal, i.e. during Narendra Deva's reign (998 A.D.).[2] These include miniatures and painted book covers.

One peculiar feature of Newar Buddhism is that the Buddhist priest called Vajracarya, does not stay in the monastery or temple but with his family and performs the rites dressed in everyday clothes. Only those who belong to the Vajracarya family can become a priest, but they must have already gone through a form of initiation called Acarya abhiseka and been married.

Another peculiarity of Newar Buddhism is its ritual and its sacred literature, which are written in Sanskrit language, because of which we can call Newar Buddhism "Sanskrit Buddhism." We have discussed about the status of Newar Buddhism elsewhere.[3]

With the collapse of Indian Buddhism, some of the Buddhists escaped from suppression in India and fled to Nepal. The Newars of Kathmandu Valley accepted them and their religious and cultural inheritance. The two groups intermarried and their religions and cultures merged to become Newar Buddhism. This happened from 9 century to 13 century A.D. They have continued to copy Sanskrit manuscripts repeatedly up to the present day. All Buddhists owe a debt to the Newars, the through whose efforts we can study these Sanskrit manuscripts today.

Manuscripts in Libraries

1.Buddhist Library, Nagoya

In the early seventies Mr. Hidenobu Takaoka, a Japanese Buddhist priest, visited the Kathmandu Valley and investigated thoroughly the status of Nepalese Buddhist culture. Lamenting the situation of the multitude of scattered manuscripts and the condition of Buddhism in Nepal, he undertook to preserve the Nepali Manuscript heritage by taking microfilms of Sanskrit and Newar Manuscripts. It took him a decade of effort to microfilm the Buddhist Manuscripts exclusively from private collections rather than certain public archives. Due to fear of theft or trafficking he kept hidden the names of the collectors and simply mentioned as A, KA, KH, GA,GH,CH, and DH. It was a judicious decision. In his catalogue he had been able to microfilm 1521 titles of Buddhist Manuscripts. There are yet number of private collectors the manuscripts that were not microfilmed yet. This was not possible because of conservative behavior from the part of the owner or for some unknown reasons.

In 1981, he published "A Microfilm Catalogue of The Buddhist Manuscript in Nepal" from Buddhist Library, Japan. In his collection of Manuscripts, the subject matter consists of Mahayana Sutras, Jataka-avadana, Sastras, Tantra, Purana literature, Strotra, Caryagita, Pujavidhi, Dharani-mantra, tantra commentaries and so forth.

2.The Asa Archives

The Asa Archives is a public library of Nepalese Manuscripts named after the late Mr. Asha Man Singha Kansakar, father of the late Mr. Prem Bahadur Kansakar (1917-1991). Mr. Kansakar was prominent activist, social worker, educationist and Newar writer who had founded several social, cultural, literary and educational institutions. The nucleus of this was donated by Prem Bahadur Kansakar to Cvasa Pasa, a premier literary association of Newar writers on August 16,1985. To this personal collection were later added the donations of valuable manuscripts and palm leaf documents by several well-wishers and friends. Among them mention should be made of Mr. Ian Alshop, an American student of Kansakar, Dharma Ratna Vajracarya, Guru Sekhar Rajopadhyaya, Rev. Hidonobu Takaoka, Gyan Ratna and Dr. Kamal Prakash Malla. Similarly, more than a dozen other donors have helped this archive with gifts from their personal collections of manuscripts.

The Archives were inaugurated by Prof. Yujiro Hayashi, the Executive Director of the Toyota Foundation, Japan on December 7,1987. It was made accessible to the public since that time. The Toyota Foundation had made a generous grant to purchase, innovate and furnish the house where it is now located. The Foundation has also supported the documentation of the manuscripts and initial operation of the archives with a fund deposited as seed money and endowment.

In this archive there are several valuable collections of palm leaf, loose-leaf pothi and folded manuscripts. There are more than 6,700 manuscripts and about 1100 palm leaf land grant documents. These manuscripts belong to various sects and genres written in different languages and scripts. Largest among these are the ritual texts, medical texts, manuals of magic and necromancy, astrology/astronomy, Vedic and Puranic texts, and Tantric texts of the êaiva, Bauddha, and êakta sects. A large number also come from the Mahayana and Vajrayana Buddhism. There are technical and symbolical drawings and architectural designs of religious and secular structures, painted covers, and book illustrations of great beauty and delicacy. Perhaps the most important component of the archives is the literary texts, hymns, songs, plays, popular narratives, didactic tales and Buddhist avadanas in the Newar language. One can find specimens of beautiful calligraphy in the collection written in plain black ink, silver and golden letters.

The Archives has also a collection of nearly all Nepal bha*a books in print, journals, magazines and newspapers in Nepal bha*a. There is also a small Nepal collection, consisting of books on Nepal in English and other languages which will be of great interest for study and research on the culture and heritage of the Nepal valley.

The archive is preparing a systematic and descriptive catalogue of all its collections. Presently, several types of temporary catalogues are available. There is a handwritten catalogue in the form of a ledger of the collection, with running numbers, classification by religion, language or genre with a workable amount of information. This is also available in the form of a card catalogue. There are at present two printed catalogues available. One was prepared by Mr. Charles M. Novak, A Catalogue of the Selected Buddhist Manuscripts in the Asa Archives, (1986). The other catalogue is the Descriptive Catalogue of Selected Manuscripts in the Asa Archives prepared by Dr. Janak Lal Vaidya and Prem Bahadur Kansakar (Kathmandu, Cvasa pasa 1991). This is a descriptive catalogue of the 547 most important manuscripts in the collection. There is also a descriptive monograph on the Asa Archives (1996), containing important speeches, and articles all edited by the librarian Mr. Raja Shakya.

In collaboration with the Buddhist Library of Japan, Nagoya, the Asa Archives is completing the digitalization of its entire collection of manuscripts. When the project is completed all the manuscripts including their paintings and illuminations will be available on CDROM.

3. Nepal Research Center

A principal task of the Nepal Research Center is to house and support the Nepal-German Manuscript Preservation Project (NGMPP). The NGMPP was established in 1970 by an agreement between His Majesty's Government of Nepal and German Oriental Society. It is a joint venture between the Department of Archaeology, the Ministry of Youth, Sports and Culture (up to 1995 it was under the Ministry of Education and Culture), His Majesty's Government and the German Oriental Society. It is designed to preserve on microfilm Nepal's extraordinary wealth of manuscripts and historical documents, thereby contributing considerably to the preservation of the country's cultural heritage and identity, as well as providing invaluable opportunities to explore virtually all aspects of its manifold literary, religious and historical traditions.

All equipments and materials necessary for the execution of the NGMPP are provided by the German Oriental Society with financial assistance from the German Research Council. In consultation with its Nepali counterpart, the society set up a photographic section in the National Archives. Run by experts and technicians provided by His Majesty's Government, it microfilmed the collections of the Nepal Archives, and develops and copies all films of the project, including those produced by a separate microfilming unit located at the Nepal Research Center. According to the agreement, one positive copy of each film, together with the original negative, remains in the National Archives, while a second positive copy is handed over to German

Oriental Society for preservation in the Staatsbibliothek Berlin PreuBischer Kulturebesitz, the former Prussian State Library.

During its first phase, from 1970 to 1975, the activities of NGMPP were limited to the collections of the National Archives. The subsequent extension of the agreement provided for the inclusion of all public libraries and private manuscript collections within the Bagmati Zone. To date, around 155,000 manuscripts with nearly five million folios have been microfilmed in the whole of Nepal.

With the second extension of the agreement, the restriction to the Bagmati zone was lifted. From 1982 onwards, the NGMPP undertook various exploratory tours and opened temporary microfilming stations in other parts of the Kingdom. Up to February 1987, the Sanskrit section alone microfilmed 2,267 manuscripts with 74,487 folios outside the Kathmandu valley, namely in Kaskikot (1982), Gorkha (1983), Janakpur (1984/85) and Rajbiraj (1986/87). It should be pointed out that, through these activities of the NGMPP, many texts have become available for the first time outside what may have been a very limited area of dissemination.

This wealth of manuscripts is not only distinguished by its exceptional range of diversity - nearly all sub-fields of Hindu and Buddhist Sanskrit literature are represented - but frequently also by the rarity and greater antiquity of individual pieces. In many cases, the microfilmed manuscripts represent the oldest available sources for a given text, and this holds true not just for the Buddhist Sanskrit texts, but also for many Vedic, Brahmaöic and Hindu works which are extant elsewhere, if at all, only in later copies.

4. The Nepal Archives

Recently, The Nepal Archives has published a catalogue of the entire Sanskrit Buddhist Manuscripts in the collection with a view to facilitate scholars and researchers. It also includes a catalogue of microfilm reels prepared by Nepal German

Manuscript Preservation Project acquired through its missiwork in the different districts of Nepal. This does not mean that the catalogue was the first of its kind. It has published several catalogues previously. One special feature of this catalogue is that it exclusively addresses Buddhist manuscripts along with additional manuscripts microfilmed in Nepal German Manuscript Preservation Project.

The number of Buddhist manuscripts in the possession of the Nepal Archives totals 889 plus the 940 acquired in different mission by the NGMPP thus the grand total of 1829 manuscripts.

Another catalogue, a catalogue of The Buddhist Tantric Manuscrips in the National Archives of Nepal and Kesar Library, deals specifically with this excellent collection of Tantric Buddhist manuscripts. This most valuable catalogue was compiled by Prof. Mitutoshi Moriguchi from Taisho University.

It would be befitting to give the classification of Buddhist manuscripts with regard to its subjects:

* Buddhist Mahayana Sutras
* Sastras:
* Avadana
* Karmakanda
* Mahatmya and Purana
* Jataka
* Katha or stories
* Tantra
* Dharani
* Strotra
* Caryagita (music)
* Paintings

5. Nagarjuna Institute

Since the inception of Buddhist Dharaö′ Input Project in 1999 Jan., Nagarjuna Inc. has input titles from 100 strotras and

80 Dharaö´s. Our aim is to input the entire collection of Dharaö´s (more than 600 titles) from the collection of Nagarjuna Inc., The Asa Archives, and The Nepal Archives. We are informed that by the end of February, The Asa Archive is giving its service to the researchers the Manuscript on Dharaö´s and Strotras to produce a CDROM version.

The Nepal Archive has already put their entire collection of Buddhist manuscripts in Microfilm, so it is a matter of purchasing the microfilms. Since resources are desperately lacking wherewith to purchase the microfilm copies, the completion of the input project has been delayed. Should funds become available, it is certain that we could complete this first phase of our input project at the end of this year.

Scripts used in Nepalese Manuscripts

Four types of script were generally used to write the Manuscripts, they are Pracalita, Newari, Ranjana, Bhujimole and Devanagari script. Among these, Newari script was used for most of the manuscripts. Ranjana is used for books used for worship such as Prajñaparamita and so forth. They were often written on Indigo-paper in gold or silver.. The Bhujimole script was used in ancient times (11th to 17th c.) and was written mostly on palm leaves. Devanagari script is used in modern times both by Hindus and Buddhist alike.

Palm-leaf Manuscript

The Sritala Palm leaves are used for writing and painting, because of their thin and flexible qualities. From early 11th to 17 century manuscripts were written on palm leaves called Tadapatra. 1084 number of rolled palm leaf manuscripts are held by the National Archives of Nepal alone. These were written during the 14th century. One of the oldest among these dates from 1334 A. D. It is excellent material for writing and remains preserved in rather excellent condition. It is safe from worms and also can be scrolled into a small bundle. Most of them are written in Bhujimole script. Most of the historical documents of early medieval period were found in these palm leaves. Some of the RPLM are also in the custody of British Library.

Rolled palm leaf manuscripts are placed in small pigeonhole boxes. These are made of straw board and bucrum. These boxes are stored inside a steel cabinet rack to protect from dust, dirt and thieves.

Experiments have demonstrated that citronella oil and polypropylene glycol relax slowly. Some force is required to open them, whereas water-based items open fully and do not need any force to open them. Cracked and weaken RPLMs are strengthened with the help of Archibond. Experiments demonstrate excellent results.

Haritalika Paper Manuscript

Haritalika is yellow in colour, has a crystalline solid structure, is odorless, water insoluble and impervious to inorganic salt. Haritalika is used in hand-made paper (Nepali paper) with some binding agents or media to make it more durable and insect resistance. Nepali hand-made papers are made from the bark of Lokta plant. It contains sheets of cellulose compound. It is creamy in color and contains some small pieces of solid dark brown raw materials due to impurity of pulp. It is supposed to be made from the bark of the Lokta plant. Microscopic study of paper clearly indicate that it contains long fibers, arranged irregularly, having a rough surface. Due to this, it offers a premium coating of Haritalika paste. The majority of hand-made papers are physically and chemically of good quality, high strength, and a strong ph factor of 7-9. These have a high value of tensile strength, folding endurance, and bursting strength.

Starch paste is prepared by using rice flour, water, formaldehyde (1:5:0.1) in a thick aluminum vessel. Nepali hand-made paper is flattened on a smooth board using a small quantity of water. Then a coating of the prepared paste described above is applied uniformly using long brushes very attentively. Another sheet of Nepali hand-made paper is placed and press over it. In this way the number of hand made papers is pasted down according to the required thickness of the paper. In freshly prepared paper, the paste is added and finely grounded Haritalika powder (2:1) mixed and stirred thoroughly in a porcelain mortar with a pestle.

The paste is coated upon a freshly prepared layer of Nepali hand-made paper with the help of a long brush and dried at room temperature. The dried paper is peeled off and trimmed as per the required manuscript size

Haritalika coated paper is used for writing valuable documents and books to protect it from biological agents that might lead to its deterioration.

It seems that this type paper is convenient for handling. That's why around 17th century most of the Nepalese manuscripts were written on handmade paper called "Nepali paper" produced in the Himalayan foothills around the 16-17 century. Since the manuscript is written on both sides, a single layer of Nepali paper is too thin to write on and not fit for writing manuscripts. It was made thick by pasting 3-5 layers of paper together. This thick, pasted paper is cut into a long rectangular shape. Nepali paper is usually given a layer of yellow coating of Hartala on one side or on both sides of the leaves for protection from worms.

Thyasaphu Paper Manuscript

The long rectangular folding books are mainly employed for rituals, Dharani recitation and Stotra gita or hymns.

Scroll Manuscript:

It is used most for writing Vamsavalis or chronicles or genealogical records of royal family.

Bound Book Manuscript

The bound book is quite new and was most probably copied from Western examples.

The importance of inputting these Sanskrit Buddhist texts into a digital format cannot be over-emphasized, for it was from these valuable Sanskrit originals that entire Mahayana and Vajrayana corpus were translated into the Chinese and Tibetan languages, and derivatively, into Korean, Japanese and Mongolian. With the Sanskrit originals in our possession, the translated versions are of secondary importance. The corpus of Sanskrit Buddhist literature found in Nepal is remarkably greater in number than the Pali literature available today. It is imperative that these Sanskrit originals should be preserved in digital format so that they are accessible to the many varieties of researchers.

35
QUR'ANIC MANUSCRIPTS WORLD WIDE

Quran is the holiest books of Muslims. It contains the language of God revealed to the Prophet through the angle Gabril. From the very spread of Islam, the disciples of the Prophet maintained the text of Quran which was revealed to him in parts. Great care was taken to maintain the accuracy of the book and to preserve it on the materials available at that time.

The purpose of the collection is to illustrate something of the history and development of Islamic calligraphy, which grew rapidly from insignificant beginnings, into a major art form the beauty of which has been unsurpassed. Interest in the art of writing was not a feature of pre-Islamic society. The Arabs were poets and storytellers of high ability who trained and improved their memories. Competitions were regularly held at which epic poems were recited and for which prizes were awarded. An alphabetic script had been invented and was used by the Phoenicians and the Nabateans mainly for the purposes of recording business transactions.

For a short period after the revelation of the Holy Qur'an the Arabs continued to follow the old oral tradition. It was only when a great number of the 'Huffaz' (trained people who had committed the Qur'an to memory) were killed in battle that it was realised that memory alone could never be accurate enough , and the Holy book would have to be written down . By 651 AD it had been recorded, codified and official copies sent to all centres of Muslim learning . It was from these copies that every future edition of the Holy Qur'an has been taken.

It was the necessity of recording the Qur'an precisely that played such a central role in beautifying the writing so that it might be worthy of divine revelations. Islamic teachings state that the Holy Book was revealed to the Prophet Mohammed (pbuh) in Arabic and so the language has the status of divine speech. In the following centuries scribes became highly trained and respected people, with the well-educated person, and that included Sultans and Emperors, considering it an honour to learn to write under the guidance of an eminent scribe.

There were a number of early Arabian scripts of two main types, a round curved one and a long straight version. The rounded script was written on materials like leather, while the straight style could be incised into wood, onto flat stones and camel bones. Because neither style was particularly attractive they were not considered suitable for recording the Qur'an.

At an early stage no vowel signs were used and so similar shaped consonants could not be easily differentiated . The Father of Arabic grammer is considered to be Abu'l Aswad Du'ali of Basra (d. 688AD) . He is thought to have invented the system of coloured dots that indicate vowel signs. Two of his students continued his work and devised a method of using these dots to differentiate between consonants and similarly shaped letters.

An outstanding scribe mentioned in Arabic sources was Qutbah al Muharrir. He is thought to have developed the four important styles known as Thuluth, Jalil, Nisf and Tumar. Many people experimented with different styles but most did not survive the test of time. Those that did are known as Al Aqlam al Sittah or The Six Pens. These six styles have survived to this day and are called Thuluth, Naskhi, Rayhani, Muhaqqaq, Riq'a and Tawqi. Naskhi and Riq'a are taught in modern schools.

The single most important development in calligraphy took place in eight century Baghdad. Abu Ali Mohammed ibn Muqlah was a Vazir to three caliphs and was not only a talented mathematician but a calligrapher as well. Using his knowledge of geometry , he designed a script that was easy to write, perfectly proportioned yet beautiful to behold. He laid down a set of rules which still apply. He used the rhombic (diamond shaped) dot , the Alif and circles as basic measurements. Before his death in 940 AD, he had succeeded in devising a set of scientific rules for calligraphy that could be applied by anyone. Ibn Muqlah is thought to have used his rules on at least six cursive. Unfortunately little of his actual work has survived though the Baghdad museum possesses a few pages of manuscript that are generally agreed to be in his hand writing.

The next outstanding calligrapher was Ibn Al Bawwab (d. 1022) who was trained by one of Ibn Muqlah's students . Ibn Al Bawwab was not just a calligrapher but also a talented artist. He gave to writing a new elegance of free flow and beauty. He mastered a number of styles but was particularly inspired by Naskhi and Muhaqqaq. He is thought to have completed sixty four copies of the Holy Qur'an , of which one has survived as well as a few pages of his secular work.

There were many talented calligraphers in the eleventh and twelfth centuries advancing the art, of which Yaqut Al Musta'simi (d. 1298 AD) should be mentioned. He invented a new way of cutting the reed pens (which are still used in calligraphy classes) and which imparted to his writing an extra dimension of beauty and grace. Yaqut Al Musta'simi is still remembered as a strict teacher who made his students practice long and hard. He 'warmed' up each day by writing two sections from the Holy Book. There is a legend about him that says during the terrible sacking of Baghdad by Ghengis Khan's Mongols (1258AD), he climbed to the top of a minaret clutching a pen and some ink, but no paper. All he had was a towel of Baalbeki linen, on which he wrote a few words on the towel in such a manner that looking at them one is seized with wonder. A delightful Persian miniature in the Freer Gallery, Washington DC, shows Al Musta'simi practising the letter Kaf while sitting at the top of the minaret. Such devotion to ones profession was both expected and essential and there are numerous tales illustrating such enthusiasm and piety.

As an art form calligraphy could be considered fully developed by the thirteenth century. It was during this period that many words such Al Kymia (Chemistry) , Amir Al Bahar (Admiral) , Aljabr (Algebra) etc. passed into the English language. Libraries flourished in the great cities such as Alexandria (Egypt), Baghdad and Cordoba in Spain. In many places the wealthy formed their own libraries.

It was considered that to train as a scribe was important and proper. The grandson of Tamerlane the Mongol, Ibrahim Sultan was an outstanding writer and to this day one of his works , a Qur'an written in gold Rayhani script (1413 AD) can still be seen. These numerous productions had the side effect of encouraging bookbinders, artists and illustrators and a very high standard of work was achieved. This outpouring of fine work reached into Europe and many artists of that period attempted to copy the designs and motifs. If paintings from the 13th/15th century are studied , one can see examples of sometimes readable attempts at Arabic writing as well as other Islamic motifs used in costume details. It was during this time that the word Arabesque entered the vocabulary of many a European country.

The Museums, Institutes & Collections described below contain Qur'ânic manuscripts from 1st century of Hijra onwards. The readers are advised to go through the cited publications to obtain more information about the nature of the Qur'ânic manuscripts.

Maktabat al-Jâmia al-Kabîr (Maktabat al-Awqâf),

The Great Mosque, Sancâ', Yemen.

The Great Mosque of Sancâ', established in 6th year of Hijra when the Prophet(P) entrusted one of his companions to build a mosque. It is considered to be the first mosque in Yemen and among the oldest in Islamic world. The mosque was extended and enlarged by Islamic rulers from time to time. The manuscript collection (ca. 7,000) of the Great Mosque is housed in three libraries in the mosque complex. The first to be established was

Al-Maktaba al-Sharqîya which was completed during the reign of al-Imâm Yahyâ Hamîd al-Dîn (1904-1948). The second to be established was Al-Maktaba al-Gharbîya which houses the manuscripts and books of Al-Hay'a al-Âmma li-l-Âthâr wa Dûr al-Kutub. Both these libraries are located in the southern side of the msoque. The Maktabat al-Awqâf, the main modern library, is housed on the second floor in the new three-story building of the Great Mosque of Sancâ'. It contains some of the rarest Islamic manuscripts in the world, including rare manuscripts of the Qur'ân. Subjects include theology, jurisprudence, Qur'ânic sciences, tafsîr, terminology of hadîth, sîrah, sciences of the Arabic langauge, lexicography, literature, poetry, history, politics, philosophy, logic, astronomy, mathematics, medicine and agriculture. Among the manuscripts in the collection is a copy of the Qur'ân reputed to be in the handwriting of Al-Imâm Alî Ibn Abî Tâlib, Zayd Ibn Thâbit and Salmân al-Fârsî, in two parts, each of 150 pages, in large unpointed Kûfic script.

In 1385 H/1965 A. D. heavy rains fell on Sancâ'. The Great Mosque was affected and the ceiling in the north west corner was damaged. During the survey, the workers discovered a large vault full of parchment and paper manuscripts of both the Qur'ân and non-Qur'ânic material. The dig at the Great Mosque in Sancâ', Yemen, had found a large number of manuscripts of the Qur'ân dating from first century of Hijra.

The UNESCO, an arm of the United Nations, had compiled a CD containing some of the dated Sancâ' manuscripts as a part of "Memory of the World" programme. In this CD there are more than 40 Qur'ânic manuscripts which are dated from 1st century of Hijra (in both Hijâzî and Kûfic scripts), one of them belonging to early 1st century. More than 45 manuscripts have been dated from the period 1st / 2nd century of Hijra. A few examples of the manuscripts from 1st, 2nd, and and 3rd centuries of Hijra can be seen at this website.

A few more examples of the 1st and 2nd century Qur'ânic

manuscripts from Sancâ' can be found in the book Masâhif Sancâ'. This book is a catalogue of an exhibition at the Kuwait National Museum, with articles by Hussa Sabah Salîm al-Sabah, G. R. Puin, M. Jenkins, U. Dreibholz in both Arabic and English. World Survey Of Islamic Manuscripts covers the catalogue of manuscripts at the Great Mosque published in various books.

1. Memory Of The World: Sancâ' Manuscripts, CD-ROM Presentation, UNESCO.
2. Masâhif Sancâ', 1985, Dâr al-Athâr al-Islâmiyyah, Kuwait.
3. Geoffrey Roper (ed.), World Survey Of Islamic Manuscripts, 1992, Volume III, Al-Furqân Islamic Heritage Foundation, London, p.p. 664-667.

Dâr al-Kutub al-Misrîyya (Egyptian National Library), Cairo, Egypt.

The manuscript collection in Dâr al-Kutub is regarded as one of the largest and most important in the world. The total number of manuscripts in this library are 50,755 out of which 47,065 are in Arabic, 996 in Persian and 2,150 in Turkish. It contains priceless and rare manuscripts from the Islamic heritage, especially from the first four centuries of hijra, as well as extremely rare illustrated manuscripts unmatched anywhere else in the world. There is a high proportion of manuscripts copied in the early centuries of Islam. It holds two of the earliest dated Qur'ânic manuscripts dating from 102 AH / 720 A. D. and 107 A. H./725 A. D.

The manuscripts of Da al Kutub cover nearly all subjects. A complete reference of catalogue of the manuscripts can be seen in:

1. Geoffrey Roper (ed.), World Survey Of Islamic Manuscripts, 1992, Volume I, Al-Furqân Islamic Heritage Foundation, London, p.p. 212-218.
2. B. Moritz, Arabic Palaeography: A Collection Of Arabic Texts From The First Century Of The Hidjra Till The Year

1000, 1905, Cairo, See Pl. 31-34 and Pl. 1-12 for 102 AH / 720 A. D. and 107 AH / 725 A. D. respectively.

3. Thomas W. Arnold & Adolf Grohmann, The Islamic Book: A Contribution To Its Art And History From The VII-XVIII Century, 1929, The Pegasus Press, p. 22.

Âstân-i Quds-i Razavî Library, Mashhad, Iran.

This library has one of the oldest (established in 861 AH/ 1457 A. D.) collection of Islamic manuscripts in the Muslim world and the most important in Iran.It has about 29,000 manuscripts in Arabic, Persian and Turkish. Of the 29,000 manuscripts it possess, 11,000 are manuscripts of the Qur'ân, thus making it the largest Qur'ânic manuscript collection in the world. It is also important in that it contains a large number of magnificent, old and illuminated Qur'ânic manuscripts, including several old Kûfic Qur'ânic manuscripts written on deer skin, other with marvellous illuminations from 3rd century Hijra (9th century A. D.) onwards, and some written by famous calligraphers. The manuscripts are catalogued in various publication as can be seen in the reference below:

1. Geoffrey Roper (ed.), World Survey Of Islamic Manuscripts, 1992, Volume I, Al-Furqân Islamic Heritage Foundation, London, pp. 481-486.

Islamic Museum, Jerusalem, Palestine.

This museum was established in 1923 by the Islamic Legal Council in Palestine. The manuscript collection of the Islamic Museum consists entirely of masâhif of the Qur'ân, numbering 644, donated over centuries to Al-Aqsâ Mosque and the Dome of the Rock. Some were presented by rulers and private individuals, and others have been donated by such Palestinian cities as Hebron and Nablus.

The Qur'ânic manuscripts vary in type, age and size. Many are rabcât (i.e., they were copied in thirty fascicles and stored in a chest, or rabca). The oldest is Kûfic, from the end of the second century after hijra, while the most recent is a copy from the thirteenth century after hijra. Sizes range from 16 x 11.5 cm. to the massive second volume of the Qur'ân of the Mamlûk Sultân Qâ't Bây (r. 872-901/1468-1496), which measures 110 x 90 cm. and is 15 cm. thick. The majority of the Qur'ânic manuscripts are splendidly illuminated and decorated , the exceptions being for the most part the copies of the late Ottoman period.

One of the most important manuscript in this collection is the Kûfic copy of the second half of the Qur'ân, the transcription of which is attributed to Al-Hasan b. Al-Husayn b. cAlî b. Abî Tâlib. The pages in this manuscript are beautifully illuminated, with each sûrah heading bearing its own distinct style of decoration; the covers are also decorated on both sides, but are of the Mamlûk period.

The museum also hold an important collection of 883 documents (855 Arabic; 28 persian) from the the 8th/14th century. The complete reference of catalogue of the manuscripts in this museum can be seen in:

1. Geoffrey Roper (ed.), World Survey Of Islamic Manuscripts, 1993, Volume II, Al-Furqân Islamic Heritage Foundation, London, p.p. 579-581.

Beit al-Qur'ân, Manama, Bahrain.

The Beit al-Qur'ân collection of Qur'ânic manuscripts is one of the most comprehensive of its type in the world. This great collection includes magnificent calligraphic works from as early as the first century Hijra (7th / 8th A. D.) to the present day, from all regions of the Islamic world, from China to Andalusian Spain. Manuscripts from 1st and 2nd century of Hijra are available at this website. It is a privately-owned collection. More information about Beit al-Qur'ân and other museums in Bahrain is also available.

The Nasser David Khalili Collection Of Islamic Art, London, United Kingdom.

The Nasser David Khalili Collection Of Islamic Art

contains the largest and most comprehensive range of Qur'ânic material in private hands. It is managed by the Nour Foundation. The entire history of Qur'ân production from the seventh to the twentieth century is covered, and includes items from centers as far apart as India and Spain. A team of distinguished academics is cataloguing the entire collection, which is to encompass a series of twenty-six volumes. The Qur'ânic manuscripts in this collection are described and illustrated in four lavish volumes. They are written in various scripts and are dated from late 1st century of Hijra onwards. The Nour Foundation in collaboration with Oxford University Press has published the collection. The references are:

1. François Déroche, The Abbasid Tradition: Qur'âns Of The 8th To The 10th Centuries AD, The Nasser D. Khalili Collection of Islamic Art Vol. I, 1992, Oxford University Press, 192 pp.
2. David James, The Master Scribes: Qur'âns of the 10th to 14th Centuries, The Nasser D. Khalili Collection of Islamic Art Vol. II, 1992, Oxford University Press, 240 pp.

   The second of four volumes cataloguing the Qur'âns, this book includes a Qur'ân that retains its original illumination by the greatest calligrapher of the Middle Ages, Yaqût al-Musta'simi. Other masterpieces include a Qur'ân written in gold from twelfth-century Iraq; the only twelfth-century Qur'ân from Valencia; and a manuscript that is possibly the earliest Qur'ân to survive from India.
3. David James, After Timur: Qur'âns of the 15th and 16th Centuries, The Nasser D. Khalili Collection of Islamic Art Vol. III, 1992, Oxford University Press, 256 pp.

   The third of four volumes cataloguing the Qur'âns in the Khalili Collection, this book includes fifteenth century Qur'ans in Iran, Egypt, Syria, Constantinople, and India as well as sixteenth century Qur'âns in Iran and India.
4. Manijeh Bayani, Anna Contadini & Tim Stanley, The

Decorated Word: Qur'âns of the 17th to 19th Centuries, The Nasser D. Khalili Collection of Islamic Art Vol. IV, 1999, Oxford University Press, 334 pp.

This two-part volume is the last of four dedicated to the Qur'âns in the Khalili Collection, and covers the period 1700-1900 and items from Islamic Africa, Ottoman Turkey, Iran, India and the Far East.

5. Nabil F. Safwat, The Art of the Pen Calligraphy of the 14th to 20th Centuries, The Nasser D. Khalili Collection of Islamic Art Vol. V, 1999, Oxford University Press, 248 pp.

The Nasser D. Khalili Collection holds examples of Islamic calligraphy that span six centuries and demonstrate the continuity of this central art form into the modern era. The holdings - nearly 300 in total - include exceptional items that feature the work of many of the most famous master calligraphers, including Seyh Hamdullah and Hafiz Osman.

Bibliothèque Nationale, Paris, France.

Successor to the old Bibliothèque Royale, the Bibliothèque Nationale has assembled collections of Islamic manuscripts formed over the centuries and regularly augmented by purchases and gifts; these collections rank among the most important in Europe and cover nearly all subjects (total ca. 12,000). Especially noteworthy are some Qurânic manuscripts of the first centuries after Hijra. These are kept in the Département des Manuscrits, Division des Manuscrits Orientaux.

The Oriental Institute Museum, University of Chicago, Chicago, United States of America.

The Oriental Institute Museum holds a decent collection of Qur'ânic manuscripts dated from second half of the first century of Hijra (classified as 1st/2nd) onwards. The manuscripts are written in Kûfic and Maghribî scripts suggesting their origin from wide geographical locations in the Islamic world. The relevent reference to look for is the following:

1.Nabia Abbott, The Rise Of The North Arabic Script And Its Kur'ânic Development, With A Full Description Of The Kur'ân Manuscripts In The Oriental Institute, 1939, University of Chicago Press.

This much-acclaimed work of Nabia Abbott has become a sort of standard text book for the students in the western world who are interested in the origins and history of Islamic calligraphy. The book begins with the origins of Arabic script and its development after the advent of Islam. The manuscripts from The Oriental Institute Museum serve as good examples to study various scripts.

The Chester Beatty Library, Dublin, Ireland.

The Islamic Collection in the Chester Beatty Library contains almost four thousand Arabic, Persian and Turkish manuscripts including many superb copies of the Qur'ân. The Islamic Collection is one of the finest in existence and is internationally renowned for the overall high quality and scope of its material. The Library houses examples of the earliest Islamic manuscripts, dated to the ninth and tenth centuries A. D., through to those produced in the early years of the twentieth century.

The Islamic Collection consists of several sub-collections. Of these, the Qur'ân Collection, comprising some 250 manuscripts, is of special importance and is rivalled only by that of the Topkapi Sarayi in Istanbul, Turkey. Manuscripts of note are a Qur'ân of 972, the earliest dated Qur'ân copied on paper, and another copied some nine centuries later for the Ottoman Sultan cAbdulmecid, the binding and illuminations of which are exceptionally exquisite. However, the real gem of the collection - and indeed one of the most treasured objects of the entire Library - is the splendid Qur'ân copied by the famed calligrapher Ibn al-Bawwâb in Baghdad in the year 1001.

The published manuscripts are in the following books:

1. A. J. Arberry, The Chester Beatty Library: A Handlist Of The Arabic Manuscripts, 1955, Vols. 1-8, Emery Walker (Ireland) Ltd., St. Margaret's Donnybrook, Dublin.
2. A. J. Arberry, The Koran Illuminated: A Handlist Of The Korans In The Chester Beatty Library, 1967, Hodges Figgis & Co Ltd., Dublin.
3. David James, Qur'âns And Bindings From The Chester Beatty Library: A Facsimile Exhibition, 1980, World of Islam Festival Trust, London.

The Institute Of Oriental Studies, Russian Academy of Sciences, St. Petersburg, Russia.

Among eighty-five thousand manuscripts in 65 living and dead Oriental languages, which are preserved in the St. Petersburg branch of The Institute Of Oriental Studies (formerly the Asiatic Museum founded in 1818), Russian Academy of Sciences, there are many rare or unique religious, historical, and scientific works awaiting their publication. The Institute of Oriental Studies has recently started a project that deals with compiling the manuscripts in the electronic format. The project, which is similar to UNESCO's "Memory of the World" programme, is called: Asiatic Museum. Treasures from St.Petersburg Academic Collection of Oriental Manuscripts (CD-ROM Series).

This institute houses one of the oldest Qur'ânic manuscripts dated to the first half of the 8th century A. D. and has been published. It has 81 large parchment folios in Hijâzî (i.e., Makkan or Madinan) script contain about 40% of the text of the Qur'ân (full texts of 22 sûrahs and fragments of another 22). The manuscript reflects changes in the orthography and "lay-out" of the sacred text. Such changes were added to the text in red ink, probably a century after the date of copying. Simultaneously, the simple gaps which were left between the preceding sûrah and the beginning of the following sûrah were filled with coloured ornaments (very interesting compositions of triangles, arcs, intertwined or intersecting lines, sometimes evocative of nomadic jewelry) with sûrah titles and information about the number of ayât. The MSS was displayed at the exhibition "Pages of Perfection" (Paris - New York - Lugano - Salzburg) in 1995-1996. Exhibited at the Musée du Petit Palais, Paris, at the Villa Favorita at Lugano, Switzerland and at the New York Metropolitan Museum of Art. The relevent publication is:

2. Efim A. Rezvan, Issue 4: One Of The Most Important Qur'anic MSS In The World, THESA Company, St. Petersburg, Russia.

Tareq Rajab Museum, Kuwait

The Tareq Rajab Museum in Kuwait has a large and important collection of Al Qur'an and manuscripts from all periods and countries (including NW China) around the Islamic world. The museum possesses some fine examples of the writings of renowned calligraphers such as Yaqut Al Musta'simi (d.1293 A.D.). Although little of his work has survived, his influence was of outstanding importance to the development of calligraphy.

Topkapi Palace Library, Istanbul

The present Topkap Palace, the home of the Ottoman sultans and the administrative center of the Ottoman Empire for four hundred years, was turned into a museum in 1924, the manuscripts, found in many pavilions and rooms, were gathered together to form the New Library. Today, the Islamic manuscripts preserved in this new library have been sorted out into categories of Arabic, Persian and Turkish. A complete catalogue was compiled and published by F.E. Karatay in 1960. The first of the Arabic catalogues contains Korans and works of Koranic commentary. These Korans and Commentaries, which have been gathered from the various pavilions, buildings and rooms of the Palace and are classified by the name of the location where they were found, number more than two thousand.

The collection of Korans, the richest to be found anywhere in the world, comprises texts of the Koran inscribed during the

7th - 19th centuries in Arabia, Ian, India, Maghrib (North Africa) and the lands dominated by the Seljuks and Ottomans. Almost all have been prepared by famous calligraphers, gilded by master gilders, and bound by the most capable bookbinders of the times. The 1600 or more Korans found in the first volume of the Arabic catalogue are preserved in the Palace Library as rare books. Among these are seven believed to be inscribed by Caliph Osman (RA), nine accredited to Caliph Ali (RA), two ascribed to Hasan and Hussein (RA) as well as many translations. There are twenty-one Turkish translations, thirty-nine Farsi translations, twenty-one Chagatay translations and one Uygur translation.

The first Korans were written on parchment in the 7th - 8th centuries in a monumental type of script called kufic. This script, whose name is derived from Kufa, an early Islamic center, is a style of Arabic script closest to pictorial design. Kufic script, most characterised with its horizontal and vertical lines, showed regional peculiarities in the 9th century. The kufic script of Iran differed from the kufic of the regions of Baghdad and North Africa. The script used in Baghdad and North Africa was more dynamic and of slighter dimension.

The first Korans written in kufic script, besides the one believed to have been recited by khaliph Osman (RA) at the moment of his death (A. H.32), are the Korans written in vertical form (M.3 M.74, for example). In addition to those written on parchment, there are those of the 9th -11th centuries inscribed on thick dark paper with sepia ink using delicate kufic lines.

Also in the Palace collection are Korans prepared in North African cities such as Ceuta and Marrakech between the 12th and 16th centuries. These are written on parchment on thick dark paper in Maghribi kufic with gilded frontispiece, illuminated surah headings, surah titles, marginal rosettes and sajdah marks.

36

FURTHER READINGS

1. Abdar Rahman. Dalil-al- marijey al-Arabiya-wa-al-murabba. Guide to Arabic Reference Books: an annotated bibliography of books in Arabic and Western languages dealing with the Arabs. Basra, 1970.
2. *Accessions List: Middle East*. v. 1- . 1962-. Cairo: Library of Congress Office, 1962.
3. Afshar, Iraj. Kitabshinasi-i-Fihrist ha-yi Nuskha ha-yi Khatt-i-Farsi dar Kitabkhanah ha-yi dunya. Tehran, University of Tehran 1958.
4. Ahamd Taymur. Nawadir al-makhtutat al-Arabiya wa-amakin wujudiah. Ed. By Salah al-Din al-Munjid. Beirut. Dar al Kitab al Jadid, 1980.
5. Ahmet Ates. Istanbul Kütüphanelerinde Farsça Manzum Eserler I. Istanbul, 1968.
6. Amcazade Hüseyin Pasa and Hekimpasa Musa Nazif Efendi Dermesi, Ankara, 1987. (The Collection of Amcazade Hüseyin Pasa and Hekimpasa Musa Nazif Efendi).
7. Amjad Ali. Oriental libraries and their collections in India. New Delhi, Ess Ess Publications, 2004.
8. Arif Naushahi. Bharat men makhtutat ki fihristen. Lahore, Maghribi Pakistan Urdu Academy, 1988.
9. Arsan, 'Ali 'Uglah, *Mushkilat fi al-Thaqafah al-'Arabiyah* (Damascus: Ittihad al-Kuttab al-'Arab, 1989), p. 179.
10. Awwad, Kurkis. Faharis al-Makhtutat al-Arabia fil-Alam. Kuwait, Ma'had al-Makhtutat al-Arabiya, 1984. (2 vols.).

11. Azerbaycan Respublikasu Tesil Nazilliyu, M.E. Rasulzadc adyna Baku Dovlet Universiteti. Kitabkhanacilig Fakultesi (The Ministry of Education of the Azerbaijan Republic Baku State University, n.a. M. E. Rasulzade. Library School). *Book/et (Baku,* 1994).

12. *Azerbaydzhanskaya Sovetskaya Entsiklopediya (Azerbaijani Soviet Encyclopedia)* v. 2 (Baku: Azerneshr, 1981).

13. B. Moritz, Arabic Palaeography: A Collection Of Arabic Texts From the first century of the Hidjra till the year 1000, 1905, Cairo, See Pl. 31-34 and Pl. 1-12 for 102 AH / 720 CE and 107 AH / 725 CE, respectively.

14. Besterman, Theodore. A World bibliography of oriental bibliographies. Revised by J. D. Pearson. Oxford and Totawa, 1975.

15. Birnbum, Eleazar. Turkish Manuscripts: cataloguing since 1960 and Manuscripts still uncataloged. (In) Journal of the American Oriental Society, 103, 1983 and 104, 1984.

16. Bordin Ruth, B and Warner Robert, M. the modern manuscripts Library, New York, The Scarecroe Press, 1966.

17. Boud' Out, A. (Dir.) *Christian pages of Egypt: manuscripts of Coptes* , 2004

18. Brhatsucipatram part I by Buddhisagara Sharma Nepal, Virpustakalaya, 1964

19. Brhatsucipatram part II by Buddhisagara Sharma

20. Brhatsucipatram part III by Buddhisagara Sharma Nepal, 1966 Brhatsucipatram part IV by Pandit Deviprasad, Nepal Rastriyapustakalaya, 1967

21. Brockelman, Carl. Geschichte der Arabischen litteratur. Leiden, Brill, 1937-1949, 5 vols; including supplement.

22. Brockelmann, Carl. Geschichte des arabischen Literatur, I-II. Leiden, 1943-1949.

23. Buddhist Manuscripts of the Bir Library, by the Sanskrit Seminar of Taisho University, Memoirs of Taisho University, No.40, 1955. Buddhist Manuscript Texts of Kathmandu, Gajin Nagao, 1963, (Japanese).

24. Buddhist Sanskrit Manuscripts: A title list of the Microfilm Collection of the Institute for Advanced Studies of World Religions.1975

25. Catalogue of Palm-leaf and selected paper Mss. belonging to the Durbar Library, Nepal by Hari Prasad Shastri, Calcutta Vol.I,1905 do, Vol II, 1905

26. Catalogue of Sanskrit Manuscripts in the British Museum, by Cecil Bendall, London,1902.

27. Catalogue of Selected Buddhist Manuscripts in Asasaphukuthi, 1986

28. Catalogue of the Buddhist Sanskrit Manuscripts in the Library of Tokai University by Yutaka Iwamoto, Proceedings of the Faculty of Letters, vol.III, Tokai University, Tokyo 1960.

29. Catalogue of the Buddhist Sanskrit Manuscripts in the University Library, Cambridge by Cecil Bendall, Cambridge 1883.

30. Catalogue of the Buddhist Tantric Manuscripts in the National Archives of Nepal and Keshar Library by Mitutoshi Moriguchi Sankibou Busshorin, Tokyo 1989.

31. Catalogue of the Sanskrit Manuscripts in the Tokyo University Library, Seiren Matsunami, Suzuki Research Institute, Tokyo 1965

32. Chakravarti, C. The study of manuscript. Festschrift of P. V. Kane. Pune, Kane Publications, 1941.

33. Collection of Muslim manscripts in Istanbul and Konya. By B. Utas. (article in) Annual Newsletter of Scandinavian Institute of Asian Studies. 1984.

34. Dalil faharis al makhtutat fil Majma al Islamiya. 2nd ed.

Amman,Al-Majma al Maliki li-Buhuth al-Haidara al-Islamia, 1986.

35. Danishpazuh, Muhammad taqi. Nuskha-ha-yi Khatti dar kitabkhana ha-yi Ittihad-i-Jamahir-i-Shuravi:guzarish va fihrist. Tehran, Danishgah-i-Tehran, Kitabkhananah-i-Markazi, 1358.

36. David Filipov, "In Azerbaijan, at First Gush: Ex-Soviet Republic Taps Promise of Caspian Oil," *Boston Globe,* 13 November 1997.

37. Dennis Kimmage, ed., *Russian Libraries in Transition: An Anthology of G/asnost Literature* (Jefferson, N.C.: McFarland, 1992), 149.

38. Descriptive Catalogue of Selected Manuscripts in the Asa Archives prepared by Dr. Janak Lal Vaidya and Prem Bahadur Kansakar Kathmandu, Cvasapasa 1991

39. Deshmukh, Revati P. A study of descriptive catalogues of Sanskrit manuscripts. Jaipur, Printwell, 1966.

40. Francis, Frank. Treasures of British Museum. London, James and Hudson, 1975.

41. Fuat Sezgin. Geschichte des arabischen Schrifttums, I-IX. Leiden, 1967-1984.

42. Geoffrey Roper (ed.), World Survey Of Islamic Manuscripts, 1992, Volume I, Al-Furqân Islamic Heritage Foundation, London.

43. Giresun Yazmalari, Ankara, 1980. (Giresun's Manuscripts. These manuscripts are preserved at the Süleymaniye Library); - Ali Nihat Tarlan Dermesi, Ankara 1981. (The Collection of Ali Nihat Tarlan. These manuscripts are preserved at the Süleymaniye Library); - Antalya Tekelioglu Dermesi, Istanbul 1983 and 1984. (The Collection of Antalya Tekelioglu. These manuscripts are preserved at the Süleymaniye Library);

44. Halit Dener. "Süleymaniye Umumi Kütüphanesi".

Istanbul: Maarif Basimevi, 1957. (The Süleymaniye Public Library).

45. Janert, Klaus Ludwig. An annotated bibliography of Indian manuscripts. Weisbadean, Franz Ateiner Verlag, 1965.

46. Kalinowski, Dir. *Divination and company in medieval China: study of the manuscripts of Dunhuang of the national Library of France and British Library*, 2003

47. Katherine van de Vate, *Books from the Arab World: A Guide to Selections and Acquisitions*, (Durham: Middle East Libraries Committee, 1988), p. 31.

48. Khalil Ismaylov, "Respublikada kitabkhana ishi yenilezekmi," ("Will Librarianship in the Republic Be Updated?") *Khayat,* 21 December 1991.

49. Khalil Sabat, *Tarikh al-Tiba'ah fi al-Sharq al-'Arabi*, al-tab'ah 2. (al-Qahirah: Dar al Ma'arif, 1966.

50. L. ¥. Medvedeva, "Fondy na tyurskikh yazykakh narodov SSSR," in *Akademiya Nauk SSSR. Institut Narodov Azii. Vostokovednye fondy krupneishikh bibliotek Sovetskogo Soiuza* (Academy of Sciences of SSSR. The Institute of the People of Asia. Oriental Collections of the Largest Libraries of the Soviet Union) (Moscow: Izdatcl'stvo Vostoznoy Literatury, 1963), 19.

51. Majallat al-Majma' al-'Ilmi al-'Arabi. Dimashq: al-Majma' al-'Ilmi al-'Arabi, 1964—. Now published under the title: Majallat Majma' al-Luqhah al-'Arabiyah bi-

52. Maktabat al-Asad (Damascus, Syria). *al-Bibliyughrafiya al-Wataniyah al-Suriyah al-Raji'ah.* Dimashq: Maktabat al-Asad, 1987—.

53. Maktabat al-Asad (Damascus, Syria). al-Bibliyuqhrafiya al-Wataniyah al-Suriyah. Dimashq: Maktabat al-Asad, 1985

54. Maktabat al-Asad, *al-Bibliyughrafiya al-Wataniyah al-Suriyah* (Dimashq: Wizarat al-Thaqafah, Maktabat al-Asad, Mudiriyat al-Tawthiq wa-al-I'lam, 1991).

55. Manuscript libraries in Istanbul. By Gunay Kut Tr. by Frologan. (article in) Current Turkish Thought 43, 1980.

56. Micro-film catalogue of the Buddhist manuscripts in Nepal Buddhist Library by H.Takaoka, Nagoya 1981

57. Monnet, N. *China, Empire of the feature: penmanships and drawings of the O C to the XIX* E *century*, 2004

58. Munzavi, Ahmad. Fihris-i-nuskhahai khatti-i-Farsi. Tehran, Regional Cultural Institute, 1969. 6 vols.

59. Munzavi, Ahmad. Fihrist-i-Mushtark-i-nuskha hyi khatt-i-Farsi-i-Pakistan. Islamabad. Maekaz-i-Tehqiqate Farsi, Iran va Pakistan, 14 cols. 1983-98.

60. Paul L. Horecky, *Libraries and Bibliographic Centers in the Soviet Union,* Slavic and East European Series, v. 16 (Bloomington: Indiana University Publications, 1959), 15.

61. Pearson, T. D. Index Islamicus supplement, 1956-1960: a catalogue of articles in Islamic subjects in periodicals and other collective publications. Cambridge, 1962.

62. Pondurangi, K. T. The wealth of Sanskrit manuscripts in India and abroad. Bangalore, 1978.

63. Pearson, J. D. and Behn, W. Index Islamicus 1976-1980. Pt. 1: Articles; Pt. 2 Monographs. London, 1983.

64. Pearson, J. D. and others. Index Islamicus 1906-1955: a catalogue of articles on Islamic subjects in periodicals and other collective publications. Cambridge, 1958

65. Pearson, J. D. Oriental Manuscripts in Europe and North America: a survey. Zug. Inter Documentation Company, 19771.

66. Richard, F. *The Persian book* , 2003

67. Ritter. "Ayasofya Kütüphanesinde Tefsir Ilmine Ait Arapça Yazmalar".

68. Romadan, Shishin. Nawadir al-makhtutat ai-Arabiya fi maktabat Turkiya. Bairut, Dar al-Kitab al-Jadid. 3 vols. 1975-82.

69. Roman, S. Development of Islamic Library collections in Western Europe and North America. London, Mansell, 1990.

70. Roper, G. T.Index Islamicus 1981-1985: a bibliography of books and articles on the Muslim world. London, 2 vols.

71. Salman Shamsi Nadvi. Hindustan ke mashriqi kutubkhane. Lucknow, 1973.

72. Samksiptasucipatram by Buddhi Sagara Sarma Nepal, Nepal Vira Pustakalaya, Samvat 2020 (A.D.1963)

73. Sanskrit Buddhist literature of Nepal by Rajendra Lal Mitra, Calcutta 1882.

74. Sarkis, Yusuf Ilyan. Mu'jam al-Matbu'at al-'Arabiyah wa-al-Mu'arrabah: wa-huwa shamil li-asma' al-kutub al-matbu'ah fi al-aqtar al-sharqiyah wa-al-qharbiyah, ma'a dhikr asma' mu'allifiha wa-lum'ah min tarjamatihim wa-dhalika min yawm zuhur al-tiba'ah il\'a nihayat al-sanah al-hijriyah 1339 al-muwafiq li-sanat 1919 miladiyah. Misr: Matba'at Sarkis, 1928-1931.

75. Shayesta Khan. Rare Arabic and Persian manuscripts in India sub continent. Patna, Khuda Bakhsh Orietal Public Library, 1995. vol. 1 (in English) vol. 2 (in Urdu).

76. Simayaka, Marqus and Yassa Abd al-Masih. Catalogue of the Copti and Arabic manuscripts in the Coptic Museum, the Partriachate, the Principal Church of Cairo and Alexandria and monastries of Egypt.. 2 vols. Cairo. 1939-42.

77. Simon Francis, ed.. *Libraries in the USSR* (Hamden: Linnet Books and Clive Bingley Ltd., 1971.

78. Storey, C. A. Persian literature: a bio-bibliographical survey. London, 1927.

79. Succinct Catalogue of the Sanskrit Manuscript in the Possession of the Faculty of letters, Kyoto University, compiled by Kiyotaka Goshima and Keiya Noguchi, Kyoto 1983

80. Sucipatram-part I by Srinarayana Prasad Sharma, Nepal 1964
81. Sulaiman Nadvi, Syed. Hijaz ke Kutubkhane (article published in) Maarif, Azamgarh. Vol. 18, 1926.
82. Tasbihi, Mohamaad Husayen. Kitabkhana ha yi Pakistan. Islamabad: Markazi-i- Tahqiqat-i-Farsi-i-Iran va Pakistan, 1977.
83. *The Middle East and North Africa (1992)*, 38th ed. London: Europa Publications Limited, 1991.
84. *The Near East National Union List*. Compiled by Dorothy Stehle under the direction of George N. Atiyeh. Washington: Library of Congress, African and Middle Eastern Division, 1988-.
85. Thomas W. Arnold & Adolf Grohmann, The Islamic Book: A Contribution To Its Art And History From The VII-XVIII Century, 1929, The Pegasus Press, p. 22.
86. Türkiyat Mecmuasi 7-8. Part II. pp. 1-93. Istanbul, 1945.
87. Venkatappaiah, V. Handbook of libraries, Archives and Information Centres in India. Ed. By B. M. Gupta. New Delhi, Aditya Prakashan. 1991.

INDEX